Pablo Tac, Indigenous Scholar

The publisher gratefully acknowledges the generous support of the Lisa See Endowment Fund in Southern California History and Culture of the University of California Press Foundation.

Pablo Tac, Indigenous Scholar

Writing on Luiseño Language and Colonial History, c. 1840

Lisbeth Haas

with Art by James Luna

Including the complete manuscript of Pablo Tac, transcribed by Marta Eguía, Cecilia Palmeiro, Laura León Llerena, Jussara Quadros, and Heidi Morse, with facing-page translation by Jaime Cortez, Guillermo Delgado, Gildas Hamel, Karl Kottman, Heidi Morse, and Rose Vekony

UNIVERSITY OF CALIFORNIA PRESS

Berkeley · *Los Angeles* · *London*

University of California Press, one of the most distinguished
university presses in the United States, enriches lives around
the world by advancing scholarship in the humanities, social
sciences, and natural sciences. Its activities are supported by
the UC Press Foundation and by philanthropic contributions
from individuals and institutions. For more information, visit
www.ucpress.edu.

University of California Press
Berkeley and Los Angeles, California

University of California Press, Ltd.
London, England

Library of Congress Cataloging-in-Publication Data

Haas, Lisbeth.
    Pablo Tac, indigenous scholar : writing on Luiseño
language and colonial history, c. 1840 / Lisbeth Haas ;
with art by James Luna ; including the complete
manuscript of Pablo Tac, transcribed by Marta Eguía . . .
[et al.].
        p.   cm.
    Includes bibliographical references and index.
    ISBN 978-0-520-26189-1 (cloth : alk. paper)
    1. Tac, Pablo, 1822–1841.   2. Luiseño Indians—
California—Biography.   3. Indian scholars—
California—Biography.   4. Luiseño Indians—History.
5. Luiseño language—Grammar.   6. Luiseño
language—Dictionaries.   I. Title.
    E99.L9.H33   2011
    979.40097'45092—dc23
    [B]   2011036636

Manufactured in the United States of America

20   19   18   17   16   15   14   13   12   11
10   9   8   7   6   5   4   3   2   1

The paper used in this publication meets the minimum
requirements of ANSI/NISO Z39.48–1992 (R 1997)
(Permanence of Paper).

I would like to acknowledge and thank our tribal leaders, then and now, for their persistence, dedication, and vision, which has enabled us to hold on to our lands and ways, without which we would not have survived as tribal communities.

James Luna

I want to acknowledge all young indigenous scholars whose writing provides critical interventions in the production of knowledge, as does the work of Pablo Tac.

Lisbeth Haas

Contents

Illustrations

Foreword

Miiyum: Hello!

We, the people of the San Luis Rey Band of Mission Indians from Ocean-side, California, are honored to have the opportunity to share the history and culture of our people. We still live on land that is the territory of our ancestors, from the ocean to the mountains. We have experienced and survived both natural and manmade challenges through ten thousand years of sustainable living.

We see ourselves as being here from the beginning of time. Our creation story is here.

Today our goal is to achieve Federal recognition. It is important to be recognized as a sovereign nation by the Federal government. We are actively engaged in this long and complicated process.

Pablo Tac, a young Indian boy from the village of Quechla, which is now the site of Mission San Luis Rey, was taken to Rome, where he was trained as a scholar. His enormously significant writings are the only primary source of Luiseño language and culture written by a Luiseño until the twentieth century.

In this book Lisbeth Haas shows how Pablo Tac transcended his own time to demonstrate the profound depth and richness of the Luiseño culture. James Luna, in his contemporary performance art at the Venice Biennale, has brought Pablo Tac to the forefront of consciousness by reenergizing the connection of the past to the present.

Pablo Tac died in Rome in 1841 without revisiting his homeland. We can only wonder how his return would have benefited our ancestors as well as contemporary Luiseño people. He is a respected Luiseño scholar and hero.

No$úun Lóovic: *My Heart is Good!*

Melvin J. Vernon, Tribal Chair
San Luis Rey Band of Mission Indians
Oceanside (San Diego County), California
February 2010

Preface

I turned to Pablo Tac's manuscript in 2000 to read the entire work on microfilm while writing an indigenous history of colonial and Mexican California. This forthcoming book places native categories of analysis and source material at the center of my thinking. But as I became familiar with Tac's writing, and read each part of the manuscript in relationship to the other, new questions emerged that took me beyond the history of California. I began to wonder about Tac's life, his studies, and the writing of the other students with whom he lived and worked in Rome. These questions led me to more archives and, ultimately, to the present book.

Much of the information about Tac's adult life and the context for his work I found by following Tac's footsteps to Italy. I went to see the original Collegium de Propaganda Fide, located next to the Spanish steps in Rome, where Tac studied and wrote from 1834 to 1841. I worked at the archives that are now housed in the newer college built on Vatican land on a hill above the Roman neighborhood of Travestere.

The manuscript that Tac wrote for Giuseppe Mezzofanti, a linguist who became the Vatican librarian and a cardinal during the time that Tac studied in Rome, became part of Mezzofanti's extensive archive. After Mezzofanti's death in 1849, the Vatican sent the archive to Bologna, his birthplace. There a large part, including Tac's manuscript, was given to the Biblioteca comunale dell'Archiginnasio. The magnificent building that has housed the Biblioteca since 1838 was originally the university of med-

icine and philosophy, built in 1563, and has the arms of noble families inscribed on its walls and ceilings. Given Bologna's formidable tradition of communal action and university education, the building became an important part of the city's dramatic array of public spaces.

I consulted Mezzofanti's archive at the Biblioteca comunale dell'Archiginnasio to read Pablo Tac's original manuscript. I also wanted to read the other grammatical studies that Mezzofanti's students and assistants compiled and copied from other sources. When I compared Tac's work to that of the others, I realized just how unique it was. Prompted by a dear friend, I decided to try to get the manuscript published in its original languages, together with English translation.

Just before I began my research in Bologna, I received a call from James Luna, a well-known contemporary Luiseño artist who lives on La Jolla Reservation. The National Museum of the American Indian had selected Luna to be its first representative at the Venice Biennale in 2005, for which he planned to produce a work in honor of Pablo Tac. Luna generously asked me to collaborate by sharing my understanding of Tac's writing and a copy of Tac's microfilmed manuscript. I watched, in turn, as Tac's work took on other dimensions through Luna's eyes in his piece *Emendatio*. (See the exhibition catalogue *James Luna: Emendatio*, ed. Truman Lowe and Paul Chaat Smith [Washington, D.C.: National Museum of the American Indian, Smithsonian Institution, 2005], which includes my essay "Pablo Tac: Memory, Identity, History," 49–53.)

Luna's work often speaks to history in the present, forming a politics of memory. Although there are no known images of Pablo Tac, Luna had his own portrait painted in the likeness of a nineteenth-century Indian scholar and titled it *James Tac*. Thus, all three—the portrait, Luna, and Tac—went to Italy. In creating the memory of Tac's presence in Italy, Luna returned Pablo Tac to the public eye there, and returned Tac's work to an international setting. The painting hung at the entry to his installation at the Biennale.

The portrait constitutes one of the many visual references Luna made during the exhibition to the connections between past and present. The fifteenth-century palace also reverberated with the words that Tac wrote in Rome, words Luna had woven into Navajo rugs. In one of the installation rooms, Luna's piece *Apparitions* appeared in video format, juxtaposing photographs of elder Luiseños taken in the early twentieth century with images of Luiseños today. Some of these pairs, through which Luna explores the dual theme of resemblance and translation, are reproduced in the present book. *Emendatio* addressed many things that

concerned Pablo Tac, things about which he wrote, such as history, words, images, attention to elders, humor, poetry, and wit. Tac's willingness to persevere, so evident in his writing, imparts a sense of assurance in a precarious time, an assurance on which both Luna and I could draw.

When James Luna and I presented a draft of this book to the San Luis Rey Band, Luna asked me to say something personal, to give people a sense of my motives in publishing the work. As a historian, my personal voice usually remains absent, and I encountered some resistance inside. Yet at our first meeting in Vista, San Diego County, in a roadside restaurant, the tribal chairman Mel Vernon asked me why I undertook this project. I told him a vivid story of my birth and being given up for adoption in the Blue Ridge Mountains. Vernon listened intently. I think it offered some potential for humanity in my approach. The experience made me favor histories that are difficult to reconstruct, and forms of knowledge that escape the dominant paradigms of an era. The beauty of history, to me, is being able to place people in the worlds they created during times of little choice, as faced by so many. That sense of having to work within narrow parameters, and of possessing little language to define one's story, joins many people together in a common dilemma. Pablo Tac addressed that dilemma well.

Today Luiseño has been decolonized as a written language. Its grammar, orthography, and syntax are developed from the spoken language, so that references to non-Luiseño speech are no longer necessary. The spellings have been revised to remove the Latin and Spanish influences found in Tac's written grammar and dictionary. Many Luiseños are now studying the written language. Tac's writing represents a different era.

Acknowledgments

Many people collaborated on this book and made it possible. I chose scholars to transcribe Tac's manuscript who love literature and language. Marta Eguía and Cecilia Palmeiro transcribed the entire manuscript with expertise, care, and perseverance. Laura León Llerena edited the Spanish-Luiseño transcription. Her work on indigenous colonial writing in Peru enabled her to better understand the intellectual world Tac formed part of as a native scholar. Jussara Quadros brought her linguistic and literary prowess to the Luiseño text to assure that it followed Tac's original writing. I also thank Karl Kottman and Heidi Morse for their transcription and translation of Latin portions of the manuscript.

The principal translators brought their poetic sensibilities and substantial knowledge of indigenous literary and cultural production, and of Spanish, Latin, and Luiseño, into the translation of Tac's writing into English. Jaime Cortez used his bilingual knowledge of Spanish and English, along with his multilingual sensibility, to render Tac's nineteenth-century Spanish into English. Guillermo Delgado captured the sound and meaning of the ethnographic sketch Tac wrote in Latin because of his knowledge of Latin, Spanish, and indigenous languages and texts. Gildas Hamel also provided gems of insight into Pablo Tac's Latin. I am very thankful to Eric Elliott for his help understanding Tac's dictionary. Elliott placed Tac's words in relationship to contemporary Luiseño, and otherwise made Pablo Tac's historic language more comprehensible. All of those who have translated Tac's writing understand the live quality and intertextuality of language.

As copy editor of the book for the University of California Press, Rose Vekony best grasped the specific literary and historical quality of Tac's writing. She tried to ensure that the transcription and translation maintained their original, indigenous, and deeply bilingual Luiseño-Spanish quality. It is a significantly better book overall because of her trained and poetic eye.

The tribal Chairman of the San Luis Rey Band of Luiseño Indians, Mel Vernon, presented a greeting to readers of this book. The San Luis Rey Band is the contemporary coastal tribe related to Tac's lineage and heritage. I am grateful that they bless this endeavor; as many Luiseño people, they kept the memory and story of Tac alive. I thank Pechanga Chàmmakilawish bilingual elementary school for allowing me to sit in on an adult language class and to see the bilingual classrooms.

I thank the Mellon Foundation for a grant that enabled me to do research at the Huntington Library in San Marino, California, where I initially worked with a microfilm of Tac's manuscript. I am grateful to the staff at the Huntington Library for their exceptional help. The community of fellows working at the Huntington in 2000–2001, when I began studying Tac's manuscript, created an environment in which ideas flourished. I am especially grateful for discussions with Maria Lepowsky and David Weber.

The Hispanic Recovery Project at the University of Houston, Texas, awarded me a grant in 2005 that enabled me to work with the original manuscript in Bologna, Italy. I thank the director of the Biblioteca comunale dell'Archiginnasio, Pierangelo Bellettini, who extended the right to publish the manuscript. I am grateful for the help of the head archivist Anna Manfroni, and I also thank Paola Foschi and other staff in the manuscript and rare book reading room at the Biblioteca comunale dell'Archiginnasio. They have created a truly beautiful place to work.

I completed my work on Tac's manuscript while a fellow at the Davis Center in Princeton University in 2008–2009. I am grateful to Gyan Prakash, then director of the Center, for making postcolonial and subaltern history a vibrant aspect of our collective thinking. I thank the American Studies Department at Princeton for the opportunity to present a paper on Tac and for the lively discussion that followed. The Davis fellows, Princeton colleagues, the librarians and library, and Jennefer Houle at the Davis Center were exceptional in the support they provided, and I thank them all.

I am grateful to my colleagues at the Tepoztlán Institute for the Transnational History of the Americas for their comments on a version

of my work concerning Tac and other indigenous scholars. I have especially benefited from discussing this project with María Josefina Saldaña. I thank her and the collective inspiration of David Kazanjian, María Elena Martínez, and David Sartorius. I benefited from the excellent comments of Florencia Mallon on one version of my essay on Tac and for helping to clarify the book project. William Taylor has been influential to my thinking throughout the process of writing about colonial and Mexican California. I thank Rose Marie Beebe and Robert Senkewicz for the innovative work they have done transcribing and publishing documents that offer new perspectives on mission history. I appreciate Fray Francisco Morales for his invitation to present this work in Cholula, Mexico, and Jeff Burns for his constant support.

The University of California, Santa Cruz, has fully supported my research and writing. I received a President's Faculty Research Fellowship from the University of California, and many generous grants from the Committee on Research to pursue work in various archives and to support the transcription and translation. A fellowship from the Institute for Humanities Research at UC Santa Cruz gave me time off from teaching and research funds to work on this and a related book. I thank those who administer the grant aid, especially Janelle Marines.

My colleagues at Santa Cruz provide important sustenance. For this project the comments of Gabriella Arredondo and Guillermo Delgado have been crucial. I am grateful to Ruby Rich for her reading of my work. Anjali Arondekar, Jim Clifford, Dana Frank, Rosalinda Fregoso, Herman Grey, Norma Klahn, Renya Ramirez, and many other dear colleagues in Latin American and Latino Studies, History, and Feminist Studies are among those whose thinking has influenced this project. I also thank my colleague Sandra Chung for her insight into Luiseño.

The University of California Press made the impressive commitment to publish this manuscript in four languages with art, and I thank them deeply. Niels Hooper, my acquiring editor, has done excellent work. I also thank the fabulous editing and design staff at the Press.

The idea of publishing Pablo Tac's manuscript as a book emerged in December of 2003, when I went to look at Tac's work in the archives of the Collegio di Propaganda Fide in Rome. Margaret Brose and Hayden White were living in Rome at the time and opened their home to me. On hearing my story about Tac and the archive, Margaret said that it sounded like a book in the making, and the idea grew. During the next few years, Margaret headed the University of California education abroad program for Italy in Bologna. There I would visit her after long days in the library,

and she would contribute her erudite and refreshing commentary on narrative, language, and poetry as I told her about Tac's work and Mezzofanti's archive. I thank Margaret and Hayden for their ideas, and for making those research trips exceptional. Dawn Lettau extended the warmth and pleasure of her home and company in Verona, for which I'm forever grateful.

Diane and Jerry Rothenberg's poetic voices are ones that have inspired me throughout my adult life. I hope they find poetry in Tac's writing. I thank my husband Chip Lord, a loving man and artist, who took photos of the original manuscript from which the text was transcribed, some of which are reproduced in this book. My deep appreciation to Sophia Zamudio-Haas, my daughter, whose belief that knowledge might change the world also inspires me.

PART ONE

Introduction

The Life and Writing of Luiseño Scholar Pablo Tac, 1820–1841

LISBETH HAAS

As a historian and scholar, Pablo Tac defied the dominant ideas expressed about Luiseños and other indigenous people under Spanish colonialism. His work used categories of analysis such as "dance" that offered an indigenous way of understanding Luiseño society during the colonial and Mexican eras in California, from 1769 to 1848. Born at Mission San Luis Rey de Francia in 1820, Tac devised a way to write Luiseño from his study of Latin grammar and Spanish, and in so doing he captured many of the relationships that existed between Luiseños during his youth. Drawing on local knowledge, traditions, and ideas, his writing leaves traces of Luiseño spiritual practice and thought, while also revealing the relations of power and authority that existed within his indigenous community.

Tac passed down a way of understanding Spanish colonialism that placed Luiseños at the center of the story. His writing about language and history has wide purposes for readers today, because it constitutes an indigenous record that recasts the past. In translating between Luiseño and Spanish in his grammar and dictionary, he identified the distinct cultural concepts expressed in each language. The vivid examples Tac used to define the words in his dictionary and Luiseño forms of speech can be read as a cultural history, narrating aspects of the Luiseño world available only through his experience.

Tac wrote his manuscript for the linguist and Vatican librarian Cardinal Giuseppe Mezzofanti while studying for the priesthood in Rome; it would become one of hundreds in Mezzofanti's collection. Tac's manu-

script, however, was unique, not only for his voice, humor, and tenacity, but also for his inclusion of a history.[1]

Tac himself created the written form of Luiseño that he used, and he translated it into Spanish and Latin. Although he made Luiseño conform to Latin grammatical constructions, his word choice and his narrative form, along with his continual translation between Luiseño and Spanish, establish an indigenous framework for understanding Luiseño. Tac emphasized Luiseño equality and power, a perspective that has no precedent in the Spanish documents produced in California during his youth.

Born into an era when indigenous people had just become citizens of an independent Mexico (which included Alta California), Tac seemed determined to integrate Luiseño language, history, and oral traditions with global processes. As a nineteenth-century cultural figure, Tac worked among international scholars in Rome. He studied with young men who similarly came from distant empires and new nations in political turmoil. This context may have reinforced the sense of Luiseño equality and dignity that he conveys. His dictionary includes words such as *alauis,* or "liberal" (fol. 110v), that are not found in later Luiseño dictionaries.[2]

Tac wrote far from his territory and tribe. It took almost a century for his work to be published, and the form of publication further distanced Tac from his language and place in history. During the 1920s the Italian linguist Carlo Tagliavini divided the manuscript into three articles that he edited and published separately, thus losing the work's internal integrity, original form, and interconnected meanings.[3] As a result, scholars questioned the accuracy of Tac's representation of Luiseño culture. Alfred Kroeber referred to a dialogue Tac wrote as something "concocted in Rome," doubting its relationship to Luiseño culture—as if the culture remained stagnant, and something apart from Tac himself.[4] Above all, discussions of the manuscript have circumvented the ideas Tac put forth, ideas that could produce new ways of seeing colonial society. Scholars read Tac's published history in a form edited to fit a standard Western narrative, and removed from the rest of the manuscript, where Luiseño words temper and qualify Tac's Spanish. To highlight the knowledge Tac presents, this book integrates Tac's words and ideas by publishing the manuscript in its original form and with English translation.

GROWING TO ADULTHOOD IN MISSION SAN LUIS REY

Mission San Luis Rey had been established in the territory of Tac's ancestors in 1798, twenty-two years before the birth of Pablo Tac. But the

Spanish presence went back farther, to the time when the Franciscans established the first missions in California beginning in 1769—the year of the birth of Tac's paternal grandmother, Pitmel. For almost thirty years Pitmel and other Luiseño people who lived in autonomous territories on the mesas and coastal valleys in western Luiseño territory witnessed the constant incursion of caravans that moved north and south through their land on El Camino Real. They also witnessed the San Diego revolt of 1775 and endured widespread illnesses even before the mission was founded. Tac noted—perhaps from oral history and official records—that five thousand people were living in Luiseño territory before the Spanish arrived (fols. 75r, 80v, 92r). Of that number, he wrote, two thousand perished from illness, leaving only three thousand (fol. 92r). Although the Spanish traveled through Luiseño territory from the presidio and mission of San Diego and all points north for nearly thirty years after 1769, their own records make no note of these illnesses. The Spanish rarely commented on the Luiseño society they passed through.

Perhaps the slow shift in power relations regionally, together with the spread of disease among Luiseños, created a "time of little choice," so that by 1795, some Luiseño leaders were willing to allow a mission to be established in their territory.[5] Indeed, a few of them had already been baptized by the late 1780s. Some Luiseños had affiliated with Mission San Diego de Alcalá, to the south, or the missions San Juan Capistrano and San Gabriel Arcángel, to the north. By 1798, the chief of Quechla—the territory of Tac's forebears—had likewise agreed to the founding of a mission within his jurisdiction. His was one of more than twenty-seven politically independent but interconnected Luiseño territories.[6]

Construction of the mission began in 1798. Inhabitants of the nearby mesas and valleys joined the church first; within a week, seventy-seven persons had been baptized, and twenty-three others had received instruction on site. Fray Fermín Lasuén wrote that "larger numbers are not admitted to instruction for it is impossible to maintain them in the customary manner because of the grave and unavoidable inconveniences," especially the difficulty of feeding a large group of new converts, five troops, two missionaries, and thirty indigenous translators and aids from San Diego and San Juan Capistrano.[7] By 1 August 1798 three principal Luiseño chiefs and their wives from neighboring villages lived at the mission and received instruction, together with twenty-nine others.[8] By early September Fray Lasuén saw the mission "progressing in spiritual and temporal matters in extraordinary and admirable ways."[9]

A blind prayer leader from Mission San Juan Capistrano, a native of

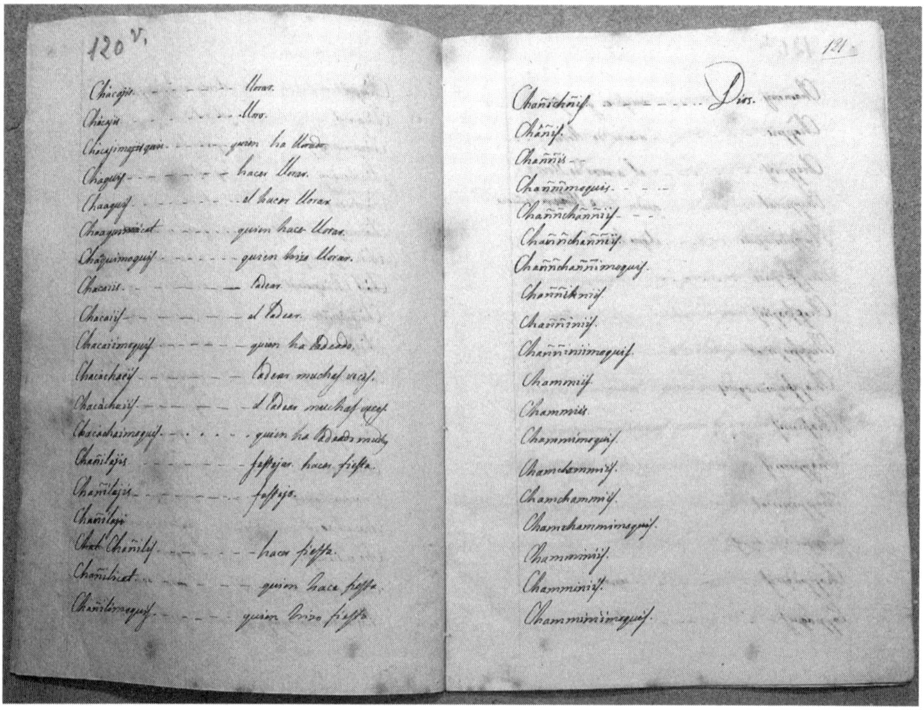

FIGURE I. *Dios* in Pablo Tac's dictionary (fols. 120v–121r). All photographs of Tac's manuscript at the Biblioteca comunale dell'Archiginnasio, Bologna, are by Chip Lord.

Luiseño territory, helped translate the prayers and doctrine into Luiseño and instructed adults "in their own language."[10] The adults attended instruction "punctually morning and evening from the very day of the foundation." The prayer leader and his cotranslators from San Juan Capistrano came from strong religious traditions, including that of Chanichñis (fig. 1).[11] These translators placed the Christianity that Luiseños accepted in baptism into a framework that offered great latitude for interpretation through their perspectives.

Pitmel, Tac's grandmother, took her son to be baptized as Pedro Alcántara Tac, on 19 October 1801, shortly after his birth. Four years later she would receive her own baptism, and the baptismal name Liberata. The family probably moved from her village to the mission village at that point. The mission had settled in Quechla, Pitmel's territory and the name of the indigenous village at the mission. When Tac writes that they called their territory Quechla, he speaks both of his ancestral land and the mission proper (fols. 65v, 78v, 92r).

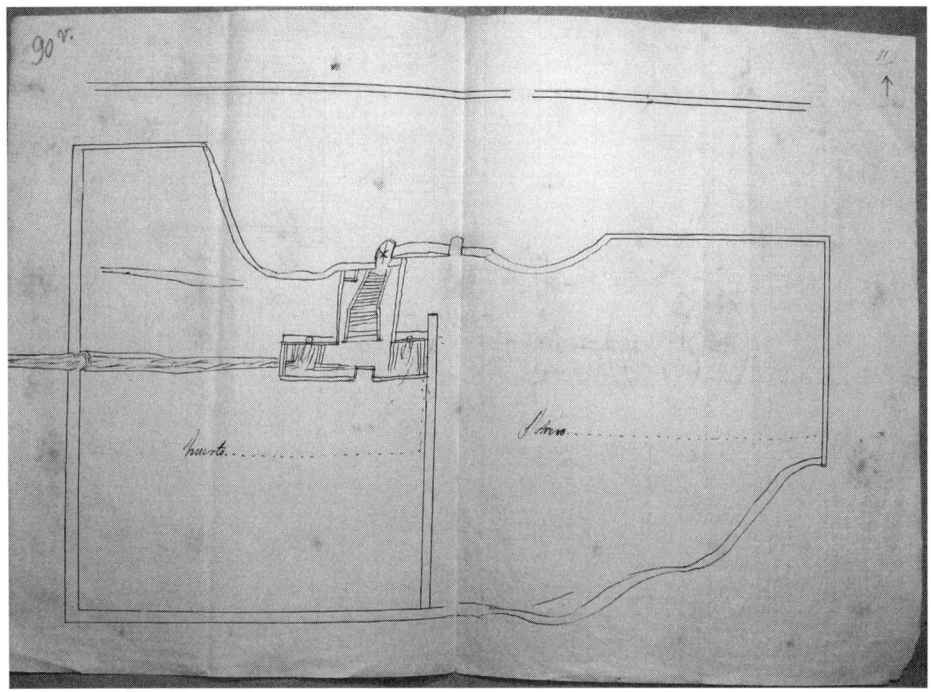

FIGURE 2. Tac's drawing of Mission San Luis Rey (fol. 90v).

The rapid rate of baptisms suggests the degree of economic, political, and physical disruption caused by the growth of colonial society in and around Luiseño territory after 1769. Within eight years of its founding, by 1806, the mission registered 1,158 people baptized—the vast majority of people who lived in the valley, in territories near San Luis Rey. Most had by then relocated to the mission (fig. 2).[12]

Tac's mother, Ladislaya Molmolix, was among those who relocated during the valley's early population shift to the mission. She came from the territory of Pumusi, to the south of San Luis Rey. Baptized on 3 July 1804, she moved to the mission sometime thereafter. There she met Pedro Alcántara Tac. They married around 1818 and would have at least six children, including Pablo Tac. They baptized their daughter Dionesia on 7 October 1819; their son Pablo on 15 January 1822; their sons Julio and José on 16 February 1827 and 1829, respectively; and their daughter Teófila on 10 January 1831. After Tac's departure his parents had a sixth child, José Fermín, baptized on 8 July 1833.[13]

Agapito Amamix, who would leave San Luis Rey and study in Rome

with Tac, likewise had parents from Quechla and Pumusi. But Agapito's mother, Gerónima Atuma Mainamman, had relocated to San Juan Capistrano before the founding of Mission San Luis Rey, as did twenty-six other people from Quechla. She left Quechla at eighteen and was baptized at Mission San Juan Capistrano on 12 September 1797. The following year, when Mission San Luis Rey was founded in Quechla, she moved back to her territory to settle at the mission. She probably became one of the first translators of Catholicism, instructing the new converts in Luiseño dialects.

Gerónima would have six children. She bore five with her first husband, Camilo Pihungani, who was also from Quechla: Gabriel (1802), María Presentación (1807), Casilda (1810), Gerónima (1813), and Camilo (1816), the last born shortly before his father died.[14] By 1820, Gerónima married the widower Vicente Amamix, who brought his daughter Evita into the household. The girl's mother, Vicenta, had died sometime between 1816 and 1820. Both Vicente and Vicenta came from Pumusi and had received masculine and feminine forms of the same name at their respective baptisms, in June and July of 1805. Gerónima and Vicente had one son, Agapito Amamix, whom they baptized on 6 August 1820. Gerónima died soon thereafter.

Left without their mother and having lost their father earlier, Gerónima's daughters moved to the girls' dormitories at the mission, while her oldest son married an indigenous woman raised at Mission San Gabriel. Agapito Amamix remained with his father and his half-sister, Evita. Vicente remarried around 1824. His third wife, Pia Chenvaugan, also a widow, came from Jalpay, a borderlands village of Ipai speakers near the ocean. Some people from her village affiliated with Mission San Diego and others with Mission San Luis Rey. Pia had been baptized at the age of six on 12 September 1810 and bore two children by her first husband, Baltasar Chapugix: Dominga (1820) and Fermín (1822). Both children, as well as her husband, died before 1824. Pia herself did not live long after her marriage to Vicente Amamix, who followed her in death a few years later. Agapito, orphaned by both parents, went to live with other young men in the *monjerio*, where he began to assist the missionary Fray Antonio Peyri.[15]

A SHADOW OF SORROW AND LAMENT

These families experienced a high degree of trauma through occasional epidemics and endemic new diseases such as syphilis, dysentery, and the flu, which left many dead. By 1835, Tac's parents, Pedro Alcántara Tac

and Ladislaya Molmolix, had lost all their children in death except Tac, then living in Rome. They stood among many families with similar losses. Agapito and his extended family of siblings saw their parents and step-parents die. Orphaned more than once, his siblings married into other mission Indian families of various descents.

"Poor and also orphaned" is how Tac translated the Luiseño word *ahicho* (fol. 109r). The pair of adjectives he brought together reveals how vulnerable Luiseño children found themselves without the network of family and the full set of ritualistic practices that had previously sustained them and enriched their future.

A shadow of sorrow and lament crosses the pages of Tac's manuscript. Tac uses the verb "to cry" relatively frequently in examples interspersed throughout the grammar. *Naṅiṡ* means "to cry" for men and adults. For a man the verb *ṅaṅiṡ* expresses a greater degree of sorrow, as in *Yaas op Naċ*, "the man cries" (fols. 69r–v. Among his grammatical examples, Tac writes, "For you he always cried" (fol. 35r) and "My mother cries for my older brother" (fol. 69r). The verb first appears toward the beginning of the grammar, in the example "There was a man who always cried," which Tac contrasts with the example of "another who always laughed" (fol. 27r). But crying reappears in many more examples, while laughter does not.

One grammatical example reads, "Why do you cry? I cry for my father who was eaten by the wolves" (fol. 97r). In an earlier example Tac writes, "They say that over there in that place there are wolves, and that they paint, write, and sing very well . . . who believes it?" (fol. 72v). The Spanish used painting, writing, and singing as a cultural basis for Christianization. Translators gave a single Luiseño word, *nauiṡ*, three equivalents in Spanish: "to signal," "to paint," and "to write" (fol. 82r). Luiseños did not have a tradition of writing, canvas painting, or melodic song. Those three activities remained associated with the Spanish. In Tac's grammatical example above, he suggested a connection between death and the Spanish through the figures of wolves. In the same set of grammatical examples Tac writes, "He said he wanted to kill all the foreigners approaching his country" (fol. 72v).

Peyri chose Tac and Amamix, both young men from among the first families who formed the mission community in Luiseño territory, for entry into the priesthood. They probably began assisting Peyri around the age of eight or nine. They continued to do so in Mexico City, home to the oldest Franciscan institutions of indigenous education in the Americas, where they first went to study.

Peyri's own departure, as well as the preparation of Tac and Amamix

for the priesthood, responded to changing conditions in Alta California after Mexican independence from Spain on 16 September 1821: Mexico announced its intention to emancipate California mission Indians from *neofía*, or their legal tie to the mission, and to secularize mission property. After turning most of the land over to the Mexican state, the missions were to become parishes. In response to this impending change, Peyri and many other missionaries expressed a desire to leave California.[16] But before he left, Peyri defended the indigenous land rights of Luiseños in the inventories he drew up of the San Luis Rey and Pala mission properties in 1822 and 1828. He stood almost alone among missionaries and settlers in Alta California to insist that Luiseños and other California Indians were the collective owners of the vast lands claimed by the mission.[17]

Tac and Amamix were originally expected to return from Mexico City to San Luis Rey, where they would be priests at the parish church that was to replace the mission. After the California territorial government finally issued the Emancipation and Secularization Decree in 1834, Luiseños, who had been politically active to establish the terms of their freedom, retained a far greater amount of land, tribal property, and power than did many California peoples following their colonial encounters. But by that time Tac and Amamix were on their way to Europe.

MEXICO CITY, 1832–34

Peyri finally received permission to return to his home in Catalonia, Spain, in 1829, and began his journey more than two years later, accompanied by Tac and Amamix. The three left the mission on 17 January 1832, sailing south from San Diego to Mexico City, their initial destination. There they settled at the Iglesia y Colegio de San Fernando, located near the northwest end of the Alameda Central, a large public park created in 1592 by Viceroy Luis de Velasco, not far from the Zócalo, at the heart of the colonial city. Franciscans founded the Iglesia y Colegio de San Fernando in 1755 to train missionaries to work with indigenous people in Mexico's north, where new missions continued to develop. Fray Junípero Serra and other missionaries who founded California missions had studied at San Fernando.

The Iglesia de San Francisco stood near the southeast end of the Alameda, built on land that Hernán Cortés had granted to the Franciscans in 1521. Its grounds held the former San José de los Naturales (1529), an open-air church that served an Indian parish near the Zócalo

and the first monastic school for indigenous scholars, established by Franciscan Fray Pedro de Gante during the same early era after the conquest. The magnificent structure of San Francisco still encompassed nearly a city block when Tac arrived in 1832, but the Franciscan college for the indigenous nobility no longer existed.[18]

Although indigenous peoples of the Spanish Americas had legal rights to education and property, and the Spanish Crown promoted the education and ordination of the native elite, many in the church sought to reserve the priesthood, with its social and economic privileges, for Spaniards and those of Spanish descent born in the colonies. At the archdiocese of Guadalajara, for example, only about 5 percent of the priests in the late colonial period identified themselves as Indian, and few of this group identified as mestizo or *casta*.[19]

Indigenous priests often claimed noble ancestry and legitimate birth. Many originated in the Indian barrios of Mexico City or the pueblos of the Valley of Mexico. They often earned a language degree (a *título de idioma*), preparing them to work with the diverse linguistic populations of Mexico. Those who held a *título de idioma* spoke at least one indigenous language in addition to either Otomi or Nahuatl, as well as Spanish and Latin. Despite their scholarly degrees, their knowledge of languages, and their vows to the priesthood, they generally remained assistants to other priests.[20] Similarly, very few convents would accept indigenous women, and then only if they came from elite families.[21] Despite the many ways Spanish colonial society excluded the indigenous elite from formal power, the rights of indigenous people to education enabled some to become scholars who documented their communities' histories, languages, and ways of seeing. Their work furthered indigenous representation and authority in the colonial Americas.

Neither Tac nor Amamix descended from ruling lineages, nor had they received advanced education at Mission San Luis Rey. Moreover, secularization threatened church property there as well. The political upheaval left the two young scholars in uncertain circumstances.[22] Thus, in February 1834 they sailed with Peyri to Spain, arriving in Barcelona on 21 June. Peyri secured their entrance to the Collegium Urbanum de Propaganda Fide in Rome, where they enrolled in early September 1834.[23]

ROME, 1834–41

Tac brought very local and specific formative experiences among his people to his scholarship. He moved across difference quite early, learn-

ing Spanish and working for Peyri. Tac and Amamix left the mission sometime after they had reached the age for induction into manhood in Luiseño
society. In Mexico they experienced life at the center of the new republic, where they could read and hear about dramatic political conflict over
the rights of indigenous citizens. They witnessed conflicts between church
and state in Mexico, Catalonia, and Rome. The political histories they
had come to know at firsthand resembled those of many students they
would meet in Rome.

Tac and Amamix enrolled at the Collegium Urbanum de Propaganda
Fide as *Cheegnajuisci in California*—"people from Quechla"—as Tac
later put it. *Quechla* at once referred to their ancestral territory and to
the land on which the mission settled (fig. 3).[24] This demarcation of origin also reflected Tac's sense that Luiseños continued to possess their ancestral territories, in contrast to the claims made by Spain and Mexico
to the land. Being identified as *Cheegnajuisci in California* acknowledged
their territory and suggested the intellectual space of affirmation that
opened for both young men in Rome.

The pope gave the congregation of Propaganda Fide the right to train
young men from poor mission regions for the priesthood. The congregation founded the Collegium Urbanum de Propaganda Fide in 1627.[25]
Students from around the world studied and lived at the large complex,
a structure that occupied a city block of Vatican land in Rome. The Collegium rose up around a central patio and had an internal courtyard for
horses and carriages. Facing the Piazza di Spagna (Plaza of Spain), with
its steps leading up to an old church overlooking Rome, the neighborhood had long been an international quarter. Foreign embassies to the
Vatican were interspersed with a dense cluster of churches, monasteries,
shops, and residences, all built on narrow streets that wound up hilly
inclines.

Twenty-nine other young men entered the college in 1834, often arriving in pairs, like Tac and Amamix, from places defined by political
conflict in former empires and new nations. They came from Albania,
Persia, Cypress, Mesopotamia, Constantinople, Bulgaria, and other areas
of the Ottoman Empire where Roman Catholics formed a minority population. Wars and rebellions from internal and external challenges to Ottoman rule engulfed many areas. Although the independence forces eventually lost, Albania, Bulgaria, and Cypress allied with Greece and rose
up against the Ottomans in the 1820s. Bulgaria experienced a growth of
national culture and language but would not gain independence from
Ottoman control until 1878.

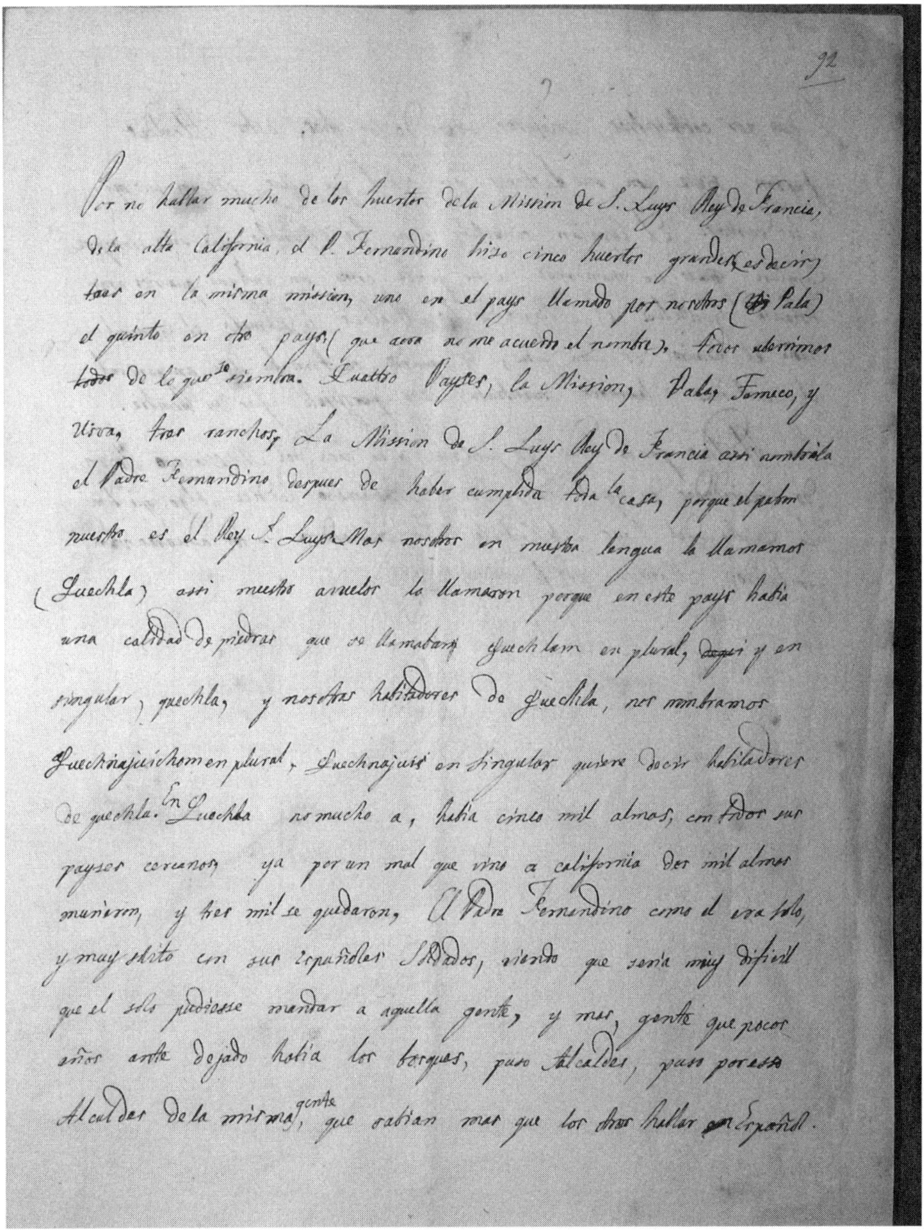

Por no hallar mucho de los huertos de la Mission de S. Luys Rey de Francia,
de la alta California, el P. Fernandino hizo cinco huertos grandes, es decir,
tres en la misma mission, uno en el pays llamado por nosotros (de Pala)
el quinto en otro pays (que aora no me acuerdo el nombre), tres tenemos
todos de lo que se siembra. Quatro Vaytes, la Mission, Pala, Temeco, y
Usva, tres ranchos, La Mission de S. Luys Rey de Francia assi nombrola
el Padre Fernandino despues de haber cumplida toda la casa, porque el patron
nuestro es el Rey S. Luys Mas nosotros en nuestra lengua la llamamos
(Quechla) assi nuestros aruelos la llamaron porque en este pays habia
una calidad de piedras que se llamaban quechlam en plural, aqui y en
singular, quechla, y nosotros habitadores de Quechla, nos nombramos
Quechnajuichom en plural, Quechnajui en singular quiere decir habitadores
de quechla. En Quechla no mucho a, habia cinco mil almas, con todos sus
payses cercanos ya por un mal que vino a California dos mil almas
murieron, y tres mil se quedaron, El Padre Fernandino como el era solo,
y muy listo con sus españoles Soldados, viendo que seria muy dificil
que el solo pudiesse mandar a aquella gente, y mas, gente que pocos
años antes dejado habia los bosques, puso Alcaldes, pues por esso
Alcaldes de la misma gente, que sabian mas que los otros hablar en Español.

FIGURE 3. *Quechla* in Pablo Tac's history (fol. 92r).

Christian populations had long existed in places like Persia (today's Iran), Mesopotamia (Iraq), and Constantinople (Istanbul). Numerous revolts consumed Persia in the wake of the government's attempt to unify the region from Tehran. Mesopotamia carried out extensive modernization around 1834. Constantinople remained on the outer reaches of the Ottoman Empire. These students had therefore seen various kinds of anticolonial movements, and attempts to form new geopolitical entities, conflicts that must have shaped their sense of political rights.

Students from impoverished circumstances came from western Europe as well, and from the Russian and British empires, where Roman Catholics formed minority populations. In their first year Tac and Amamix had classmates from Dalmatia, Scotland, Dublin, and Byelorussia, and even Charleston (South Carolina), Baltimore, and Cincinnati. Dalmatia, long part of the Venetian Republic, suffered the political and economic tensions common in other areas of Italy, and by 1815 it belonged to the Austro-Hungarian Empire. Scotland sent two students from poor families. The students from Dublin knew the civic strife of the movement for Irish Catholic independence from the Anglican United Kingdom. Byelorussia, with a long history of cultural nationalism, engaged in insurrection against Russia during the early nineteenth century.

Three native youths from the United States studied at the Collegium during these years along with Tac. The college's roster of students listed Patritius Lynch, a Cherokee (designated *Cheraw*) from the Carolinas, who enrolled in 1834. He began his studies in the first year of theology, an advanced course.[26] Iacobus MacCollion and Guilielmus Monfort, both from the Ohio Territory (Cincinnati), began their studies in 1832.[27] Long-established Jesuit missions existed among the indigenous and settler populations in the former French possessions of the Mississippi Valley and Great Lakes region. Indigenous-French trade relations initially structured the colonial economy, but violent conflicts and U.S. nation building brought migration into an area where many indigenous populations had predominated.[28]

China had sponsored Jesuit priests in its court for centuries, and two students came from China: Franciscus Leang, from Canton, began his studies in the more advanced class of rhetoric; Ioachimus Huo, from Huguang, studied advanced Latin.[29] Unlike the famous John Hu from Canton, who arrived in Europe with a Jesuit missionary in the 1720s but ended up in a French psychiatric hospital, these young men arrived prepared to be scholars and priests.[30]

Peyri reported that the Collegium welcomed the two Luiseños for be-

ing "from distant lands, indigenous and of legitimate birth, and well mannered," although this wording may have reflected Peyri's own concerns.[31] Tac and Amamix's fellow students, who like them came from minority populations in former empires and new nations, might have understood the limits of colonial perspectives more readily than Peyri, offering Tac a dialogue and a space to conceptualize his place as a Luiseño, and as an author, in Rome.

The students all had different levels of schooling, and most would return home as priests working among religious minorities in Islamic and Protestant societies. During their first year at the college, Tac and Amamix studied closely with nine students who also began their course work in Latin grammar, including young men from Baltimore, Bulgaria, Constantinople, Mesopotamia, Ireland, and Cypress.

Other students began with the more advanced classes of rhetoric, humanities, and philosophy. Tac later took those classes as well. Amamix studied Latin grammar in 1834 and 1835, but he fell ill and eventually was sent to convalesce in Tusculano, a monastery held by the order just outside Rome. Unfortunately, Agapito Amamix died on 26 September 1837, almost three years after enrolling in the college, and was buried in the subterranean crypt of the monastery church.[32] Although Tac had lost his companion, and his last contact with anyone who spoke Luiseño, he left no record of his response to this loss.

Tac continued to study Latin until 1838. By then literate in Latin, Spanish, and Luiseño, as well as fluent in vernacular Italian, he took yearlong courses in Latin on rhetoric (1838–39), humanities (1839–40), and philosophy (1840). On 2 February 1839 Tac made his first vows to join the priesthood. He survived a life-threatening fever but died in December 1841.

CARDINAL MEZZOFANTI'S ARCHIVE

As Tac studied, he wrote. He produced his manuscript for Cardinal Mezzofanti, the Vatican librarian and linguist who worked with Tac and other young men from around the world. In 1814 he began to work for the Vatican in Rome. In 1833 the pope appointed him custodian of the Vatican Library. He received the title of cardinal in 1838.[33] In Rome, he collected the writing of the students with whom he worked, and he also had assistants copy language fragments and manuscripts for his archive. Mezzofanti set up multilingual poetry readings with students and kept copies of poems in languages as diverse as English, Ethiopian, Russian, Swiss, and Tac's *californensis,* as Mezzofanti called Luiseño.[34]

Mezzofanti possessed "the mimetic faculty. The languages that he learned, he generally learned by the ear."[35] Excellent oral ability, pitch, and understanding of grammatical constructions enabled him to speak many languages, and he encouraged their expression and writing. Mezzofanti's knowledge of the various languages he archived differed in degree and depth. The fact that Tac wrote notes to Mezzofanti in Spanish and Latin suggests that those languages, rather than Luiseño, constituted their means of communication.[36] In collecting this material, Mezzofanti acted as an Enlightenment thinker and curator of colonial pasts. He supported the recording of unwritten languages, and he preserved fragments of the past that form part of the colonial archive of the church.

Mezzofanti's language files held grammars and dictionaries—often partial—as well as poetry and prayers in languages that included Chinese, Danish, Greek, French, English, Arabic, and Italian. He also had manuscripts in most of the world's languages, including Latin, Kichwa, Tagalog, Turkish, Valencian, and Persian, and a range of other materials, such as a copy of a dissertation about a Mexican codex belonging to the University of Bologna.[37]

Other indigenous languages from the Americas in Mezzofanti's collection include Algonguin, with a catechism in the language, sixty-two pages of grammatical notes in Algonquin and French, a thirty-two page grammar in Algonquin and Italian, and an eleven-page *Dictionnaire algonquin*.[38] The grammars and dictionary appear to have been copied by more than one person; the first-person narration and personal voice found in Tac's writing are absent.

A fourteen-page Aymara grammar from 1844, by contrast, could have been written by an Andean student. It presents carefully written Aymara grammar, mostly translated into Italian, with some pages translated into French.[39] But the Quechua grammar, like the majority of grammars, lacks the voice of a native speaker. It includes notes on Quechua translated mostly to French, and fourteen pages of a Quechua-Spanish dictionary.[40] More than one person contributed to the notes, which scribes copied from written sources. The archive also has files with words for God, the saints, and prayers in Luiseño and other American languages, or *lingue americane*.[41]

Tac's manuscript is unique among Mezzofanti's language files for its author's sustained personal relationship to the language he recorded and to the project of writing. While other students and aides to Mezzofanti had produced partial grammars and dictionaries, none offered anything near the length and depth of Tac's work. Nor did other language files in-

FIGURE 4. Each folio in Tac's manuscript is one of four sides of a larger, folded paper, numbered with a simple number on the front (recto folios) and a number plus "v" on the back (verso folios). The Vatican eagle is emblazoned in the thin paper.

clude a history, as Tac does. Tac's large file contains an exceptional array of material, including the grammar, historical and ethnographic writing, a dialogue, and a prayer (fig. 4).

KNOWLEDGE AND TRUTH

Tac wrote a statement to Mezzofanti that characterized his personal voice and revealed something about his intent and process of writing.

> I have taught Your Excellency all that I know about this language; and if something is missing, as I believe it is, which happens many times when one writes, at another time it can be finished. I would have liked to teach you more, but who can teach others what they don't know? So what I knew, I taught; what I didn't know, I've left out. It is better to be quiet than in speaking to tell lies.
>
> Now it is necessary to collect all the papers and once again begin to write the rules as we are able. (Fol. 96r; see fig. 5)

If Tac expressed doubt about the thoroughness of his rendition of Luiseño grammatical rules, which constituted a mode of analysis that he

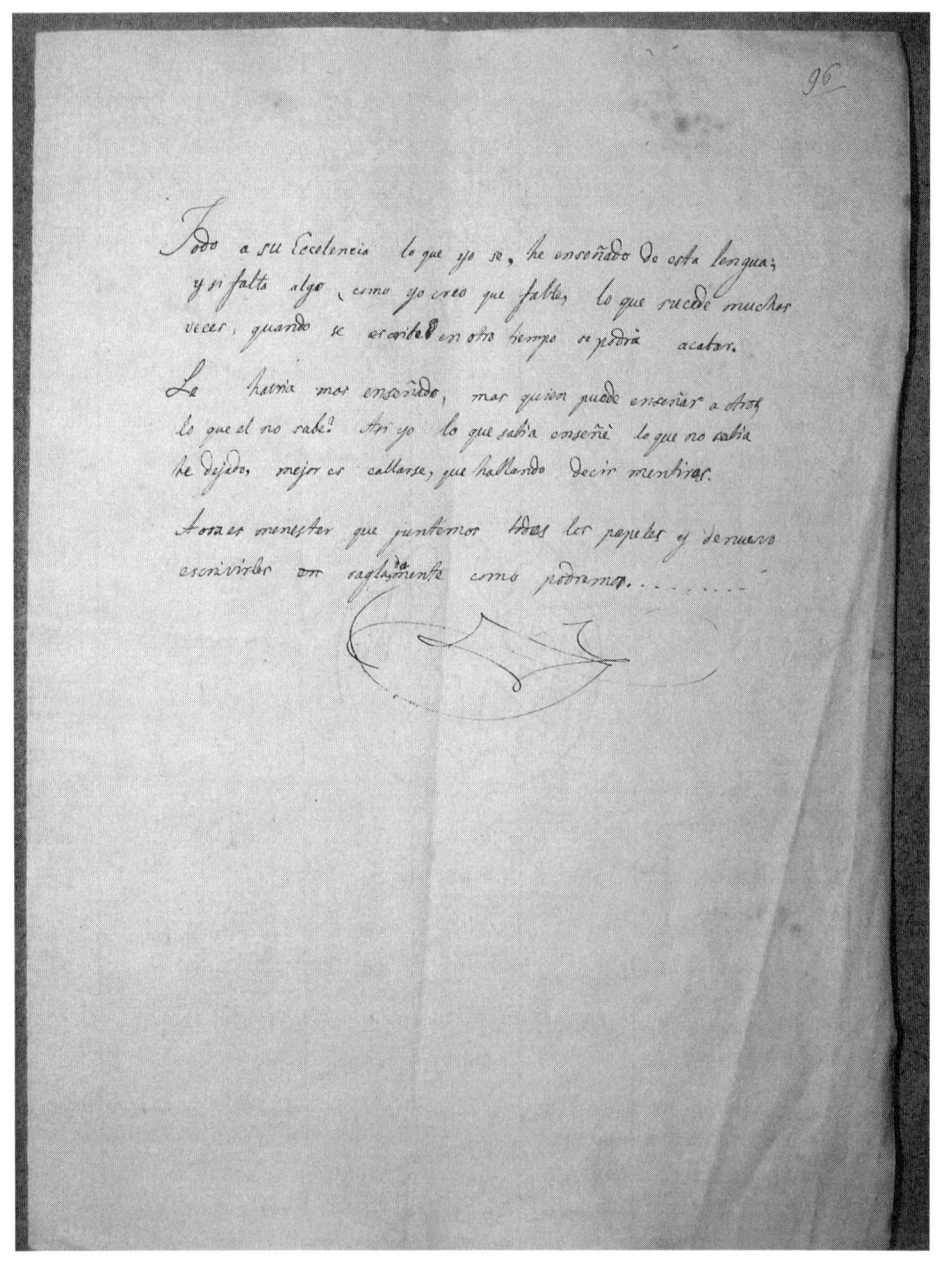

FIGURE 5. A note that Tac wrote to Cardinal Mezzofanti, occupying half a folio (fol. 96r).

learned in Rome, those hesitations did not extend to his presentation of history. Tac's note to Mezzofanti also has a playful element characteristic of his humor. After implying he has written everything he knows, he proceeds "to collect all the papers and once again begin to write the rules." The passage hints at the haphazard order in which he seems to have written the manuscript.[42]

Above all, Tac's paragraph above speaks to the way truths and lies remained a central concern to him. Baptized as an infant, Tac grew up in the new republic of Mexico, a nation that extended equality and citizenship to the indigenous majority. He lived through an extraordinary decade of political upheaval and change, as people tried to shift away from the colonial relations that often persisted long after Mexican independence. Tac witnessed the collapse of Spanish political dominance in California, the end of the Spanish Empire in Mexico, and the political chaos in Catalonia, Spain. He saw the contending claims for power that consumed new republics like Mexico. He watched as Luiseño elders made demands for the return of their land, claimed it as their own, and exercised their legal rights. Those experiences seem to have given Tac a radical sense of indigenous equality: a perspective that equality existed within (and despite) difference.[43]

His sense of equality within difference reveals a native politics, expressions of which existed in indigenous communities throughout the new Republic of Mexico. As indigenous ideas about equality and other rights took shape, they were often at odds with the definitions that became dominant. For the national elite, equality came to mean an expectation of sameness with regard to a certain type of citizen. This definition excluded women of all backgrounds and cast doubt on indigenous equality, given the difference that Indian scholars and politicians articulated. The Mexican nation began to discuss "the Indian question" as if those articulations of difference might somehow challenge indigenous qualifications for citizenship.[44]

In writing, Tac sought to situate himself beyond the deceptive representations of Luiseños that often came from the missionaries and from Mexican and military officials both before and after Mexico declared indigenous equality. Tac's history, for example, focuses on the knowledge, power, and skills held by Luiseño elders—characteristics that Peyri, at the mission since 1798, had failed to see in 1814. Peyri wrote that the natives "never had any men among them distinguished for wisdom or for letters." Surprisingly unable to comprehend the most elementary aspects of Luiseño thought, Peyri asserted that "as to the origins of these

Indians, we know nothing; nor is there any tradition in that regard among the Indians." Peyri relegated the dances and other rituals that indigenous people performed to "superstitious practices" that he called "infirmities, idolatries, and witchcraft." He confessed that he could "only manifest my ignorance regarding their practices. For they will not reveal more about these than they can help. Peyri lamented that although the missionaries tried to dissuade the Christian Indians of their beliefs and practices, "they always remain Indians."[45]

THE GRAMMAR AND DICTIONARY

Against the grain of this kind of colonial writing, Tac asserted the power held by Luiseño elders and newer authority figures who, as Tac did with writing, found ways to move between cultures and leave a record of their influence. In the first pages of his manuscript, Tac uses the Latin verb *flectere*, "to bend," to signify translation; this indicates how difficult his task would be (fol. 2r). Tac begins his grammar in Latin and Luiseño and ends it with an ethnographic sketch of California Indians in Latin. He uses the Latin diacritics established at the beginning of the manuscript, where he writes out the Luiseño alphabet (fols. 1r, 3r, and 19r), as well as Spanish phonetics and orthography with some influence of Italian, to produce Luiseño sounds in writing. His use of diacritics and his spelling of certain Luiseño and Spanish words is, however, inconsistent. The inconsistency is especially notable is the dictionary, where Tac writes Luiseño with Spanish diacritics instead of the Latin ones used in the grammar.

Latin proved too far a stretch from Luiseño, and Spanish predominates over Latin in the manuscript. The history, interspersed in the grammar, is written solely in Spanish, Tac's second language. Of course, Tac's nineteenth-century Spanish differs from contemporary Spanish, and Luiseño is no longer written as he wrote it either. Tac's is the only grammar and dictionary that translates between Spanish and Luiseño; subsequent works translate between English and Luiseño.

It is important to consider Tac's Spanish-Luiseño grammar and dictionary in the context of the role of grammar in the formation of empires, new nations, and tribal sovereignty. The construction of a Spanish grammar proved crucial for the Spanish Empire to unite itself as an administrative and cultural unit. At the same time, as words, people, and goods traveled back to Europe, Spanish took on borrowings from Nahuatl and other indigenous and Caribbean languages. The writing of indigenous

grammars also sustained the empire as it created a native lingua franca. Nahuatl and Otomi become standard indigenous languages throughout Mexico.[46] The clergy studied them and spread their use. On the one hand, native scholars formed part of the cast of scribes and translators involved in the creation of the empire through the written word. On the other, without a written grammar, indigenous societies remained less able to document their histories and claim their legal rights.

Tac records the translations made before his birth, when his elders first began to render Luiseño and Spanish mutually intelligible, translating the prayers and catechism into their native language, both orally and in writing. The imposition of Spanish and Catholicism produced vast changes in indigenous societies in California and the Americas, as well as seemingly irreparable losses to indigenous languages.[47] Yet many scholars emphasize the influence indigenous translators had in representing their languages and defining the words that entered them. Writing about the first major evangelization in central Mexico after the conquest of Tenochtitlán in 1521, Louise Burkhart emphasizes the dialogue that took place between two cultures and systems of thought when Nahuatl scholars worked with Spanish missionaries to translate Christian doctrine. Because Nahuatl named a different set of objects and ideas than in Latin or Spanish, and did so in accordance with a particular ideology, translation gave Christian thought a new and distinct form.[48]

William Hanks has shown how Mayan translators and populations responded to Spanish, turning a language of domination around to make it speak to their interests and visions.[49] After studying missions in many areas of the world, Lamin Sanneh concluded that "mission is translation." Sanneh asserts that Christianity cannot escape the cultural framework of the people it seeks to convert, so that the religion assumes the features of the cultures under conversion.[50] Vincent Rafael has found that in the Philippines, Tagalog speakers used translation "less as a process of internalizing colonial-Christian conventions than of evading their totalizing grip by repeatedly marking the differences between their language and interests and those of the Spaniards." He concludes that it took two centuries for Tagalog conversion to coincide with, rather than simply circumvent, Spanish intentions.[51]

This process allowed the meaning of Spanish words to give way to native ideas and understandings, as is particularly evident in the dictionary words that Tac records relating to the world of the sacred. In his history Tac states in Spanish that Luiseños gave their allegiance to *Dios* (meaning God). But *Dios* is translated in his dictionary and written in the Luiseño

grammar as *Chanichñich,* a central figure in a set of indigenous ritual prac-tices and beliefs alive throughout Southern California during the colonial era and the nineteenth century.[52] (Note the distinct spellings of *Chanich-ñich* on fols. 2v, 24r, and 35v, for example, as Tac developed his Luiseño orthography.) Not only was *Dios* equated in translation with *Chanichñich,* but the thought and practices surrounding *Chanichñich* persisted along-side Catholicism and often imparted new meaning to it.

For the native population one of the means to power after Spanish set-tlement was dance, a practice through which the body produced knowl-edge, hope, and healing.[53] The dictionary illustrates how translators brought dance into the daily life of Luiseño Christians. The noun *cheiis* meant "the act of dressing" and also referred to the *cheiat,* a headpiece of precious feathers worn for important dances (fol. 126v). Wearing the clothing made at the mission and purchased through trade constituted a symbol of being Christian. Using the noun *cheiis* for the Christian prac-tice of dressing would have brought remembrance of dance ritual into the daily language at the missions. In the early twentieth century, Luiseño speakers again used the word *cheiis* only for dance regalia; it no longer referred to the general act of dressing.[54]

Tac's dictionary records many words related to dance. He defines the noun *aluiis* as "the act of looking up" (fol. 110r). Dancers looked up in Chanichñich dance. The dictionary records fourteen additional entries re-lated to *aluiis,* or looking up (fols. 110r, 110v). The word *caquis* meant mimicking the caw of the raven, a sacred bird in Luiseño religion con-nected to Chanichñich ritual. Dance, song, and other ceremonies required the voice of the raven. The many forms based on this word included "to order that one mimic the caw of a raven," "person who ordered [the caw of a raven] be mimicked," and "person who made the caw of a raven many times." Nine noun and verb forms existed for the practice (fols. 119r–v).

Frequent traces of the Luiseño sacred world appear in Tac's dictio-nary, where many words have a ceremonial meaning, even though Tac translates them with a simple Spanish equivalent.[55] *Assuot* refers to the golden eagle; Tac translates it as "eagle," leaving the sacred word un-written (fol. 112v). He translates *chàcajis* as "to cry," even though the word refers to deep sorrow expressed through ritualistic weeping (fol. 120v). Tac translates *chappiis* as "the act of rain stopping," words re-lated to ceremonial power rather than mere descriptions (fol. 121v). He translates *chuiis* as "to burn," but it refers to cremation of the dead, prac-ticed widely before the Christian era (fol. 136v). The Spanish replaced Luiseño cremation with Christian burials whenever possible.

FIGURE 6. Tac's drawing of an eagle dancer (fol. 105r; the dance is described on 106v).

Though the word *aś* refers both to domesticated animals and to the shaman's familiar, a supernatural figure that imparts knowledge and skills, Tac translates *aś* as "animal" (fol. 112r). Yet it is important to know that during the colonial period horses and cows—both introduced into the New World—became shaman's familiars, along with the native animals. The metamorphosis of domesticated animals associated with Spanish dominance into shamans' spirits suggests an appropriation of Spanish power.

Many words, such as *aś* and *chocorris,* had religious significance that could not be conveyed in Spanish. The word *chocorris,* "to make like a mountain or wooded hill," for example, had five related forms, including *chocorrimocuis,* which, extrapolating from similar entries in the dictionary, would mean "person who makes them act like a mountain or wooded hill" (fol. 134v). But Spanish culture had no equivalent practice, and Tac gave no translation for the related forms that he wrote in Luiseño. In rendering the meaning of words, Tac both revealed things and left silences.

Tac's remarkable Luiseño-Spanish dictionary illustrates the care with

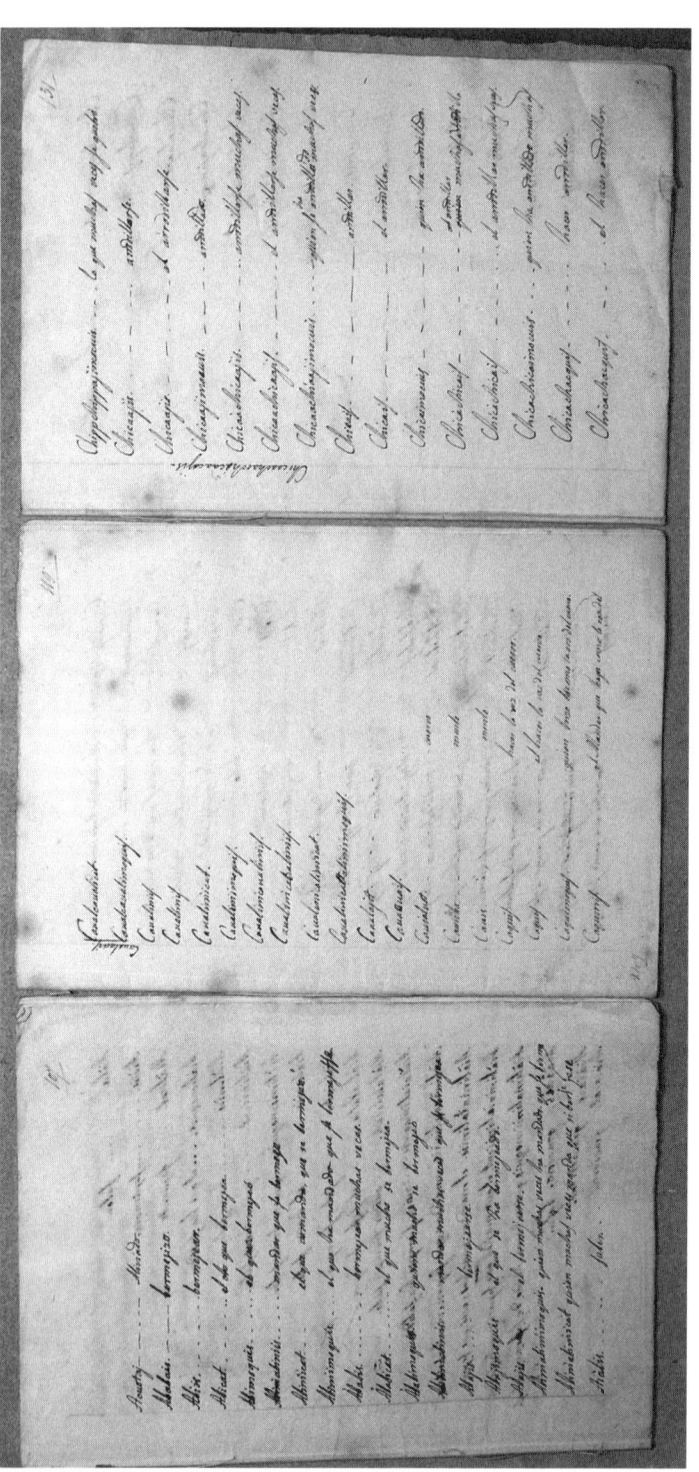

FIGURE 7. Tac's three dictionary booklets, each carefully held together by linen threaded through the pages on the left side.

which he selected entries and wrote them out. It consists of three discrete booklets, listing Luiseño words more or less alphabetically from *A* through *Cu* (fig. 7). He carefully bound each one with white linen on the left side. Each booklet contains about twenty-five pages (fols. 107r–142v). Luiseño words, in rough alphabetical order, run down the left side of the page. Tac meticulously drew dashed lines to the Spanish equivalents on the right. Tac listed approximately two thousand Luiseño words but left about one fifth of them untranslated. About two hundred separate words are translated, while the rest are either related to translated nouns and verbs or are not translated.

The dictionary also records the way Tac made Luiseño conform to Spanish. Luiseño has no infinitive. Verbs always relate to the person who conducts the action rather than to the action itself. Tac devised infinitives for each verb. He also provided multiple forms of usage. The number of ways that he represented a verb or noun suggests that some words and actions remained more prominent in his memory. These words may also have been frequently used during the 1820s.

Linguists and anthropologists have favorably evaluated Tac's dictionary and grammar. Sandra Chung writes that Tac's view of Luiseño "corresponds reasonably well with what we know from the later descriptions."[56] She notes that his writing also illustrates some grammatical rules and uses simplified or eliminated since Tac's time. Alfred Kroeber found Tac's "attention to grammatical details," and the information he supplies, to be in "substantial accord or exact identity" with subsequent grammars in the areas he covered.[57]

These comments confirm the accuracy that Tac achieved, but his grammar and dictionary have wider purposes for readers today. They speak to the ethnohistory of Luiseño society under Spanish domination and to the equality Tac established when moving between different linguistic systems. His explanations for the differences between Spanish and Luiseño illustrate two distinct ways of understanding and relating to society, politics, and culture. The elaboration of those differences suggests that Luiseños continued to organize themselves around particular relationships and practices despite Spanish colonialism.

WRITING HISTORY

I call the part of Tac's manuscript that is written in Spanish and titled "Conversion de los San Luiseños" a history of Luiseños under colonial rule, because history concerns questions of power.[58] Tac told a story about

his people's conversion that emphasized different forms of power that they held in the past and present, notwithstanding statements about the defeat of his ancestors by the Spanish. His historical narrative is circular and repetitive. It begins with the abbreviated title "Conversion of the Sanl," at the top of folio 59r , and an apparently truncated discussion of dance. Tac then turns to "The Ball Game" (fig. 8).

The overall form Tac uses to write the history defies Western linear thought. It may reflect the influence of a Luiseño narrative style by which histories are sung in stories that are repeated, with variations, in order to articulate concepts and precepts.[59] Tac presents an idea rarely found in missionary writing in California: that Luiseños retained forms of power through their leaders, and that they continued to possess their territories and produce the wealth of the mission. Those who held authority included the elected alcaldes who, by Spanish law, represented their respective indigenous constituents.[60] Traditional leaders who inherited their position by lineage and those who became leaders because of the knowledge and skills they had continued to hold power. Tac focuses on traditional leaders, including political and ritual leaders and the father and mother in their home, in his stories "On the Dance of the Indians" (fols. 104r–106v) and "What is Done Each Day" (fol. 66r). He focuses on traditional and new authority in the story "The Ball Game." Tac begins with the remark, "Now let us look at the games, that here serve the San Luiseños . . . and how well they serve us" (fol. 59r), implying that the games offer sustenance to individuals and the community that derived from indigenous culture. Tac also gives a detailed portrait of the mission, including the names of indigenous territories where the mission had fields and pastures. The stories he tells focus on the ordering of indigenous labor, daily life, ceremony, knowledge, and hierarchies at the mission among Luiseños and between Luiseños, Spaniards, and the missionary.

In the overarching history of conversion, the traditional authority of a central Luiseño leader forms the core of the story about the encounter between Spaniards and Luiseños. Tac emphasizes three times that the leader's friendship is what enabled the Spanish to settle (fols. 63r, 75r, 78r). In the third version of the story about "Conversion," Tac gives a traditional Spanish historical explanation for the settlement of Luiseño land, but he repeats his story of encounter thereafter (fols. 78r, 80r). Like other native scholars, Tac worked in dialogue with Spanish historical narrative, inserting his own history and place of origin.[61] Tac also portrays the relative loss of authority of the former political leaders. At the end of the history, he writes of the Luiseño leader who had been crucial to

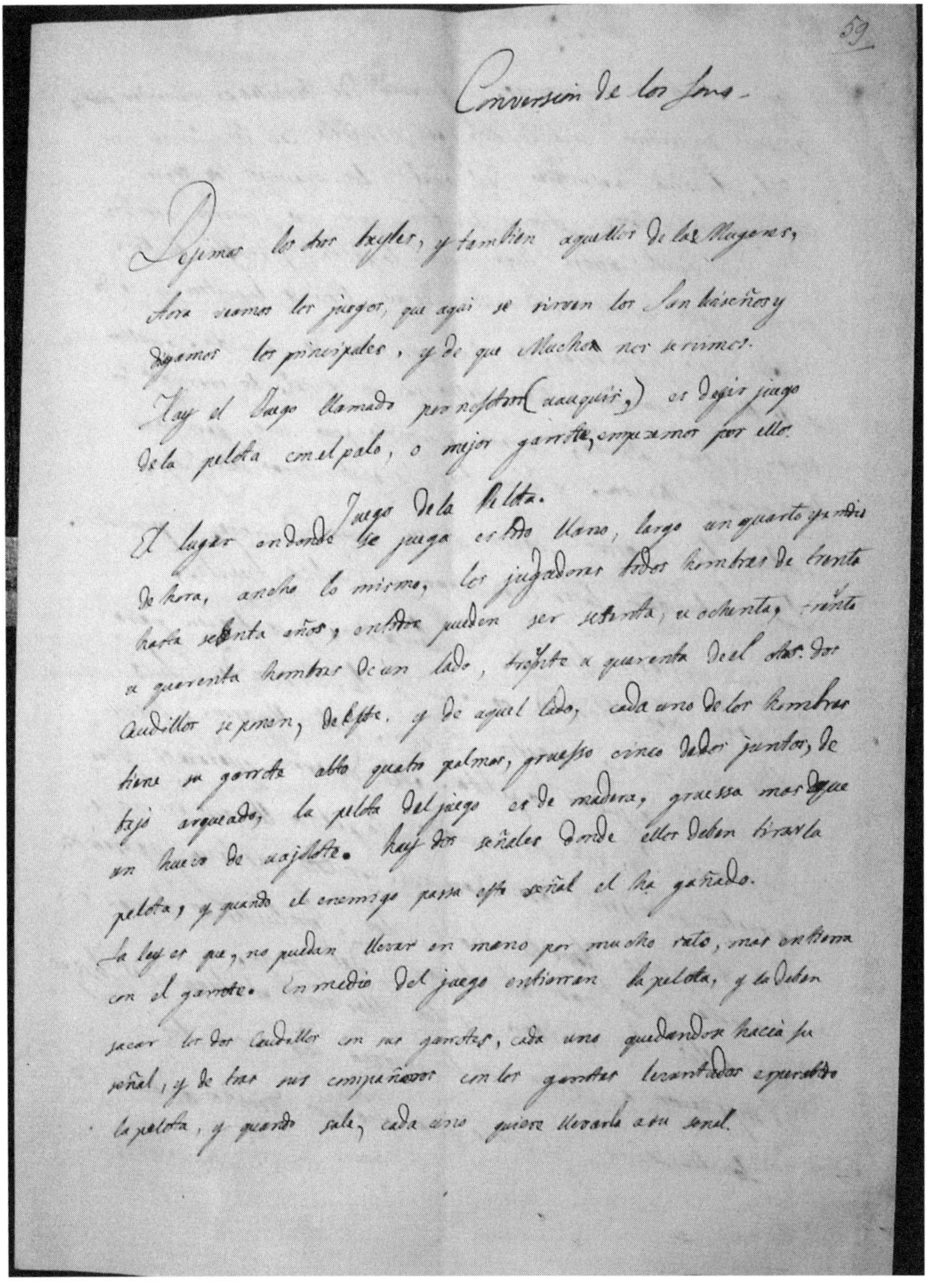

59

Conversion de los Sns-

Dejemos los dos bayles, y tambien aquellos de las Mugeres,
Ahora veamos los juegos, que aqui se sirven los San Luiseños y
digamos los principales, y de que Muchos nos servimos.
Hay el Juego llamado por nosotros (uauquis,) es decir juego
dela pelota con el palo, o mejor garrote, empezamos por ello.

Juego dela Pelota.

El lugar en donde se juega es todo llano, largo un quarto y medio
de hora, ancho lo mismo, los jugadores todos hombres de treinta
hasta setenta años, entodos pueden ser setenta, u ochenta, treinta
u quarenta hombres de un lado, treinta u quarenta de el otro. dos
caudillos se ponen, de este, y de aquel lado, cada uno de los hombres
tiene su garrote alto quatro palmos, gruesso cinco dedos juntos, de
bajo arqueado, la pelota del juego es de madera, gruessa mas que
un huevo de uajolote. hay dos señales donde ellos deben tirar la
pelota, y quando el enemigo passa esta señal el ha gañado.
La ley es que, no pueden llevar en mano por mucho rato, mas en tierra
con el garrote. En medio del juego entierran la pelota, y la deben
sacar los dos caudillos con sus garrotes, cada uno quedandose hacia su
señal, y de tras sus compañeros con los garrotes levantados esperando
la pelota, y quando sale, cada uno quiere llevarla a su señal.

FIGURE 8. The first folio of Tac's history, "Conversion of the San Luiseños," with a description of the ball game (fol. 59r).

Spanish settlement: "The Captain dressed like the Spaniards, still remaining a Captain but not ordering his people, as in older times." Instead, the alcaldes had assumed he position of intermediaries and conveyed the missionary's orders to the population (fol. 92v).

Tac's history, set in Quechla, includes the ball field, the locus of the dance, and an Indian home in the mission village. Such places seldom figured in other documents written during the era and never took precedence as significant spaces.[62] In these spaces Tac shows that native authority presided, and people found access to formal power, emotional sustenance, and indigenous ways of relating. Tac's events focus on indigenous people, rarely on Spaniards, unlike Western histories, in which Indian-Spanish relations are often foregrounded. Tac works with his own categories in introducing these spaces. Like other indigenous writers, he offered categories of analysis specific to the concerns of his history and language.

Tac writes about dance a number of times (fols. 59r, 61r, 61v, 104r–106v; see fig. 9).[63] His sections on dance celebrate the ritual authority and knowledge of village singers and other village elders. Dance offered an ongoing way for indigenous populations at the missions to continue to access power despite the political losses they suffered to the Spaniards. Fray Gerónimo Boscana of Mission San Juan Capistrano, just north of Mission San Luis Rey, similarly emphasized the constant presence of dance. He wrote of dances that lasted for days on end. "Hardly a day passed without some portion of it being devoted to this insipid and monotonous ceremony," Boscana wrote. "As on all the feast days of the Indians, dancing was the principal ceremony."[64] Like Peyri, his contemporary at Mission San Luis Rey, Boscana wrote of dance taking place for every conceivable reason, including the attempt to rectify existing conditions through its spiritual and political uses.

Tac writes of three specific dances, two of them for men only and one with older men and women. He notes that women had their own dances but does not elaborate on them, because they are outside his realm of experience and field of knowledge. Within the tradition that Tac knew from indigenous California, dance produced knowledge and could regenerate power. The figure Chanichñich had given Luiseños and Juaneños some of the most important dances performed during the colonial and Mexican eras. Chanichñich conveyed the laws and established rites and ceremonies for the preservation of life through dance.[65] In a broader sense, dance rendered the spiritual world into corporal existence.

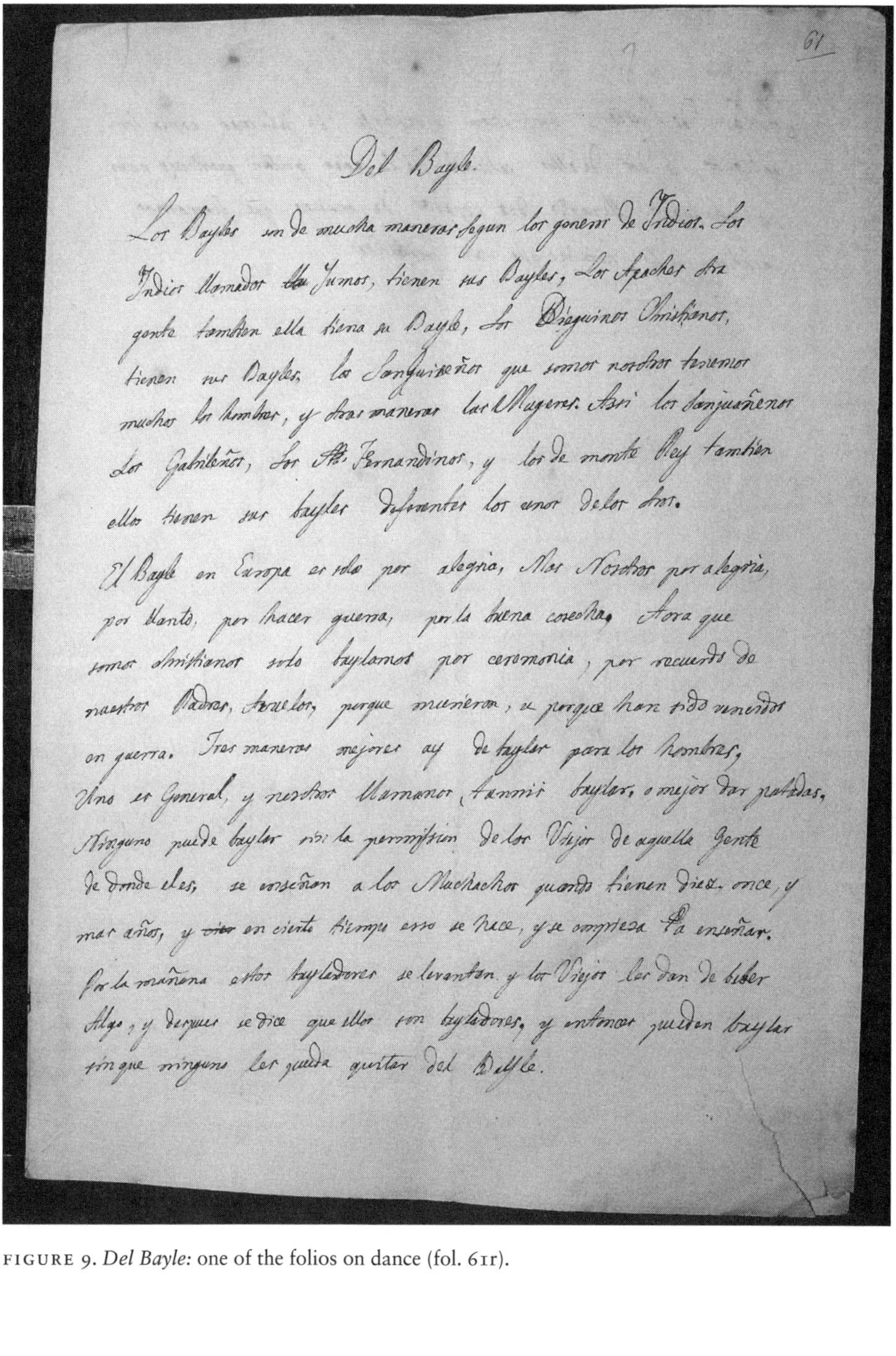

Del Bayle.

Los Bayles son de mucha maneras segun los genero de Indios. Los Indios llamados tha Yumos, tienen sus Bayles, Los Apaches esta gente tambien ella tiene su Bayle, Los Dieguinos Christianos, tienen sus Bayles, los Sanjuiseños que como nosotros tenemos muchos los hombres, y otras maneras las Mugeres. Asi los Sanjuaneños los Gabileños, los S.n Fernandinos, y los de monte Rey tambien ellos tienen sus bayles diferentes los unos delos otros.

El Bayle en Europa es ido por alegria, Mas Nosotros por alegria, por llanto, por hacer guerra, por la buena cosecha, Aora que somos Christianos solo baylamos por ceremonia, por recuerdo de nuestros Padres, Abuelos, porque murieron, o porque han sido vencidos en guerra. Tres maneras mejores ay de bayler para los hombres, Uno es General, y nosotros llamanos tannir baylar, o mejor dar patadas. Ninguno puede bayler sin la permision de los Viejos de aquella gente de donde eles; se enseñan a los Muchachos quando tienen diez, once, y mas años, y en cierto tiempo esso se hace, y se empieza la enseñar. Por la mañana estos bayladores se levantan, y los Viejos les dan de beber Algo, y despues se dice que ellos son bayladores, y entonces pueden bayler sin que ninguno les pueda quitar del Baile.

FIGURE 9. *Del Bayle:* one of the folios on dance (fol. 61r).

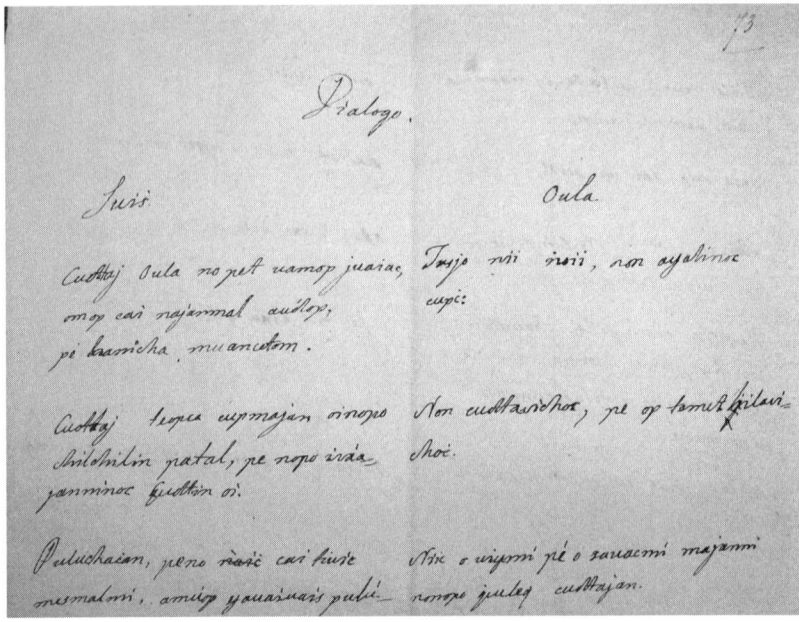

FIGURE 10. The opening of the dialogue between rabbit and blood, in Luiseño (fol. 73r).

Tac's historical imagination embraces forms of relating to the world through the transmutation of people and things, and the animation of the natural and animal worlds. Tac relates a dialogue between a rabbit and blood, in which the two go hunting (figs. 10 and 11). The rabbit refers to his own changeable state: "I am a rabbit, my name is, but I am not a true rabbit" (fol. 74r). Both blood and rabbit have human qualities, logic, and lifeways. Tac's ways of perceiving history rely on non-Western assumptions about reality.

Tac suggests he is not an expert when writing an ethnographic sketch about California Indians for Mezzofanti in Latin (fols. 152r–153v). His sketch describes eight different groups of people, including those from missions San Fernando, San Diego, San Luis Rey, San Juan Capistrano, San Gabriel, and Santa Barbara. He also comments on the Apaches and Yuma. Tac emphasizes that his knowledge is based on opinion; his remarks reflect common ideas about Apaches in Mexico during his era. Tac wrote to Mezzofanti:

> Your Eminence, I have put forth an individual opinion on the characteristics of the Californians, down to language differences (insofar as it seemed to me to be true). If some expert will perhaps deny it to be true, whether by adding

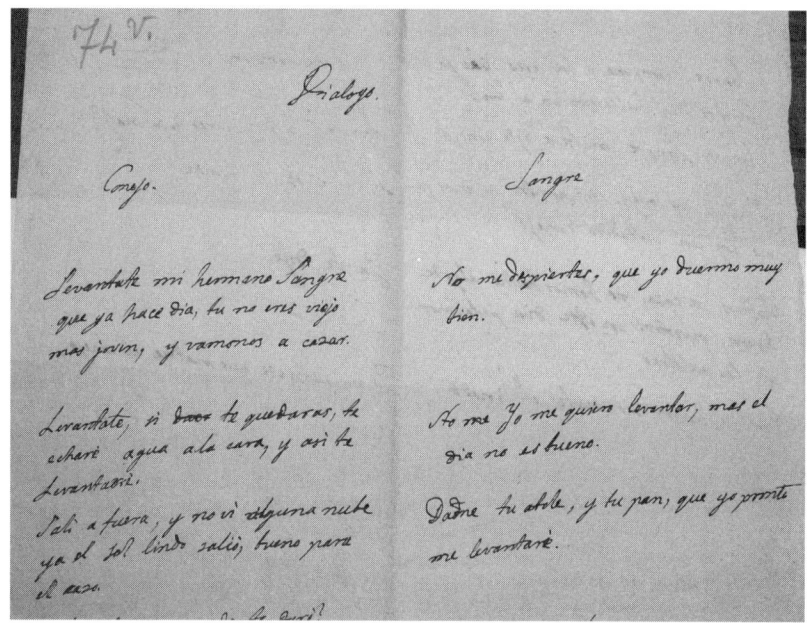

FIGURE 11. The opening of the dialogue between rabbit and blood, in Spanish (fol. 74v).

or subtracting as much as seems to him wrong, I regret it and shall accede to their claim, go by whatever is said, and change my opinion. (Fol. 152v)

Still interested in truth, as in his previously quoted statement to Mezzofanti about writing, Tac seems to be resisting the kinds of information Mezzofanti wanted. He appears reluctant to engage in the production of knowledge that requires assumptions about culture and facts that Tac did not possess.

Tac's writing conforms to many of the qualities found in other indigenous sources. James Lockhart and other historians working with Nahuatl documents argue that indigenous writing prioritized different categories, events, and places.[66] The idea of Spanish conquest, for example, is virtually absent in native records, and it does not appear as "conquest" in Tac's narrative. Indeed, he implies more than once that the Spaniards were lucky the Indians allowed them to stay. Rather than describe communities living in fear or overwhelmed by the violence of Spanish intervention and settlement, indigenous writers and oral historians emphasized, as Stephanie Wood has found, "pride in their own leadership and ancestry . . . the moments in history that strengthened their com-

munities and autonomy, that pointed to their own heroism and even their own conquests."[67]

The narrative structure of native histories generally differs from that of Western history. Native histories are usually "encoded in physical space," such as the social geography of indigenous places that Tac establishes.[68] Indigenous writers speak of intertribal relations and emphasize the rise of new political authority within their communities. They often relate the past through myth and ritual, condense time frames, and conflate time and space. Tac's writing shares these qualities.

Along with leadership and local knowledge, land rights are a frequent subject of indigenous colonial documents. Tac repeatedly spoke of Quechla, the mission settlement, as his ancestral land. In colonial Mexico indigenous scribes documented their communities' titles to ancestral land in *títulos primordiales*. The *títulos* recorded the land rights those communities held in former and new towns after the native population recovery began in the 1650s. Written in indigenous languages and primarily for native communities, these accounts were effectively municipal histories, presenting indigenous towns deeply engaged in the service of their patron saints that had been adopted after the Spanish invasion. Yet the *títulos* and other native documents minimized the effects of Spanish settlement, instead describing unbroken pasts.[69]

TO CONCLUDE

Pablo Tac's writing offers a sense of the "ongoing production of Indian histories" that Phillip Deloria and others discuss as taking place in native communities.[70] Tac conveys the oral histories of his youth and knowledge of his culture through his narratives and discussion of language. Other indigenous writers from across the Americas have likewise presented the critical discourse, theory, and concepts to define native experience, but Tac's record has no parallel in California history.[71]

Unfortunately, Tac never returned home to his tribe; he died of a virus in Rome on 13 December 1841. The death registry lists his place of origin as "Californiensis (Mexicanus) ex Missione St. Ludovici Regis."[72] Recall that when he entered the college in 1834, the registrar marked his origins as *Cheegnajuisci*, a word for his tribal land where the mission settled. By 1841, the mission had been secularized and made the property of the Mexican state, and the Luiseño place name had been erased from the official record in Mexico and in Rome. Whereas the Luiseño place reference *Cheegnajuisci* left a trace of the precolonial and

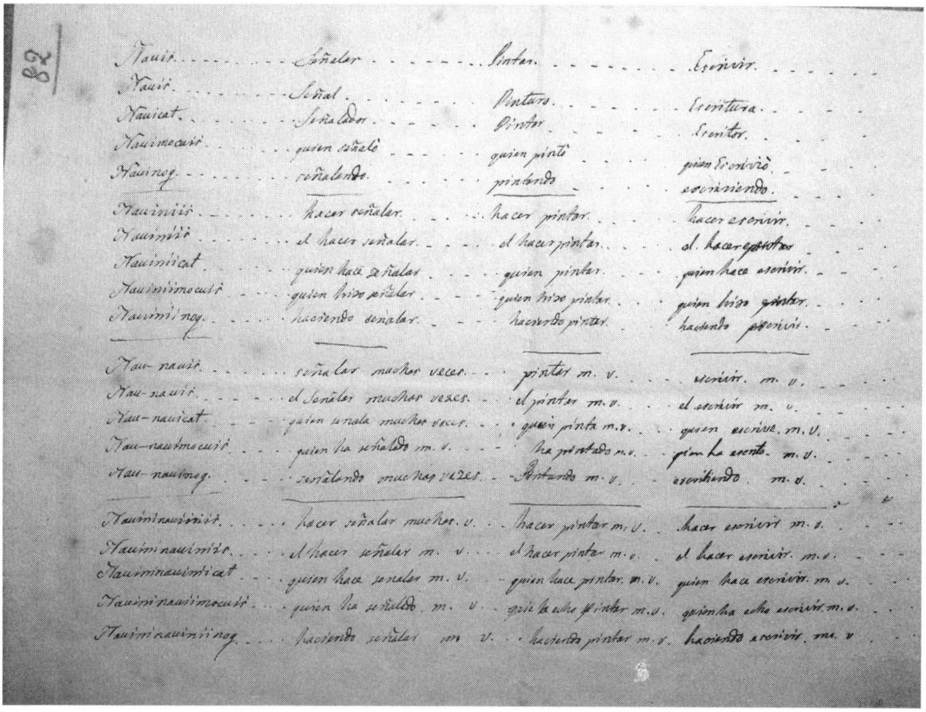
82

Nauiŝ	Señalar	Pintar	Escribir
Nauiŝ	Señal	Pintura	Escritura
Nauicat	Señalador	Pintor	Escritor
Nauimocuiŝ	quien señalò	quien pintò	quien escribiò
Nauinoq	señalando	pintando	escribiendo
Nauiniiŝ	hacer señalar	hacer pintar	hacer escribir
Nauiniiŝ	el hacer señalar	el hacer pintar	el hacer escribir
Nauiniicat	quien hace señalar	quien pintar	quien hace escribir
Nauiniimocuiŝ	quien hizo señalar	quien hizo pintar	quien hizo escribir
Nauiniinoq	haciendo señalar	haciendo pintar	haciendo escribir
Nau-nauiŝ	señalar muchas veces	pintar m. v.	escribir. m. v.
Nau-nauiŝ	el señalar muchas veces	el pintar m. v.	el escribir m. v.
Nau-nauicat	quien señala muchas veces	quien pinta m. v.	quien escribe m. v.
Nau-naumocuiŝ	quien ha señalado m. v.	ha pintado m. v.	quien ha escrito m. v.
Nau-naunoq	señalando muchas veces	pintando m. v.	escribiendo m. v.
Nauininauiniiŝ	hacer señalar muchas v.	hacer pintar m. v.	hacer escribir m. v.
Nauininauiniiŝ	el hacer señalar m. v.	el hacer pintar m. v.	el hacer escribir m. v.
Nauininauiniicat	quien hace señalar m. v.	quien hace pintar m. v.	quien hace escribir m. v.
Nauininauiimocuiŝ	quien ha señalado m. v.	quien ha echo pintar m. v.	quien ha echo escribir m. v.
Nauininauiniinoq	haciendo señalar m. v.	haciendo pintar m. v.	haciendo escribir m. v.

FIGURE 12. A folio in Tac's grammar giving Spanish translations of the Luiseño word *nauiŝ* and related terms (fol. 82r).

contemporary world of the 1820s and early 1830s in which Tac grew up, *Californiensis* does not. Further erasures of things native, and of indigenous pasts, occurred during the era of nation building. Moreover, Tac's death follows an all-too-common pattern among native scholars, diplomats, and translators who traveled to Europe: many died there, and their bodies never returned home. Although Tac is buried in Rome, his unique contribution remains because he took up the mandate of *nauiŝ*. *Nauiŝ* is a Luiseño verb that translates to Spanish as *señalar* (to sign, mark), *pintar* (to paint), and *escribir* (to write) (fol. 82r; fig. 12). Each of those three verbs had long histories in Western traditions, but in Luiseño culture, European painting and writing were introduced to signal new things. Luiseños painted in the precolonial era for other purposes. To signal change, they gathered, stored and passed knowledge through sand and rock painting, through oral formulaic patterns of storytelling, and through dance and healing ceremonies. Writing Luiseño gave Tac the ability to leave a sign about these Luiseños' cultural pro-

ductions, concepts, and language at a time when his homeland seemed to be receding from him.

Tac wrote during an era when other indigenous scholars were likewise putting their oral languages into writing.[73] The Cherokee scholar Sequoyah developed a Cherokee writing system in 1808, which the Cherokee nation adopted in 1821. Many Cherokees wrote to defend their land and political autonomy and to stop their forced removal from the South during the 1830s.[74] Under very different circumstances, prominent Hawaiian cultural figures—teachers of dance, song, and memory traditions who wrote down their languages for Hawaiian royalty in the nineteenth century—became some of the foremost translators of the Bible. Since they were among the most knowledgeable about their own societies, they often moved most easily between worlds.

Because of the importance of literacy in contemporary life, indigenous scholars continue to write down their languages today, but they and nonnative scholars now give new answers to the questions about how to write, standardize, and represent the languages visually.[75] Contemporary Luiseño is written to conform to the mandates and thought processes embodied in the language itself. In contemporary Luiseño the word *ahíichu* (Tac's *ahicho*) still refers to an orphan or abandoned child, but it also defines abandonment and loneliness, described in one dictionary through examples from the song *Nótma pí 'ahíichumay tamáawumal* (literally, "my mouth is lonely," meaning "I have no one to talk to").[76] These new definitions and spellings point out the vast differences in the worlds out of which written Luiseño emerged. In Tac's nineteenth-century writing, words have Latin and Spanish linguistic frameworks and reflect other colonial restraints. Contemporary Luiseño, in contrast, is spelled and conceptualized for writing and translation in a format that reflects Luiseño linguistic logic and current social norms.

The current language, which is being studied widely by Luiseños today, conforms to the sounds and visual signs chosen for Luiseño rather than ones used in English.[77] Contemporary Luiseño stands outside and apart from a colonial framework. Current Luiseño-English dictionaries and grammars refuse the structure and assumptions of the Western dictionary.[78] The written language, as well as its translation, is built around Luiseño concepts, linguistic practices, and historical speech.

The contemporary language seeks to avoid "bending" the words and sounds as Tac had to when he wrote. A simple example shows how Tac's word *ajajot* (109r), defined as Spanish *sabroso,* changed in form but per-

sisted in the language to describe delicious things. The contemporary equivalent word is written '*áx'aa-t,* meaning "fine (of food), yummy," and '*áx'axwut,* "delicious." An older pronunciation of this modern word is '*áx'aat,* approximating the sound of Tac's word.[79] Tac's work thus speaks to the present, as well as to the past.

NOTES

1. Prose Lingua Californese, "Studi grammaticali sulla lingua della California," n.d., Fondo Speciale Giuseppe Mezzofanti, cartone III, fascicolo 1, Biblioteca comunale dell'Archiginnasio, Bologna (hereafter BCAB).

2. For linguistic studies and dictionaries of Luiseño, see A. L. Kroeber, *Notes on Shoshonean Dialects of Southern California* (Berkeley: The University Press, 1909); P. S. Sparkman, *Culture of the Luiseño Indians* (Berkeley: The University Press, 1908), 187–234; William Bright, ed., *A Luiseño Dictionary* (Berkeley: University of California Press, 1968); Villiana Hyde, *An Introduction to the Luiseño Language* (Banning, CA: Malki Museum Press, 1971); and Villiana Calac Hyde and Eric Elliott, *Yumáyk yumáyk = Long Ago* (Berkeley: University of California Press, 1994).

3. Tagliavini edited the history portion of the manuscript substantially, which he then published as Carlo Tagliavini, "L'Evangelizzazione e i costumi degli Indi Luiseños secondo la narrazione di un chierico indigeno," *Proceedings of the Twenty-third International Congress of Americanists, 1928* (Lancaster, PA: Science Press, 1930), 633–48. He edited and published the grammar as *La lingua degli Indi luiseños (Alta California) secondo gli appunti grammaticali inediti di un chierico indigeno,* Biblioteca dell'Archiginnasio, ser. 2, no. 31 (Bologna, 1926). The dictionary he published under the title "Frammento d'un dizionarietto Luiseño-Spagnuolo scritto da un indigeno," *Proceedings of the Twenty-third International Congress of Americanists,* 905–17. See also Carlo Tagliavini, *Scritti minori* (Bologna: Pàtron Editore, 1982), a compendium of all Tagliavini's publications, celebrating fifty years of his work.

4. A. L. Kroeber and G. W. Grace, *The Sparkman Grammar of Luiseño,* University of California Publications in Linguistics 16 (Berkeley: University of California Press, 1960), 177.

5. See Randall Milliken, *A Time of Little Choice: The Disintegration of Tribal Culture in the San Francisco Bay Area, 1769–1810* (Menlo Park, CA: Ballena Press, 1995). Millikin uses the term "a time of little choice" to identify the effect of Spanish colonization on tribal society. Steven Hackel similarly traces that process in Monterey, California, in his *Children of Coyote, Missionaries of Saint Francis: Indian-Spanish Relations in Colonial California, 1769–1850* (Chapel Hill: University of North Carolina Press, 2005).

6. John Johnson found more than a hundred places of origin listed in the San Luis Rey Mission census, but the core population came from twenty-seven settlements. See his *Descendants of Native Communities in the Vicinity of Ma-*

rine Corps Base Camp Pendleton: An Ethnohistoric Study of Luiseño and Juaneño Cultural Affiliation—Final Report (Camp Pendleton: U.S. Marine Corps, 2001), 6.

7. Fray Lasuén to Don Diego de Borica, 20 June 1798, in Donald Cutter, ed., *The Writings of Mariano Payeras* (Santa Barbara, CA: Bellerpohon Books, 1995), 2:86–87.

8. Fray Zephyrin Engelhardt, *San Luis Rey Mission* (San Francisco: James H. Barry Company, 1921), 16.

9. Fray Lasuén to Fray Pedro Lull, 4 September 1798, in Cutter, *Writings,* 2:92.

10. Fray Lasuén to Don Diego de Borica, 20 June 1798, in Cutter, *Writings,* 2:87.

11. Fray Gerónimo Boscana wrote the only contemporaneous study of indigenous society during the colonial and Mexican periods in California, apart from Pablo Tac's work. In it, Boscana attempts to explain the history and beliefs surrounding Chinigchinich. See *Chinigchinich: A Revised and Annotated Version of Alfred Robinson's Translation of Father Gerónimo Boscana's Historical Account of the Belief, Usages, Customs, and Extravagancies of the Indians of This Mission of San Juan Capistrano Called the Acagchemem Tribe,* ed. John P. Harrington (Banning, CA: Malki Museum Press, 2005).

12. Mission San Luis Rey's baptismal and death registries are lost, but two *padrones* (or censuses) exist. This material is from Padrón I, Mission San Luis Rey, 1816. See Johnson, *Descendants,* 11.

13. Each received a number when registered for baptism: nos. 3340, 3896, 4738, 5003, 5196, and 5460, respectively.

14. Padrón I, Mission San Luis Rey, 1816.

15. All from Padrón II, Mission San Luis Rey, 1836.

16. 19 November 1822, Mission San Carlos Fray Mariano Payeras complied the list. Cutter, *Writings,* 337–38.

17. Fray Antonio Peyri to Superior Guvierno de este Territorio, 23 December 1827, Mission San Luis Rey, Santa Barbara Mission Archive.

18. Pilar Gonzalbo Aizpuru, *Educación y colonización en la Nueva España, 1531–1821* (Mexico City: Universidad Pedagógica Nacional, 2001); Gómez Canedo Lino, *La Educación de los marginados durante la época colonial: Escuelas y colegios para indios y mestizos en la Nueva España* (Mexico City: Porrúa, 1982).

19. *Mestizo* generally referred to Indian-Spanish descent, while *casta* implied some African descent. Neither category was fixed in meaning; both could differ by place and change over time. See María Elena Martínez, *Genealogical Fictions: Limpieza de Sangre, Religion, and Gender in Colonial Mexico* (Stanford, CA: Stanford University Press, 2008), and Ilona Katzew, *Casta Painting: Images of Race in Eighteenth-Century Mexico* (New Haven, CT: Yale University Press, 2004). See also William B. Taylor, *Magistrates of the Sacred: Priests and Parishioners in Eighteenth-Century Mexico* (Stanford: Stanford University Press, 1996), 87, 568n80.

20. Taylor, *Magistrates,* 96 and 573n125.

21. Margaret Chowning, for example, mentions one convent for Indian women

in Valladolid. See Chowning, *Rebellious Nuns: The Troubled History of a Mexican Convent, 1752–1863* (New York: Oxford University Press, 2006), 29, 57n37.

22. By the late eighteenth century the Crown insisted on the education of all Indian youth in Spanish and other subjects, but parishes and missions often lacked the funds to offer sustained schooling.

23. Letter from Antonio Peyri to Don Estevan Anderson, 16 April 1836, Vallejo Collection, C-B 3:1, Bancroft Library, University of California, Berkeley. The council of Mexico inquired about Tac, who left Mexico at the age of thirteen of fourteen, with the destination of the Collegium. Letter from Sig. Stagno. Torreno, Barcelona, to Sig. Torlonia, Rome, 31 January 1853, Collection MPRF 57, Propaganda Fide, Archives of the University of Notre Dame.

24. They were listed among 111 students at the Collegii in the *Catalogus Alumnorum Collegii Urbani, qui ab anno MDCCCXIX ad annum MDCCCXXXVII* (Rome: Collegii Urbani, 1837), Archive of the Collegium of Propaganda Fide, Rome (hereafter CPF). "Tac Paulus" appears on p. 6 and "Amomix Agapitus" on p. 22.

25. See Karl Kottman, "Pablo Tac's Vocal Remembrance of 'Californian,' " *California Mission Studies Association Boletín* 22, no. 2 (2005).

26. Entries in the *Catalogus Alumnorum,* CPF.

27. A letter introduced them as young Indian men. 15 May 1832, *Scriture riferite nei Congressi, America Centrale dal Canada all'Istmo di Panama,* 10 (1829–32):729–30, Czneirrató, CPF.

28. French priests still dominated the diocese in most areas of the Ohio Territory during the 1830s. See *Scritture riferite nei Congressi, America Centrale dal Canada all'Istmo di Panama*12 (1837–40): 323, CPF.

29. Entries in the *Catalogus Alumnorum,* CPF.

30. See Jonathan D. Spence, *The Question of Hu* (New York: Alfred Knopf, 1988). John Hu, though wise in his ability to strategize his own survival, had lacked the background and support to undertake scholarship.

31. Letter from Peyri to Anderson, 16 April 1836.

32. Engelhardt, *San Luis Rey,* 86. See the notice of Amamix's illness in *Catalogus Alumnorum,* 22, CPF.

33. K. Stolz (handwritten in pencil on the title page), *Biografia del Cardinale Giuseppe Mezzofanti, Bolognese* (Bologna: Tipografia Governativa Alla Volpe, 1850).

34. Index for the Fondo Speciale Manoscritti Mezzofanti, BCAB.

35. Thomas Watts, "On Dr. Russell's *Life of Cardinal Mezzofanti,*" *Transactions of the Philological Society, 1859* (Berlin: Asher and Co., 1860), 243.

36. C. W. Russell, *The Life of Cardinal Mezzofanti* (London: Longman, Brown and Co., 1858), suggests that Mezzofanti actually knew all those languages—for which no evidence exists. See also Nicholas Wiseman, *Recollections of the Last Four Popes and of Rome in their Times* (New York: Joseph F. Wagner, n.d. [c. 1850s]).

37. *Catalogo della Libreria dell'Eminentissimo Cardinale Giuseppe Mezzofanti—compilato per ordine di lingue da Fillippo Bonifazj* (Rome: Tipografia dei Fratelli Pallotta, 1851), and Lingua messicana, Fondo Speciale Giuseppe Mezzofanti, cartone IV, fascicolo 2, BCAB.

38. "Lingua Algonchina," Manoscritti Mezzofanti, cartone II, fascicolo 14, BCAB.

39. "Lingua Amhara. Savori in prosa. Studi grammaticali," Manoscritti Mezzofanti, cartone II, fascicolo 15, BCAB.

40. "Lingua Kichua," Manoscritti Mezzofanti, cartone IV, fascicolo 1, BCAB.

41. "Il Pater noster, l'Ave Maria ed il credo in più di 30 lingue dell'America Meridionale," "Varia" Green Notebook, Fondo Speciale Giuseppe Mezzofanti, cartone VII, fascicolo misc. 1, BCAB. The prayers in Luiseño are in the last folder, no. 9.

42. When Mezzofanti's archive arrived at the Biblioteca comunale dell'Archiginnasio in Bologna, the archivists numbered the pages in the order found. This volume follows the archival order.

43. This is a key subject in my book *Saints and Citizens: Indigenous Histories of Colonial Missions and Mexican California* (forthcoming from University of California Press).

44. See Manuel Ferrer Muñoz and María Bono López, eds., *Pueblos indígenas y estado nacional en México,* (Mexico City: Universidad Nacional Autónoma de México, 1998).

45. Frayes Antonio Peyri y Francisco Suñer, "Preguntas y respuestas," 12 December1814; Santa Barbara Mission Archive.

46. See David Rojinsky, Companion to Empire: A Genealogy of the Written Word in Spain and New Spain, c. 550–1550 (Amsterdam: Rodopi, 2002).

47. José Rabasa, *Writing Violence on the Northern Frontier* (Durham: Duke University Press, 2000).

48. Louise Burkhart, *The Slippery Earth: Nahua-Christian Moral Dialogue in Sixteenth-Century Mexico* (Tucson: University of Arizona Press, 1989.)

49. William F. Hanks, *Converting Words: Maya in the Age of the Cross* (Berkeley: University of California Press, 2010).

50. Lamin Sanneh and Joel A. Carpenter, eds., *The Changing Face of Christianity: Africa, the West, and the World* (New York: Oxford University Press, 2005); and Lamin Sanneh, *Translating the Message: The Missionary Impact on Culture* (Maryknoll, NY: Orbis Books, 1989), 93.

51. Vincent Rafael, Contracting Colonialism: Translation and Christian Conversion in Tagalog Society under Early Spanish Rule (Ithaca, NY: Cornell University Press, 1988), 211.

52. Boscana, *Chinigchinich,* xv.

53. See Lisbeth Haas, " 'Raise your sword and I will eat you': Luiseño Scholar Pablo Tac, ca. 1841," in *Alta California: Peoples in Motion, Identities in Formation, 1769–1850,* ed. Steven W. Hackel (Berkeley: University of California Press, 2010), 79–110.

54. See Eric Elliott, "Dictionary of Rincón Luiseño" (PhD diss., University of California, San Diego, 1999). Elliott spells it *chéeya-t.*

55. Eric Elliott included these same words in his dictionary of Luiseño (ibid.) and offered a more in-depth interpretation of their religious significance. Elliott, interview by Lisbeth Haas, 13 January 2007.

56. Sandra Chung, "Remarks on Pablo Tac's *La Lingua degli Indi Luiseño,*" *International Journal of American Linguistics* 40, no. 4, pt. 1 (October 1974): 297.

57. A. L. Kroeber and George W. Grace, *The Sparkman Grammar of Luiseño*, University of California Publications in Linguistics 16 (Berkeley: University of California Press, 1960). They, as other linguists, used Tagliavini's *Studio grammaticale*, which offers an edited version of the grammar.

58. See Joanne Rappaport, *The Politics of Memory: Native Historical Interpretation in the Colombian Andes* (Durham, NC: Duke University Press, 1998). On native historians, see Philip J. Deloria, "Historiography," in *A Companion to American Indian History*, ed. Philip J. Deloria and Neal Salisbury (Oxford: Blackwell, 2002), 6–21.

59. Raymond White, "Religion and Its Role among the Luiseño," in *Native Californians: A Theoretical Retrospective*, ed. Lowell Bean and Thomas Blackburn (Ramona, CA: Ballena Press, 1976), 356.

60. On the alcaldes see Steven Hackel, "The Staff of Leadership: Indian Authority in the Missions of Alta California," *William and Mary Quarterly* 54, no. 2 (1997): 347–377.

61. See Rolena Adorno, *The Polemics of Possession in Spanish American Narrative* (New Haven, CT: Yale University Press, 2007); also Tejaswini Niranjana, *Siting Translation: History, Post-Structuralism, and the Colonial Context* (Berkeley: University of California Press, 1992).

62. Steven Feierman is among scholars who look at the value of popular theorizing of history as implicit in Tac's work. See Feierman, *Peasant Intellectuals: Anthropology and History in Tanzania* (Madison: University of Wisconsin Press, 1990).

63. See Haas, " 'Raise your sword.' "

64. Boscana, *Chinigchinich,* 57.

65. Ibid., 34–35.

66. See James Lockhart, *The Nahuas after the Conquest: A Social and Cultural History of the Indians of Central Mexico, Sixteenth through Eighteenth Centuries* (Stanford, CA: Stanford University Press, 1992). This approach has shaped more than a generation of scholars. Lockhart and others began with simple translation and analysis of everyday kinds of legal writing. See Arthur Anderson, Frances Berdan, and James Lockhart, *Beyond the Codices: The Nahua View of Colonial Mexico* (Berkeley: University of California Press, 1976); and James Krippner-Martinez, *Rereading the Conquest: Poverty, Politics, and the History of Early Colonial Michoacán, Mexico, 1521–1565* (University Park: Pennsylvania State University Press, 2001).

67. Stephanie Wood, *Transcending Conquest: Nahua Views of Spanish Colonial Mexico* (Norman: University of Oklahoma Press, 2003), 19–20. Wood finds an exception in the anguished report on the Spanish invasion from a small town called Santo Tomás Ajusco that presented fear along with sadness, anger, and a pragmatic view of defeat.

68. Rappaport, *Politics of Memory,* 21.

69. Almost all scholars concerned with native peoples in Mesoamerica discuss the primordial titles, which were not limited to central Mexico. For a discussion of the scholarship, see Stephanie Wood, "The Cosmic Conquest: Late-Colonial Views of the Sword and Cross in Central Mexican Títulos," *Ethnohistory* 38, no. 2 (Spring 1991): 191.

70. Deloria, "Historiography," 15.

71. Robert Warrior, *The People and the Word: Reading Native Nonfiction* (Minneapolis: University of Minnesota Press, 2005).

72. From the Registro del Collegio Urbano, cited by Tagliavini, "Evangelizzazione," 634.

73. Robert Warrior emphasizes the crucial role of the nonfiction tradition in native writing, beginning with William Apess. Warrior, *The People and the Word: Reading Native Nonfiction* (Minneapolis: University of Minnesota Press, 2005). Also see Barry O'Connell, *On Our Own Ground: The Complete Writings of William Apess, a Pequot* (Amherst: University of Massachusetts Press, 1992).

74. See Renya Ramirez, "Henry Roe Cloud: A Granddaughter's Native Feminist Biographical Account," *Wicazo Sa Review* 24, no. 2 (2009): 77–103; Maureen Konkle, *Writing Indian Nations: Native Intellectuals and the Politics of Historiography, 1827–1863* (Chapel Hill: University of North Carolina Press, 2004); and David J. Carlsson, *Sovereign Selves: American Indian Autobiography and the Law* (Urbana: University of Illinois Press, 2006).

75. See, for example, Félix de Guarania, *Ñe'ẽrekokatu ha ñe'ẽ morangatu: Gramática y literatura guarani* ([Fernando de la Mora, Paraguay]: Ateneo de Lengua y Cultura Guaraní, 2004).

76. Pablo Tac, fol. 109r; and Eric Elliott, interview by Lisbeth Haas, 13 January 2007. See Elliott, "Dictionary of Rincón Luiseño."

77. Eric Elliott helped devise the contemporary orthography with Luiseño consultants. Contemporary Luiseño now forms part of the bilingual program at Pechanga Reservation for the Pechanga band of Luiseño Indians.

78. See, for example, the contemporary Luiseño dictionary by Hyde and Elliott, *Yumáyk yumáyk*.

79. The pronunciation is from Eric Elliott (unpublished ms., January 2004).

Fasten Your Seat Belts, Prepare for Landing

The Travels of Payomkowishum Art Warriors

JAMES LUNA

I am on my way to Venice to make art. I stare out of the jet plane window as we cross over the Alps and the border between Switzerland and Italy. I think that it is amazing how mankind can learn to exist in most any environment and create a culture within that territory. I wonder about history and why there seems to be only one history, the history of the dominant Western world—when there so are many histories growing at once all over the world.

I have chosen Pablo Tac, a fellow Payomkowishum from the coast, to be my subject for the exhibit. In 1832 Pablo was selected to travel to Rome to attend a Catholic missionary school with an international student body trained to spread the Catholic religion to their respective peoples. He was no doubt considered a high-level student who could achieve the goals of that institution, but he went beyond those goals and devised an alphabet of our language, which I feel is of major importance for people to know and understand, as it dispels the common misperception of us as simple hunter and gathers and elevates us to scholars. Venice seems like the perfect world stage to present Pablo, given its association with Catholicism and Western expansion.

Working as a visual artist of some stature, I know the importance of the written word in Western culture. To write, and to be written about, holds high value in the Western world—you become validated . . . you exist.

Can we talk?

FIGURE 13. James Luna with his grandmother Rebecca Trujillo Osuna, before his First Communion, 1958. Photo courtesy James Luna.

I don't consider myself a visual artist alone but also a commentator on cultures: one who approaches these subjects in various creative ways and who has been given a gift to see, listen, and comment—in that order. I think the bestowed title of an "American Indian ceremonial clown" is the best description for what I am—that is, a satirist and commentator with a special gift of gab.

So my tribal brother, Mr. Pablo Tac, crossed these same waters but in a slow-moving sailboat at a different place and time. He, I believe, came voluntarily, because I believe he also had come to understand that he was given a gift (maybe several gifts) of writing and understanding its power. His gift enabled him to come see the "other" world, to experience the places where those strangers came from, to learn more of the way they thought, what they believed, and to learn more of how and why they expressed themselves in written form.

Side note: Pablo is part of an ongoing cultural revelation of who we really are and what we are to American culture. The dominant culture seems comfortable perceiving Indian people as renegades, not as cultures of high concepts and technology. In 1911 Mr. Ishi (Yahi, Yana) emerged from the wild and was immediately given the title of the "Last Wild

FIGURE 14. Communion portrait with boys from Luna's neighborhood in Fountain Valley, 1958. Photo courtesy James Luna.

California Indian." Confined in the museum of the University of California, Berkeley, he was studied head to toe and observed from all angles. He was asked for his thoughts on a high point of Western culture, and he responded that he felt that the match was the best that Western culture could have done. Pretty smart guy! I bring this up to remind you that as cultures we see things differently and should try to understand this, and perhaps consider where these things come together, first, and where they part, second.

Pablo arrives in Rome, where he is to study so that someday he will be sent back to the other world to spread the word of Jesus and the high ideals and ways of the Western world. But in his ensuing education, and under supervision, he responds to questions about life as a native. He responds with a series of written thoughts and visual pictures as to how he saw the world. He explains in simple but emotional terms what it meant to be Indian at that moment in history.

In his writing there is a slightly veiled anger toward the Spanish, and he doesn't use the word God or Jesus but the Luiseño word for the creator! This was another place where Pablo and I come together. I resisted being a Catholic, I resisted by questioning and not fully participating in

FIGURE 15. Luna as director of the La Jolla Indian Education Center, with children and staff, 1978. Photo courtesy James Luna.

the rites of after-school catechism and let my fear of priests and nuns develop to the point of disrespect. Why did I resist? I felt that religious beliefs did not go with the real experiences I saw taking place around me, such as family and community dysfunction; native theory and pop culture just didn't fit with the strict and supernatural teaching of the church. In religion studies we were not afforded the right to question, and through intimidation and fear we were expected to believe. Nothing else made my sense of the world seem questionable, and those questions made it clear that there was more than one world: mine and theirs. Pablo came from a culture that was not tarnished; as the world he knew was singular, there was nothing else to compare it to until the Spanish arrived. I cannot help but feel that each day he was faced with philosophical questions about existence, and that writing was his savior, enabling him to quell the anger of domination.

Note on tribal peer pressure: I think of the many tribal people who have supported my art efforts, but I also know that with each success come critical reviews by the cultural police and others bitter for not having lived their dreams as Pablo and I. I don't think our culture has changed

much in the way of envy. That is a product of the "have not" mentality, which many of us Indians have to live down. So there are those among our people who think we left them, who don't understand our talents or our motives and think the worse of us for becoming "one of them," one of the oppressors. Little do they know the lonely times we face, of being truly alone, being and feeling different, and living confused and angry. We carry on because no matter what, we understand the importance of what we have been gifted to do. My elders—people from only a generation before me—who went away to boarding school returned home with basic grammar skills and new talents of manual labor skills. They were shunned by some for "having changed," or shunned for having applied and accepted these new ideas. There was little sympathy or understanding of the forced learning that went on in the government schools. But at the core of this thinking was fear of the demise and partial losses of the Indian way as they knew it. I cannot help but think of the controversy that Pablo would have stirred if he had returned home.

Here is the stratosphere in which Mr. Tac and I come together as tribal brothers.

I think that despite time and place, we are a living and thriving culture within a culture. Our land base has certainly changed, but some of us still live where we have always lived; we know and can identify our cardinal points of the world, the plants and animals that have made it through and share our environment to this day. Most importantly, we continue to survive. Though it was not our intent, Pablo and I are voices for our people: we inform, teach, and defend our culture to others as well as to our people. We are cultural warriors.

My silence of thought is broken.

The voice on the plane's intercom says, "We are starting our descent. Please fasten your seat belts, turn off your electronic equipment, and prepare for landing."

I am arriving in the Old World to do my duty as a culture warrior and as a tribal citizen of the Payomkowishum nation. I wonder for a moment if Pablo was thinking the same thought as his ship anchored.

FIGURE 16. James Luna, *Apparitions: Past and Present*, 2003.

a. William Benson (Pomo), basket maker, 1931. Photo courtesy James Luna.

b. James Luna, La Jolla Reservation. Photo by Mark Velasquez.

FIGURE 17. James Luna, *Apparitions: Past and Present*, 2003.

a. Luiseño man, Saboba Reservation, 1897. Photo courtesy James Luna.

b. James Luna, La Jolla Reservation. Photo by Mark Velasquez.

FIGURE 18. James Luna, *Apparitions: Past and Present*, 2003.

a. Jose Albañas, La Jolla spiritual leader, 1932. Photo courtesy James Luna.

b. James Luna, La Jolla Reservation. Photo by Mark Velasquez.

FIGURE 19. James Luna, *The Spirit of Motherhood Is Alive*, 2005

a. Luna's great-grandmother Maria Apish Trujillo (Luiseño), with his grandmother Rebecca Trujillo Osuna as a child, 1906. Photo courtesy James Luna.

b. Luna's sister Jennifer Nelson (Luiseño/Sioux), with her daughter Kathlyn "Coffee" Nelson (Luiseño/Sioux/Kumeyaay). Photo by Mark Velasquez.

FIGURE 20. James Luna, *Apparitions 1,* 2004. The backdrop portrays Ipai Mesa Grande elders waving rattles and feather wands during rites held in 1907. Left to right: Joe Agua, Rafel LaChappa, Narciso La Chappa, Tuer Santo Peña, and Antonio Maces. Standing in the foreground, left to right, are Roger Rose (Caddo/Witchita), James Luna (Luiseño), Ty Morritti (Luiseño), Willie Nelson (Luiseño), and Raymond Lafferty (Ipai). Photo courtesy James Luna.

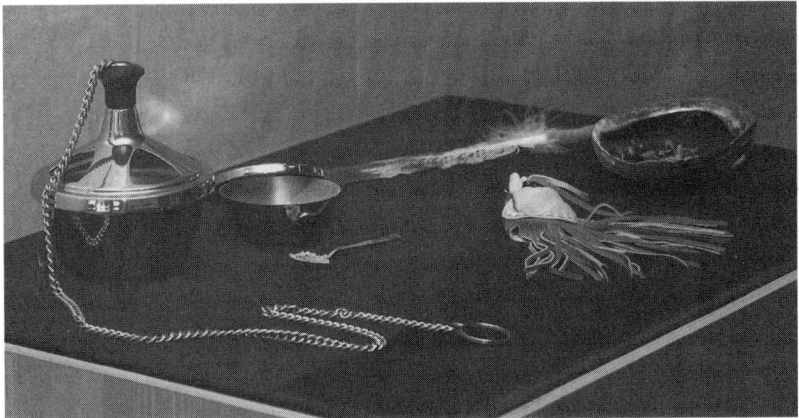

FIGURE 21. James Luna, *Emendatio*, Venice Biennale, 2005. Courtesy National Museum of the American Indian, Smithsonian Institution; photos by Katherine Fogden.

    a. *(facing page, bottom)* Luna's chapel for Pablo Tac.

    b. *(above, top)* The altar and display case in Luna's chapel for Pablo Tac.

    c. *(above, bottom)* One of two display cases in Luna's chapel for Pablo Tac.

PART TWO

The Manuscript

Pablo Tac's Luiseño Grammar and History

This book attempts to provide an exact reproduction of Pablo Tac's writing as found in his manuscript at the Biblioteca comunale dell'Archiginnasio, Bologna. In the present section (grammar and history), Tac's Latin, Spanish, and Luiseño text is transcribed on the left-hand pages, with English translation of the Latin and Spanish on the right-hand pages. In the following section (the dictionary), the text and translation appear in separate columns of the same page. Italic is used only for Luiseño; Latin and Spanish are in roman type. Throughout, folio numbers of the manuscript are given in the margins of the page. Footnotes are added only as needed for clarity.

The grammar and spelling remain Tac's own; they are neither standardized nor made to conform to contemporary usage. Tac's writing can speak to a range of questions that could have been precluded by efforts to introduce consistency or rearrange the order of things. Tac's Spanish is modern, but it predates the standardized use of some letters and accents. His Latinization of Luiseño and his translation between Luiseño and Spanish in the grammar and dictionary are unique to his writing and era. Contemporary Luiseño has another structure and logic.

Prima
Linguae Californensis Rudimenta
a P. Tak proposita.

I.

Californienses omnibus fere quibus Hispani litteris utuntur. Sed peculiares sibi sonos superposito quibusdam litteris puncto signare ~~commoverunt~~ commode possunt

a . b . c . ċ . d . e . g . h . i . j . l . ll . m . n . ñ . ṅ . o . p . q . r . s . ṡ . t . u . y .

Desunt Litterae = *f . k . z .*

ċ, effertur cum aspiratione.

ṅ, aequat *ng.*

ṡ, = *sc,* seu *ch.* Gallorum.

Prima

Nomina genera carent, duas pro omnibus caribus habent terminationes, at plurati numero adiiciunt *m,* vel *om.*

Ex duplici pluralis numeri terminatione duplex agnoscitur declinatio quarum altera singularem numerum littera vocali concludit, altera consonanti terminatur.

PRIOR DECLINATIO.

Nom. *yula.* capillus.

Gen. *yula.*

Dat. *yulai*

Acc. *yulai*

Voc. *yula.*

PLURALITER

Nom. *yulam.*

Gen. *yulam.*

Dat. *yúlami.*

1r

First
Rudiments of a Californian Language
proposed by P. Tak

I.

Californians make use of nearly all the letters the Spaniards do. But by placing a mark over certain letters they are able to properly inscribe sounds particular to themselves.

a . b . c . ċ . d . e . g . h . i . j . l . ll . m . n . ñ . ṅ. o . p . q . r . s . ṡ . t . u . y.

These letters are missing: *f, k, z.*

ċ is aspirated.

ṅ equals *ng.*

ṡ = *sc,* or the *ch* of the Gauls.

First

Nouns lack gender. They have two endings for all familiar forms; and those things plural in number add *m* or *om.*

1v

For both [declensions], the plural is expressed using an ending of a plural number. One concludes the singular using a vowel, and the other ends in a consonant.*

FIRST DECLENSION.

NOMINATIVE: *yula.*   hair

GENITIVE: *yula.*

DATIVE: *yulai*

ACCUSATIVE: *yulai*

VOCATIVE: *yula.*

PLURAL

NOMINATIVE: *yulam.*

GENITIVE: *yulam.*

DATIVE: *yúlami.*

---

*This sentence (*Ex duplici . . . terminatur*) is very difficult to make sense of. Tac seems to be observing that the plurals of both declensions are similar, whereas the singulars differ in that the first declension ends with a vowel and the second declension ends with a consonant.

Acc. *yúlam.*

Voc. yulam.

Sic flectuntur

Pala   aqua

Quicha. domus.

Huǹla. ventus.

Ejla. terra.

E. pes.

Aui. pinguis. (Dat. *auiyi* = interposito *y.* Acc. *auiyi*)

yo. mater.

yu. Caput.

Secunda declinatio

N.   *Hunuot.*   ursus

Gen. *Hunuot.*

Dat. *Hunuoti*

Acc. *Hunuoti*

Voc. *Hunuot.*

Pluraliter

Nom.   *Húnuotom*

Gen. *Hunuotom*

Dat. *Hunuotǝmi*   subduct *o**

Acc. *Hunutǝmi*

Voc. *Hunutom*

Eodem modo flectuntur.

Quaàl   vermis – musca.

Chilcuat. vas.

Momat. mare.

---

*The original word is unclear.

ACCUSATIVE: *yúlam.*

VOCATIVE: *yulam.*

2r   Thus they are translated.*

Pala. water

Quicha. house.

Huṅla. wind.

Ejla. earth.

E. foot.

Aui. fat (plump) (DATIVE: *auiyi* = with *y* placed in the middle. ACCUSATIVE: *auiyi*)

yo. mother.

yu. head.

SECOND DECLENSION

NOMINATIVE: *Hunuot.*   bear

GENITIVE: *Hunuot.*

DATIVE: *Hunuoti*

ACCUSATIVE: *Hunuoti*

VOCATIVE: *Hunuot.*

PLURAL

NOMINATIVE: *Húnuotom*

GENITIVE: *Hunuotom*

DATIVE: *Hunuotəmi* remove the *o*

ACCUSATIVE: *Hunutəmi*

VOCATIVE: *Hunutom*

2v   In the same way these are translated

Quaàl   worm – fly.

Chilcuat.   vessel

Momat.   sea

---

*Literally "bent" or "twisted."

Animadverte

Nomen = *chaṅichṅiṡ*. Deus,
eique similia dum flectuntur amittere litteram ultimam *ṡ*, ————————*

Nom. *Chaṅichṅiṡ*. Deus.
Gen. *Chaṅichṅiṡ*.
Dat. *chaṅichṅi~~chi~~* suffecto *ch*.
Acc. *Chaṅichṅi~~chi~~*.
Voc. *chaṅichṅiṡ*.

N. *Uàis* caro.
Gen. *Uaɨs*
Dat. *Uai*
Acc. *Uai*
Voc. *Uaiṡ*

PLURALITER.

Nom. *Uaȯm*.
Gen. *Uaom*.
Dat. Acc. *Uaɨmi*
Voc. *Uaɨm*.

3r

Prima Linguae Californiensis Elementa a P. Tac proposita.

1.

Californienses /*Quechṅajuichom*/ omnibus fere quibus Hispani litteris utuntur. Sed peculiares sibi sonos superposito quibusdam litteris puncto signare commode possunt.

a . b . c . ċ ċa . d . e . g . h . i . j . l . ll̶ . m . n . ñ̶ . ṅ . o . p . q q̇ . r . s . ṡ . t . u . y .

Desunt litterae *f . k . ñ . z . x ll, ċa*

at *ċ ċa* effertur cum aspiratione.

ṅ aequat *ng*.

ṡ = *sc*, seu *ch* Gallorum.

*Two words are crossed out here.

Observe

Noun = *chaṅichṅiṡ*. God,

and yet resemblances for it are bent to drop the final letter *ṡ*.

NOMINATIVE: *Chaṅichṅiṡ*. God.

GENITIVE:. *Chaṅichṅiṡ*.

DATIVE: *chaṅichṅi~~ch~~i* is sufficient [without the] *ch*

ACCUSATIVE: *Chaṅichṅi~~chi~~*.

VOCATIVE: *Chaṅichṅiṡ*.

NOMINATIVE: *Uàis*. flesh.

GENITIVE: *Uais*

DATIVE: *Uai*

ACCUSATIVE: *Uai*

VOCATIVE: *Uaiṡ*

PLURAL.

NOMINATIVE: *Uaȯm*.

GENITIVE: *Uaom*.

DATIVE [AND] ACCUSATIVE: *Uaɨmi*

VOCATIVE: *Uaɨm*.

3r The First Language of California: Principles proposed by P. Tac

1.

Californians /*Quechṅajuichom*/ make use of nearly all the letters the Spaniards do. But by placing a mark over certain letters they are able to properly inscribe sounds particular to each letter.

a . b . c . $\dot{c}^{\dot{c}a}$ *. d . e . g . h . i . j . l . ~~ll~~ . m . n . ~~ñ~~ . ṅ . o . p .* $q^{\dot{q}}$ *. r . s . ṡ . t . u . y .*

These letters are missing: *f, k, ñ, z, x, ll, ċa*

furthermore, $\dot{c}^{\dot{c}a}$ is aspirated.

ṅ equals *ng*.

ṡ = *sc*, or the *ch* of the Gauls.

2.

Nomina genera carent. Duas pro omnibus caribus habent terminationes, at plurati numero adiiciunt *m.* vel *om.*

Ex duplici pluralis numeri terminatione duplex agnoscitur declinatio, quarum altera singularem numerum vocali littera concludit, altera consonanti.

Prima declinatio.

Nom. *Yúla.* Capillus.

Gen. *Yúla.*

Dat. *Yulai*

Acc. *Yulai*

V. *Yula.*

Pluraliter

N. *Yulam* – Capilli.

Gen. *Yulam*

Dat. *Yúlami.*

Acc. *Yúlami.*

Voc. *Yulam*

Similiter flectuntur =

Pála – aqua.

Quicha – domus. *Kicha.*

Huṅla. ventus.

Ejla. terra.

Tota. petra.

Mota. mus.

Húla. sagitta.

E. pes.

Auí. pinguis. Dativ. *auiyi.*

Yò. mater.

Nà. pater.

Yú. caput.

2.

Nouns lack gender. They have two endings for all familiar forms, and
3v for those things plural in number add *m* or *om*.

For both [declensions], the plural is expressed using an ending to a
plural number. One concludes the singular using a vowel, the other
using a consonant.

FIRST DECLENSION

NOMINATIVE: *Yúla.*   hair.

GENITIVE: *Yúla.*

DATIVE: *Yulai*

ACCUSATIVE: *Yulai*

VOCATIVE: *Yula.*

PLURAL

NOMINATIVE: *Yulam*   hairs.

GENITIVE: *Yulam*

DATIVE: *Yúlami.*

ACCUSATIVE: *Yúlami.*

VOCATIVE: *Yulam*

4r These are translated similarly =

Pála   water.

Quicha house. *Kicha.*

Huṅla. wind.

Ejla. earth.

Tota. stone.

Mota. mouse.

Húla. arrow.

E. foot.

Auí. fat.   DATIVE: *auiyi.*

Yò. mother.

Nà. father

Yú. head.

4v   ## SECUNDA DECLINATIO

N.   *Húnuot.*   Ursus.

Gen.   *Húnuot.*

Dat.   *Húnuoti.*

Acc.   *Húnuoti.*

V.   *Hunuot.*

PLURALITER.

N.   *Húnuotom* – Ursi.

G.   *Húnuotom.*

Dat.   *Húnuotmi.*

Acc.   *Húnuotmi.*

V.   *Hunuotom.*

Eodem modo flectuntur

Ċuà-ál.   vermis – musca.

Chílcuat – vas.

Auàl.   canis

Coláuot.   lignum.

5r   ## NOMINA I. DECLINATIONIS.

Tota.   Petra.

Mota.   mus.

ċma.   frons.

ma.   manus

Pula.

hula,   sagitta

Pala,   aqua

5v   ## NOMINA 2. DECLINATIONIS

Mamajis   amor.

Not.   Rex.

chat.   noctua.

tamàt.   dens, os,

ueiiṡ.   lingua.

musiṡ.   barba.

4v ## SECOND DECLENSION

NOMINATIVE: *Húnuo*t   bear

GENITIVE: *Húnuot*

DATIVE: *Húnuoti*

ACCUSATIVE: *Húnuoti*

VOCATIVE: *Hunuot*

PLURAL.

NOMINATIVE: *Húnuotom*   bears

GENITIVE: *Húnuotom.*

DATIVE: *Húnuotmi*

ACCUSATIVE: *Húnuotmi*

VOCATIVE: *Hunuotom*

In the same way these are translated:

Ċuà-ál.   worm – fly.

Chílcuat – vessel.

Auàl.   dog

Coláuot.   wood.

5r ## NOUNS OF THE FIRST DECLENSION.

Tota.   Stone.

Mota.   mouse.

ċma.   forehead.

ma.   hand

Pula.

hula,   arrow

Pala,   water

5v ## NOUNS OF THE SECOND DECLENSION

Mamajis   love.

Not.   King.

chat.   owl.

tamàt.   tooth, mouth,

ueiiṡ.   tongue.

musiṡ.   beard.

naċmais. naċmaiŝ.   auris.

jarat. guttur.

al. pectus.

mat. brachium.

sulàt. unguis.

tajauiŝ. corpus.

atáj. homo.

Pronomina quse Personam significant

6r

I.

Non   ego

No. mei

niiq. mihi. *noi.*   me

PLUR.

chaom.   Nos.

cham nostrum

chamiq. nobis.   ᵃᶜ·*chami.* nos.

2.

Om. Tu.

o. tui

oiq. Tibi.   *oi.* te

PLUR.

Omom.   Vos.

om. vestrum

omòmiq. vobis

Omomi vos

nacmais. nacmais. ear.

jarat. throat.

al. breast.

mat. arm.

sulàt. finger.

tajauis. body.

atáj. man.

Pronouns that indicate person*

6r

1.

Non. I

No. my

niiq. me.†   *noi.* me‡

PLURAL

Chaom. We.

cham. our

chamiq, us.   ac.*chami.* us.

2.

Om. You.

o. your

oiq. You.§   *oi.* you**

PLURAL

Omon. You.

om. your

omòmiq. you

Omomi. you

---

  *Numbers 1 and 2 list the personal pronouns and number 3 lists the demonstrative pronouns. Unless noted otherwise, the general order of cases here for both singular and plural is as follows: (1) nominative, (2) genitive, (3) dative and ablative, and (4) accusative.

  †Dative singular.

  ‡Accusative or ablative singular.

  §Dative singular.

  **Accusative or ablative singular.

3.

Po. Ille

po. illius.

Poiq. Illi *poi.* illum

PLUR.

Pomon. Illi.

Pom. Illorum

Pomòmiq. Illis. *pomòmi.* illos.

6v
Nomina numerorum.

Supùl. unus.

Ueh. duo.

Pài, tres.

Uasà. Quattuor.

Mahár. quinque.

Deinde.

Mahàr pe supùl. quinque at unus. sex.

Mahàr pe uéh. 5 + 2

Mahàr pe pài. 5 + 3

Mahàr pe uasà. 5. + 4

Uehcom mahàr. decem. bis quinque*

Uehcom mahàr pe supùl. undecim. bis quinque et unus.

uehcom mahàr pè ueh. duodecim.

uehcom mahàr pè pai. tredecim.

uehcom mahàr pe uasà. quatuordecim.

Pài com mahar. quindecim.

Uasà com mahar. viginti.

7r *Nešmal.* vetula.

Eheṅmal. passer, at avis.

---

*In the first example of *uehcom,* the letters *om* are crossed out, with *com* written above. In the four following examples, the letter *c* is written above the word in between the letters *h* and *o*.

3.

Po. That

po. that.

Poiq. That*   *poi.* that

PLURAL

Pomon. Those.

Pom. Those

Pomòmiq. Those.   *pomòmi.* those.

6v   The names of the numbers.

Supùl. one.

Ueh. two.

Pài. three.

Uasà. four.

Mahár. five.

Next.

Mahàr pe supùl. five plus one. six.

Mahàr pe uéh. 5 + 2

Mahàr pe pài. 5 + 3

Mahàr pe uasà. 5 + 4

Uehcon mahàr. ten. twice five

Uehcom mahàr pe supùl. eleven. twice five plus one.

uehcom mahàr pè ueh. twelve.

uehcom mahàr pè pai. thirteen.

uehcom mahàr pe uasà. fourteen.

Pài com mahar. fifteen.

Uasà com mahar. twenty.

7r   *Neṡmal.* old woman.

     Eheṅmal. sparrow, bird.

---

*Dative singular. This entry presents no option for the ablative singular *[illo]*.

Uácat. ensis proprius illium gentis.
　　laus. gloria. decus. honos.*

Yejiṡ. ~~Lein~~ – Superbia.

Anàmmat. piscis.

Ċauialuot. Corvus

Cajàl. Coturnix, Gallina.

Asuot. aquila.

hunuot. ursus.

Facat. tigris.

Momat mare.

Siquínabal pecunia.

humcat. penna.

cut. lumen ~~lu~~

Femet. Sol. dies. lux.

Notbat Culter.

Sucat. Cervus. Cervus.

Mòmat. Mare.

Fòmauot tonitru fulmen

10r

Verba

Modus Infinitus Verborum erit *ṁ.ṡ.*

ayál-iṡ. scire. Haec littera mutatur *ṁ-ċ.* pro Indicativi tempore presenti *ṁ* Singulari numero, *ṁ uon, ṁ* numero plurali, nisi infinitus erit in *jiṡ.*

Pro reliquis temporibus et modis aliis mutationibus obnoxia est, ut ex paradigmate patebit.

Notandum est = Pronomina Personarum quae vocibus verbi praemittuntur, pro temporum ac modorum varietate immutari.

---

*This line is written to replace the crossed-out word below.

Uácat. a sword characteristic of that clan or tribe.

    praise. glory. distinction. honor.

Yejiṡ. ~~Lein~~ pride.

Anàmmat. fish.

Ċauialuot. raven

Cajàl. quail, hen.

Asuot. eagle.

hunuot. bear.

Facat. tiger.

Momat sea.

Siquínabal money.

humcat. feather.

cut. light ~~lu~~

Femet. sun, day, light.

Notbat knife.

Sucat. deer. deer.

Mòmat. sea.

Fòmauot thunder, thunderbolt

Verbs

The Infinitive Mode of Verbs will be *ṁ.ṡ.*

ayál-iṡ. To know. This letter is changed *ṁ-ċ.* according to the present indicative. *ṁ* [for] singular, *ṁ uon,* and *ṁ* [for] plural, unless the infinitive ends in *jiṡ.*

For the remaining tenses and modes it is subject to other changes, so that it lies open to the paradigm.

To be noted = Personal pronouns that are placed in front of verb forms indicate the tense and mode to be changed.

Paradigma.

Ayál-iŝ.   scire.

INDICATIVUS.

TEMPUS PRAESENS.

SINGULARIS NUMERUS.

Non ayal-ič.   ego scio.   *Om òp ayál-ič,*   tu scis.   *umálop aỳálic.*

PLUR. NUMERUS

chaomcha ayáliuon.   nos scimus.
omóm om ayáliuon.   vos scintis.
Uonálompom ayáliuon.   illi sciunt.

IMPERFECTUM.

Non il ayál-icuos,   ego sciebam.
Óm opil ayál-icuos.   tu sciebas.
Uonalopil ayál-icuos.   ille sciebat.
Plur. *Chaomchamil ayálicuos.*   sciebámus.
Omómomil ayál-icuos.   vos sciebatis.
Uonalomil ayál-icuos.   illi sciebant.

PERFECTUM.

Non il ayál-aj.   ego scivi.
Om opil, ayál-aj.   tu scivisti.
Uonalapil ayál-aj.   ille scivit.
Plur. *chaomchamil ayál-aj.*   scivimus.
omómomil ayál-aj.   vos scivistis.
uonálomil ayál-aj.   illi sciverunt.

FUTURUM.

Nonopo ayál-in.   ego sciam.
Omopo ayál-in.   tu scies.
Uonalpo ayál-in.   ille sciet.
Plur. *chaomchapo ayál-in.*   nos sciemus.
omomom ayál-in.   vos scietis.
Uonálomo ayál-in.   illi scient.

Paradigm

Ayál-iš   to know.

INDICATIVE.

PRESENT TENSE.

SINGULAR.

Non ayal-ič.   I know.   *Om óp ayál-ič,*   you know.   *umálop aỳálic.*

PLURAL

chaomcha ayáliuon.   we know.
omóm om ayáliuon.   you know.
Uonálompom ayáliuon.   they know.

IMPERFECT.

Non il ayál-icuos,   I used to know.
Óm opil ayál-icuos.   you used to know.
Uonalopil ayál-icuos.   he/she used to know.
PLURAL: *Chaomchamil ayálicuos.*   we used to know.
Omómomil ayál-icuos.   you used to know.
Uonalomil ayál-icuos.   they used to know.

PERFECT.

10v

Non il ayál-aj.   I knew.
Om opil, ayál-aj.   you knew.
Uonalapil ayál-aj.   he/she knew.
PLURAL: *chaomchamil ayál-aj.*   we knew.
omómomil ayál-aj.   you knew.
uonálomil ayál-aj.   they knew.

FUTURE.

Nonopo ayál-in.   I shall know.
Omopo ayál-in.   you shall know.
Uonalpo ayál-in.   he/she shall know.
PLURAL: *chaomchapo ayál-in.*   we shall know.
omomom ayál-in,   you shall know.
Uonálomo ayál-in.   they shall know.

IMPERATIVUS.

Ayáli om.   scito tu.

Plur. *Ayáliumcha.*   sciamus

Ayáliyam.   sciatis.

PRAESENS CONJÙNCTIVUS ET IMPERFECTUS.

No ayálicala.   cum scirem.

O ayal-icala.   cum scires.

Po ayal-icala.   cum sciret.

Plur. *cham ayálicala.*   cum sciremus.

om ayalicala.   cum sciretis.

Pom ayál-icala   cum scirent.

11r   ## CONJÙNTIVUS.

No ayálipi.   ut sciam.

O ayálipi.   ut scias.

Po ayalipi.   ut sciat.

Plur. *cham. ayálipi.*   ut sciamus.

om ayálipi.   ut sciatis.

Pom ayálipi.   ut sciant.

IMPERFECTUM.

No ayálipi.   ut scirem.

O. ayálipi.   ut scires.

P. ayálipi.   ut sciret.

Plur. *cham ayálipi,*   ut sciremus.

om ayálipi.   ut sciretis.

Pom ayalipi.   ut scirent.

INFINITUS.

Ayális.   scire, etiam doctrina.

PARTICIPIUM PRAESENS.

Ayálicat,   sciens. vel doctor.

PART. PRAETERT.

Ayál-imocuis̀.   qui scivit.

IMPERATIVE.

Ayáli om. you know

PLURAL: *Ayáliumcha.*   we know.

Ayáliyam. you know.

PRESENT SUBJUNCTIVE AND IMPERFECT

No ayálicala.   when I knew.

O ayal-icala.   when you knew.

Po ayal-icala.   when he/she knew.

PLURAL: *cham ayálicala.*   when we knew.

om ayalicala. when you knew.

Pom ayál-icala   when they knew.

11r   SUBJUNCTIVE

No ayálipi.   so that I may know.

O ayálipi.   so that you may know.

Po ayalipi.   so that he/she may know.

PLURAL: *cham. ayálipi.*   so that we may know.

om ayálipi.   so that you may know.

Pom ayálipi.   so that they may know.

IMPERFECT.

No ayálipi.   so that I might know.

O. ayálipi.   so that you might know.

P. ayálipi.   so that he/she might know.

PLURAL: *cham ayálipi,*   so that we might know.

om ayálipi.   so that you might know.

Pom ayalipi.   so that they might know.

INFINITIVE.

Ayális.   to know, also knowledge.

PRESENT PARTICIPLE.

Ayálicat,   knowing. for example, a teacher.

PAST PARTICIPLE

Ayál-imocuiṡ.   known.

GERUND.

Ayál-icanoq. sciendo.

En esta manera pondremos todos los otros verbos, como sigue:

Ċayàu-iś, lavar.	*Ċayàu-ċayau iś,* lavar muchas vezes
Ċayau-iś, lavadura,	*Ċayàu-ċacayau-iś,* el lavar muchas vezes
Ċayaù-ican, yo lavo,	*Ċayàu-ċayau-ican,* yo lavo muchas vezes
Ċayàu-ajnil, yo lavè	*Ċayau-ċàyàu-ajmil,* lav muchas vezes
Ċayau-in, lavarè,	*Ċayau-ċàyàu-in,* lavaré muchas vezes
Ċayau-i, lava tu.	*Ċayau-ċàyaù-i,* lava tu muchas vezes
No Ċayàu-icàla, quando yo lavaba	*No Ċàyàu-ċayàu-icala,* quando yo lavaba mu =*
No Ċayaù-ipi, para que yo lave	*No Ċayaùcayauipi,* para que yo muchas vezes lave.
Ċayàu-icat, el que lava, lavandera	*Ċayàu-cyauiċat,* quien lava muchas vezes.
Ċayau-imocùiś, el que ha lavado	*Ċayau-ċayauimoċuiś,* el que ha lavado muchas vezes.

Ċayau-imocuicbom. los que lavaron   los que muchas vezes han lavado.

Ċayàu-inoq. lavando   *Ċayaù-ċayauinoq* lavando muchas vezes.

Aquí sigue el verbo que ya por sí manda y que de todos los verbos casi se halla y se explica en Español: hacer lavar, o mandar para que se lave.

Ċayaù-imican   hago lavar, o mando que se lave

Ċayàu-imiċuormil   hazía lavar, o mandaba paraque lavassen

Ċayàu-imiinichoċuoś,   quería mandar paraque lavassen.

Ċayàu-iniajmil   hise lavar, mandè para que lavassen.

Ċayàu-iniinopo.   harè lavar, mandarè para que laven.

Ċayau-inii,   haz que laven, o manda para que laven.

No Ċayauniicàla,   quando yo hazía lavar.

No Ċayaù-ipi,   para que yo mande que se lave.

Ċayau-iniiś,   hazer, mandar, para que laven.

---

*Incomplete in the original.

GERUND.

Ayál-icanoq. knowing.

12r In this manner we will put all the other verbs as follows:

Ċayàu-iṡ,	to wash	*Ċayàu-ċayau-iṡ,*	to wash many times
Ċayau-iṡ,	[the] washing	*Ċayàu-ċacayau-iṡ,*	the act of washing many times
Ċayaù-ican,	I wash	*Ċayàu-ċayau-ican,*	I wash many times
Ċayàu-ajnil,	I washed	*Ċayau-ċàyàu-ajmil,*	I washed many times
Ċayau-in,	I will wash	*Ċayàu-ċàyàu-in,*	I will wash many times
Ċayau-i,	you wash	*Ċayàu-ċàyaù-i,*	you wash many times
No Ċayàu-icàla,	when I used to wash	*No Ċàyàu-ċayàu-icala,*	when I used to wash many times
No Ċayaù-ipi,	so that I wash	*No Ċayaùcayauipi,*	so that I wash many times
Ċayàu-icat,	one who washes, laundress	*Ċayàu-cyauiċat,*	one who washes many times
Ċayau-imocùiṡ,	one who has washed	*Ċayau-ċayauimoċuiṡ,*	one who has washed many times
Ċayau-imocuichom.	those who washed	those who have washed many times.
Ċayàu-inoq.	washing	*Ċayaù-ċayauinoq,*	washing many times

Here follows the verb that is in itself an order, and that can be found in almost all the verbs and explained in Spanish as "to have it washed" or "to order that one wash it."

12v *Ċayaù-imican* I have it washed, *or* I order that one wash it.

Ċayàu-imiċuormil I used to have it washed, *or* I used to order that they wash.

Ċayàu-imiinichoċuoṡ I wanted to order that they wash.

Ċayàu-iniajmil I had it washed, I ordered that they wash.

Ċayàu-iniinopo I will have it washed, I will order they wash.

Ċayau-inii make them wash, *or* order that they wash.

No Ċayauniicàla when I used to have it washed.

No Ċayaù-ipi so that I can order that one wash it.

Ċayau-iniiṡ to have [them wash], to order that they wash.

Ċayau-iniiṡ,   el hazer para que se lave

Ċayaù-inicat.   el que manda para que se lave.

Ċayaùiniicatom.   los que mandan para que se lave.

Ċayaù.inimocuis,   quien mandó para que se lavassen.

Ċayaù-iniimocuichom,   los que han mandado para que lavassen.

Ċayau-icànoq.   ~~lavando~~ haziendo lavar, etc.

El verbo *mocñais* repite la primera silaba en el passado como el verbo *tosñais*, mandar haciendo, *momocanil,* yo matè. Ayer mate a dos osos: *uajammil uehmalmi hunuotmi mòmocan.*

13r   Passivo

Ċayau-acàn,   Yo me lavo

Ċayaucùasmil,   me lavaba yo

Ċayaùamil,   yo me lavè,

Ċayauajànopo,   yo me lavarè.

Ċayaù aj.   lava te tu.

No Ċayauacàla,   quando yo me lavaba.

No Ċayauajpi,   para que yo me lave.

Ċayauajiṡ   lavarse.

Ċayauajis,   el lavarse.

Ċayauajimocuis,   el que se lavó.

Ċayau ajimocuichom,   los que se lavaron.

Ċayauacanoq   lavandome, etc.

14r   Preposicìones

Las preposiciones en esta lengua se metten detras o adelante. y son las que siguen

Amulo

Amúlo   adelante

Echi   sobre

Ṅa   en

Êṡ   con. de compañía

Ċayau-iniiṡ   the ordering that one wash it.

Ċayaù-inicat   he who orders that one wash it.

Ċayaùiniicatom   they who order that one wash it.

Ċayaù.inimocuis   the person who ordered that they wash it.

Ċayaù-iniimocuichom   those who have ordered that they wash it.

Ċayau-icànoq   having washed, etc.

The verb *mocñais* repeats the first syllable in the past, like the verb *tosñaiṡ*, to order doing, *momocanil,* I killed. "Yesterday I killed two bears": *uajammil uehmalmi hunuotmi mòmocan.*

13r   THE PASSIVE*

Ċayau-acàn   I wash myself

Ċayaucùasmil   I used to wash myself

Ċayaùamil   I washed myself

Ċayauajànopo   I will wash myself

Ċayaù aj.   wash yourself

No Ċayauacàla   when I used to wash myself

No Ċayauajpi   so that I wash myself

Ċayauajiṡ   to wash oneself

Ċayauajis   the act of washing oneself

Ċayauajimocuis   one who washed himself

Ċayau ajimocuichom   those who washed themselves

Ċayauacanoq   washing myself, etc.

14r   Prepositions

In this language the prepositions are placed behind or in front. And they are those that follow:

AMULO

Amúlo   in front

Echi   on

Ṅa   in

Êṡ   with. as company

---

*The reflexive is shown instead.

Tal   con. mas de istrumento

Mañai   por. de causa

Ejña   abbajo. en tierra

Ivai   de aqui.

Yvà   aqui.

Yváña   aqui, en este lugar.

Yvañai   de aqui.

Uonà   allà

Uonài   de alli.

Uonaña   allà, por alla

Uonaiċ   a allà

Yváiċ   a aquí.

Yo soy àdelante, de mi Cavallo, *Non amúlo no aiṡ,* y tambien, *Amúlon no aiṡ.* No vas che el està adelante, *càiso touc amúlo po aucala* Mete sobre tu sombrero, *tabùni echi o yumpi.*

La preposicion *ña* no se antepone al nombre, mas se pone despúes. y se pone asi si el nombre termina en vocal la prep. *ña* se añade p.e. en la mano. *màña.* mas se el nombre termina, en consonante, la consonante se quita p.e. en el cielo, *tùpaña.* Cielo se dice *tùpaṡ.* mas se quita la *ṡ.* quando se añade -*ña.*

Si el nombre substant. tiene despues desì un adjèct. todos dos congen la -*ñ.* p.e. en el lindo Cielo *yauàiuaña tupaña, yauaiuaṡ,* es el adject. y *tupaṡ* su adjet.

La prep. *ña,* quando se añade a los nobres, de dos sillabas, como p.e. *pala, yula. quicha* y mas. la segunda sillaba se quita, como p.e. en el agua. se dice *paña,* en la casa mya. no queria, *pala, quicha. yùla. hùla pùla* y en otras pocas palabras se hace esta mutacion, mas comunemente se deja como es la palabra, etc.

hula - flecha

16r   *Uórapil ċauiñai. xl ċauiñaopil uova.*

Uórapil. bajó. *Ċauicha.* monte. *ñai.* desde.

Tal with. but as instrument

Mañai for. as cause

Ejña below, in the ground

Ivai from here

Yvà here

Yváña here, in this place

Yvañai from here

Uonà there

Uonàí from there

Uonaña there, over there

Uonaic̀ to there

Yváic̀ to here

"I am in front of my horse": *Non amúlo no aiś,* and also *Amúlon no aiś.* "Don't go because he is in front": *càiso touc amúlo po aucala.* "Put on your hat": *tabùni echi o yumpi.*

The preposition *ña* is not put before the word, but after it. And it is placed like this: if the word ends in a vowel, the preposition *ña* is added; for example, "in the hand": *màña.* But if the word ends in a consonant, the consonant is dropped; for example, "in the sky": *tùpaña.* "Sky" is said *tùpaś,* but the *ś* is dropped when *-ña* is added.

If the substantive word has an adjective after it, both take on the *-ñ.* For example, "in the beautiful sky": *yauàiuaña tupaña. Yauaiuaś* is the adjective and *tupaś* is its adjective.*

When the preposition *ña* is added to words with two syllables, for example, *pala, yula, quicha,* and more, the second syllable is taken away. For example, *paña* means "in the water"; "in my house," "I didn't want to": *pala, quicha. Yùla, hùla, pùla,* a few other words make this mutation. More commonly the word is left as it is, etc.

hula arrow

16r   *Uórapil c̀auiñai. ~~xl~~ c̀auiñaopil uova.*

     Uórapil. came down. *C̀auicha* mountain. *nai.* from.

---

*Tac surely meant that *tupaś* is its subject rather than "its adjective."

O *cámayompom hicuajon o quig*

Tus hijos.　　corren　tu *quicha*. casa.　*quig*.
　　　　　　　　　　　　　　　　　　　　casa.

17r　*atájom*　hombres

pom. ellos. *cai* no.

tiù-tiniuón. puedan ver

tucbaṅa. en la noche.

túcbat. noche

na. ṅga. en

yúbajotṅa. yúbajot. escura. *ṅa*. en.

pumlop fuerte.

atáj hombre

chiùchiniċap vence.

no mi.

pausonompom. compañeros míos.

pauioṅ compañero.

pom mío

ájṅaichapo chapo terminacion

ajna mañana

cháom nosotros

tacnáyajan moriremos

pè y

mo parélxes.*

auóm otros.

chami à nosotros

napin enterraran

---

*Illegible word in the original.

O *cámayompom hicuajon o quig*
Your children. run your house. *quig.*
house.

17r *atájom* men

pom. they *cai* no.

tiù-tiniuón they can see

tucbaña in the night

túcbat night

na. nga in

yúbajotṅa. yúbajot dark. *ṅa.* in.

pumlop strong

atáj man

chiùchiniċap vanquish

no my

pausonompom my companions.

pauioṅ companion.

pom mine

ájṅaichapo short termination

ajna tomorrow

cháom we

tacnáyajan we will die

pè and

mo [illegible word]

auóm others.

chami to us

napin they will bury

Prima
Linguae Californensis Rudimenta
a P. Tak proposita.

1.

Californienses *Quechñajuichom* omnibus fere quibus Hispani litteris utuntur: Sed peculiares sibi sonos superposito quibusdam litteris puncto signare commode possunt.

a . b . c . ċ . d . e . g . h . i . j . l . ll . m . n . ñ . ṅ . o . p . q . r . s . ṡ . t . u . y .

desunt litterae *f . k . ñ . z .*

ċ. effertur cum aspiratione

ṅ . aequat ng.

ṡ = sc. seu *ch* Gallorum.

2.

Nomina genera carent, duas pro omnibus caribus habent terminationes, at plurati numero adiiciunt m, vel om.

Ex duplici pluralis numeri terminatione duplex agnoscitur declinatio, quarum altera singularem numerum littera vocali concludit, altera consonanti terminatur.

Prior declinatio

PRIOR DECLINATIO

N.   *Yúla.*   Capillus.

G.   *Yula.*   Capilli.

D.   *Yulai.*   Capillo

Ac.   *Yulai.*   Capillum.

V.   *Yula.*   Capille.

PLURALITER.

N.   *Yulam.*   Capilli.

G.   *Yulam.*   Capillorum.

D.   *Yúlami.*   Capillis.

Ac.   *Yulami.*   Capillos.

V.   *Yulam.*   Capilli.

First
Rudiments of a Californian Language
proposed by P. Tak

1.

Californians *Quechñajuichom* make use of nearly all the letters the Spaniards do. But by placing a mark over certain letters they are able to properly inscribe sounds particular to themselves.

a . b . c . ċ . d . e . g . h . i . j . l . ll . m . n . ñ̇ . ṅ . o . p . q . r . s . ṡ . t . u . y .

These letters are missing: *f . k . ñ . z* .

ċ is aspirated.

ṅ equals *ng.*

ṡ = *sc* or the *ch* of the Gauls.

2.

Nouns lack gender. They have two endings for all familiar forms; and for those things plural in number add *m* or *om.*

For both [declensions], the plural is expressed using an ending of a plural number. One concludes the singular using a vowel, and the other ends in a consonant.

First declension.

FIRST DECLENSION.

NOMINATIVE: *Yúla.* hair.

GENITIVE: *Yula.* of hair.

DATIVE: *Yulai.* to/for hair

ACCUSATIVE: *Yulai.* hair.

VOCATIVE: *Yula.* hair

PLURAL.

NOMINATIVE: *Yulam.* hairs.

GENITIVE: *Yulam.* of hairs.

DATIVE: *Yúlami.* to/for hairs.

ACCUSATIVE: *Yulami.* hairs.

VOCATIVE: *Yulam.* hairs.

Sic flectuntur.

Pala. aqua.

Quicha. domus. *Kicha.*

Huǹla. ventus.

Ejla. terra.

Tota. petra.

Mota. mus.

Húla. sagitta.

É. pes.

Aui. pinguis.

   Dat. *auiyi.* interposito *y.*

   Ac. *auiyi.*

Yò. *Mater.*

Nà. *Pater*

Yú *caput.*

20r   SECUNDA DECLINATIO

N. *Húnuot.* Ursus.

G. *Hunuot.* Ursius

D. *Húnuoti.* Urso

Ac. *Hunuoti.* Ursum.

V. *Hunuot.* Urse.

PLURALITER

N. *Húnuotom.* Ursi

G. *Hunuotom.* Ursorum.

D. *Hunuotmi.* Ursis.

Ac. *Hunuotmi.* Ursos.

V. *Hunuotom.* Ursi.

Eodem modo flectuntur

Cuà-al, vermis. seu musca.

Chilcuat. vas.

Auàl. canis.

Coláuot. lignum.

Thus they are translated.

Pala. water.

Quicha. house. *Kicha.*

Huṅla. wind.

Ejla. earth.

Tota. stone.

Mota. mouse.

Húla. arrow.

É. foot.

Aui. fat, plump

    DATIVE: *Auiyi.* With the '*y*' placed in the middle

    ACCUSATIVE: *Auiyi.*

Yò. Mother.

Nà. Father.

Yú. head.

20r SECOND DECLENSION

    NOMINATIVE: *Húnuot.* bear.

    GENITIVE: *Hunuot.* of the bear.

    DATIVE: *Húnuoti.* to/for the bear.

    ACCUSATIVE: *Hunuoti.* bear.

    VOCATIVE: *Hunuot.* bear.

PLURAL

    NOMINATIVE: *Húnuotom.* bears

    GENITIVE: *Hunuotom.* of the bears.

    DATIVE: *Hunuotmi.* to/for the bears

    ACCUSATIVE: *Hunuotmi.* bears.

    VOCATIVE: *Hunuotom.* bears.

In the same way these are translated

Ċuà-al. worm. also fly.

Chilcuat. vessel.

Auàl. dog.

Coláuot. wood.

Animadvert

Nomen = *Chańichniś*. Deus, eique similia dum flectuntur amittere litteram ultimam *ś* solent.

N. *Chańichńiś* Deus

G. *Chańichńiś*.

Đ.

A. *Chańichni*.

V. *chańichni*.

Chańichnis

N. *Uaiś* caro.

G. *Uais*. carnis.

D. *Uai*. carni.

Ac. *Uai* carnem.

V. *Uaiś*. caro.

PLURALITER.

N. *Uaóm*. carnes

G. *Uaóm*. carnum.

D. *Uaómi*. carnibus.

Ac. *Uami*. carnes.

V. *Uaóm*. carnes.

NOMINA SECUNDAE DECLINATIONIS.

Mámajis. amor, et voluntas,

Not. dux. vel Rex.

chat noctua.

Tamàt. os. oris. vel dens.

Uéyiś. lingua.

Músiś. barba.

Náimaiś. auris.

járat. guttur.

Al. pectus.

mat. bracchuim, et manus.

sulat. unguis.

tájauiś corpus.

Observe

Noun = *Chańichńiś*.   God and yet resemblances for it are bent to drop the final letter *ś*, as is usual.

NOMINATIVE: *Chańichńiś* God

GENITIVE: *Chańichńiś*.

~~DATIVE~~

ACCUSATIVE: *Chańichni*.

VOCATIVE: *chańichni*.

Chańichnis.

NOMINATIVE: Uaiś. flesh.

GENITIVE: *Uais* of flesh

DATIVE: *Uai*. to/for flesh

ACCUSATIVE: *Uai*. flesh

VOCATIVE: *Uais* flesh

20v PLURAL.

NOMINATIVE: *Uaóm*. flesh

GENITIVE: *Uaóm*. of flesh.

DATIVE: *Uaómi*. to/for flesh

ACCUSATIVE: *Uami*. flesh.

VOCATIVE: *Uaóm*. flesh.

NOUNS OF THE SECOND DECLENSION.

Mámajis. love, and inclination.

Not. leader. or King.

chat little owl.

Tamàt. mouth. of the mouth. or tooth.

Uéyiś. tongue.

Músiś. beard.

Náimaiś. ear.

járat. throat.

Al. breast.

mat. arm, and hand.

sulat. finger.

tájauiś. body.

Atàj.   homo incognitus

~~*Yasis.*~~   ~~homo.~~   ~~*yaàs*~~

Suǹàl.   mulier.

Amáyamal.   puer. vel juvenis

Najánmal   senes

Yot.   magnus.   *yot*

Neṡmal.   vetula.

Eheǹmal.   passer, et avis.

uácat.   ensis noster.

Yejis. yejis.   Laus. saepe superbia.

Pronomina
quae Personam significant.

21r

I.

N.   *Non.*   ego

G.   *No.*   mei

D.   *Nòiq.*   mihi.

Ac.   *Noi.*   me.

PLURALITER.

N.   *Chaom.*   nos.

G.   *cham.*   nostrum.

D.   *chámiq.*   nostris.

Ac.   *chámi.*   nos.

2.

N.   *Om.*   tu.

G.   *o.*   tui.

D.   *oiq.*   tibi.

Ac.   *oi.*   te.

PLUR.

N.   *Omòm.*   Vos.

G.   *om.*   vestrum.

Atàj. unknown man [stranger].

~~*Yasis.*~~ ~~man.~~ *yaàs*

Suñàl. woman.

Amáyamal. children. or youths

Najánmal old people

Yot. great. *yot*

Neśmal. old woman.

Eheñmal. sparrow, and bird.

uácat. our sword.

Yejis. yejis. praise, also pride.

Pronouns
that indicate person

1.

NOMINATIVE: *Non.* I

GENITIVE: *No.* my

DATIVE: *Nòiq.* to/for me

ACCUSATIVE: *Noi.* me.

PLURAL

NOMINATIVE: *Chaom.* we.

GENITIVE: *cham.* our.

DATIVE: *chámiq.* to/for us.

ACCUSATIVE: *chámi.* us.

2.

NOMINATIVE: *Om.* you.

GENITIVE: *o.* your.

DATIVE: *oiq.* to/for you.

ACCUSATIVE: *oi.* you.

PLURAL

NOMINATIVE: *Omòm.* you.

GENITIVE: *om.* your.

D. *omómiq* vobis.

Ac *omòmi.* vos.

3.

N. *Po.* ille.

G. *Po.* illuis.

D *Poiq.* illi.

Ac. *Pói.* illum.

PLUR.

Pomom Pomòm. illi. illae.

G. *Pom.* illorum. illarum.

D. *Pomòmiq.* illis.

Ac. *Pomómi.* illos. illás.

Nomina numerorum.

Supùl. unus. 1

Ueh. duo. 2.

Pai. tres. 3.

Uasá. quatuor. 4.

Mahár. quinque. 5.

Deinde.

Supul. pes mahar. 6.

unus, et quinque. VI.

Ueh pe mahar. 7

duo, et quinque VII.

Pai pe mahar. 8.

tres, et quinque. VIII.

Uasá pe mahar. 9.

quatuor, et quinque. IX.

Ueh con mahar. X. 10

bis quinque. X

Ueh con mahar. pe supul. 11.

bis quinque et unus. XI.

DATIVE: *omómiq.* to/for you.

Accusative: *omòmi.* you.

3.

NOMINATIVE: *Po.* that.

GENITIVE: *Po.* of that.

DATIVE: D. *Poiq.* to/for that.

ACCUSATIVE: *Pói.* that.

PLUR.

Pomom Pomòm. those

GENITIVE: *Pom.* of those

DATIVE: *Pomòmiq* to/for those

ACCUSATIVE: . *Pomómi.* those.

Names of the Numbers

Supùl. one. 1

Ueh. two. 2.

Pai. three. 3.

Uasá. four. 4.

Mahár. five. 5.

Next.

Supul. pes mahar. 6.

one, and five. VI.

Ueh pe mahar. 7.

two, and five. VII.

Pai pe mahar. 8.

three, and five. VIII.

Uasá pe mahar. 9.

four, and five. IX.

Ueh con mahar. X. 10

twice five. X

Ueh con mahar. pe supul. 11.

twice five and one. XI.

Ueh con mahar. pe ueh.   1 2.

bis quinque et duo.   XII.

Ueh con mahar. pe pai.   1 3

bis quinque et tres.   XIII.

Ueh con mahar pe uasá.   1 4.

bis quinque et quatuor.   XIV.

22r   *Pai con mahar.*   quindecim.   1 5.

ter quinque.   XV.

Pai con mahar pe supul.   1 6.

ter quinque et unus.   XVI.

Pai con mahar pe ueh.   1 7.

ter quinque et duo.   XVII

Pai con mahar pe pai.   1 8.

ter quinque et tres.   XVIII.

Pai con mahar pe uasá.   1 9.

ter quinque et quatuor.   XIX.

Uasà con mahar.   20.

quater quinque.   XX.

Uasá con mahar pé supul.   XXI.

Uasà con mahar pe ueh.   XXII

Uasà con mahar pe pai.   2 3.

Uasà con mahar pe uasà.   2 4.

~~quinquies et quatuor.~~

quater quinque et quatuor.   XXIV.

Uasà con mahar pe mahar.   2 5.

quater quinque et quinque.   XXV.

Usque ad sex numerum semper numerare solemus, a sex usque ad mille numeris hispanorum utimur, siquis autem ut nos hic numera-

22v   rimus usque ad quinque et viginti numerum Numerare vellet, posset.

Ueh con mahar. pe ueh. 12.

twice five and two. XII.

Ueh con mahar. pe pai. 13.

twice five and three. XIII.

Ueh con mahar pe uasá. 14.

twice five and four. XIV.

22r   *Pai con mahar.* fifteen. 15.

thrice five. XV.

Pai con mahar pe supul. 16.

thrice five and one. XVI.

Pai con mahar pe ueh. 17.

thrice five and two. XVII

Pai con mahar pe pai. 18.

thrice five and three. XVIII.

Pai con mahar pe uasá. 19.

thrice five and four. XIX.

Uasà con mahar. 20.

four times five. XX.

Uasá con mahar pé supul. XXI.

Uasà con mahar pe ueh. XXII.

Uasà con mahar pe pai. 23.

Uasà con mahar pe uasà. 24.

~~five times and four~~

four times five and four. XXIV.

Uasà con mahar pe mahar. 25.

four times five and five. XXV.

We are always accustomed to count to the number six, we make use of the numbers of the Spaniards from six to a thousand; however, indeed, it is desirable, if possible, to count all the way to five and twenty in order
22v   that we might measure in this way.*

---

*In other words, it is desirable to count to twenty-five in Luiseño using different combinations of *supùl, ueh, pai, uasá,* and *mahár.*

Primera declinación.

La primera declinación termina en *a, e, i, o, u.* El Nominat., el genit. y el ablat. son iguales, el dat. y el acusat. son diferentes de los otros tres casos quando el nombre termina en *a* en el nominat., el dat. y el acusat. añaden una *i*, sea en el num. singular que en el plural. Para hacer el numero plural, es menester añadir una *m* como se vee de bajo

SINGULAR

N. *pala* agua	N. *cuta* sauco	N. *quicha* casa
G. *pala*	G. *cuta*	G. *quicha*
D. *palai*	D. *cutai*	D. *quichai*
Ac. *palai*	Ac. *cutai*	Ac. *quichai*
Ab. *pala*	Ab. *cuta*	Ab. *quicha*

PLURAL

N. *palam*	N. *cutam*	N. *quicham*
G. *palam*	G. *cutam*	G. *quicham*
D. *palami*	D. *cutami*	D. *quichami*
Ac. *Palami*	Ac. *cutami*	Ac. *quichami*
Ab. *palam*	Ab. *cutam*	Ab. *quicham*

SINGULAR

N. *mota* raton	N. *huṅla* viento	N. *ejla* tierra
G. *mota*	G. *huṅla*	G. *ejla*
D. *motai*	D. *huṅlai*	D. *ejlai*
Ac. *motai*	Ac. *huṅlai*	Ac. *ejlai*
Ab. *mota*	Ab. *huṅla*	Ab. *ejla*

PLURAL

N. *motam*	N. *huṅlam*	N. *ejlam*
G. *motam*	G. *huṅlam*	G. *ejlam*
D. *motami*	D. *huṅlami*	D. *ejlami*
Ac. *motami*	Ac. *huṅlami*	Ac. *ejlami*
Ab. *motam*	Ab. *huṅlam*	Ab. *ejlam*

First Declension

The first declension ends in *a, e, i, o, u*. The nominative, genitive, and ablative are the same, while the dative and the accusative are different from the other three cases. When a noun ends in *a* in the nominative, the dative, and the accusative, add an *i*, whether singular or plural in number. To make a number plural, it is necessary to add an *m*, as you see below.

SINGULAR

N. *pala* water	N. *cuta* elder tree	N. *quicha* house
G. *pala*	G. *cuta*	G. *quicha*
D. *palai*	D. *cutai*	D. *quichai*
Ac. *palai*	Ac. *cutai*	Ac. *quichai*
Ab. *pala*	Ab. *cuta*	Ab. *quicha*

PLURAL

N. *palam*	N. *cutam*	N. *quicham*
G. *palam*	G. *cutam*	G. *quicham*
D. *palami*	D. *cutami*	D. *quichami*
Ac. *Palami*	Ac. *cutami*	Ac. *quichami*
Ab. *palam*	Ab. *cutam*	Ab. *quicham*

SINGULAR

N. *mota* mouse	N. *huṅla* wind	N. *ejla* earth
G. *mota*	G. *huṅla*	G. *ejla*
D. *motai*	D. *huṅlai*	D. *ejlai*
Ac. *motai*	Ac. *huṅlai*	Ac. *ejlai*
Ab. *mota*	Ab. *huṅla*	Ab. *ejla*

PLURAL

N. *motam*	N. *huṅlam*	N. *ejlam*
G. *motam*	G. *huṅlam*	G. *ejlam*
D. *motami*	D. *huṅlami*	D. *ejlami*
Ac. *motami*	Ac. *huṅlami*	Ac. *ejlami*
Ab. *motam*	Ab. *huṅlam*	Ab. *ejlam*

<u>en *e*</u>

SINGULAR	PLURAL
N. *è* pie	N. *e*
G. *è*	G. *em*
D. *ei*	D. *emi*
Ac. *ei*	Ac. *emi*
Ab. *è*	Ab. *em*

23v

<u>en *i*</u>

SINGULAR	PLURAL
N. *aui* gordo	N. *auim*
G. *aui*	G. *auim*
D. *auiyi*	D. *auimi*
Ac. *auiyi*	Ac. *auimi*
Ab. *aui*	Ab. *Auim*

<u>en *o*</u>

SINGULAR	PLURAL
N. *yò* madre	N. *yom*
G. *yò*	G. *yom*
D. *yoi*	D. *yomi*
Ac. *yoi*	Ac. *yomi*
Ab. *yò*	Ab. *yom*

<u>en *u*</u>

SINGULAR	PLURAL
N. *yù* cabeza	N. *yum*
G. *yu*	G. *yum*
D. *yui*	D. *yumi*
Ac. *yui*	Ac. *yumi*
Ab. *yù*	Ab. *yum*

Segunda declinación.

La segunda declinación termina en *t, l, h, ṡ, r, m*, y casi se puede decir que ~~tambien la segunda y la primera~~ no sea segunda declinación, mas que sea una unica declinación, que es la primera, mas porque algunos nombres de esta declinación no figuren la regla que dejimos, particularmente los nombres que terminan en *s* como *chañichñiṡ* y otros más.

in *e*

SINGULAR		PLURAL	
N.	*è* foot	N.	*e*
G.	*è*	G.	*em*
D.	*ei*	D.	*emi*
Ac.	*ei*	Ac.	*emi*
Ab.	*è*	Ab.	*em*

23v

in *i*

SINGULAR		PLURAL	
N.	*aui* fat	N.	*auim*
G.	*aui*	G.	*auim*
D.	*auiyi*	D.	*auimi*
Ac.	*auiyi*	Ac.	*auimi*
Ab.	*aui*	Ab.	*auim*

in *o*

SINGULAR		PLURAL	
N.	*yò* mother	N.	*yom*
G.	*yó*	G.	*yom*
D.	*yoi*	D.	*yomi*
Ac.	*yoi*	Ac.	*yomi*
Ab.	*yò*	Ab.	*yom*

in *u*

SINGULAR		PLURAL	
N.	*yù* head	N.	*yum*
G.	*yu*	G.	*yum*
D.	*yui*	D.	*yumi*
Ac.	*yui*	Ac.	*yumi*
Ab.	*yù*	Ab.	*yum*

Second declension

The second declension ends in *t, l, h, s̓, r*, and *m*. One could almost say that there is no second declension, but that there is one sole declension, which is the first one, except that some nouns in this declension do not follow the rule we stated, particularly the nouns that end in *s*, like *chan̓ichn̓is̓* and a few others.

SINGULAR

N. *hunuot*	oso		N. *chilcuat*	vaso		N. *momat*	mar
G. *hunuot*			G. *chilcuat*			G. *momat*	
D. *hunuoti*			D. *chilcuati*			D. *momati*	
Ac. *hunuoti*			Ac. *chilcuati*			Ac. *momati*	
Ab. *hunuot*			Ab. *chilcuat*			Ab. *momat*	

PLURAL

N. *hunuotom*		N. *chilcuatom*		N. *momatom*	
G. *hunuotom*		G. *chilcuatom*		G. *momatom*	
D. *hunuotomi*		D. *chilcuatomi*		D. *momatomi*	
Ac. *hunuotomi*		Ac. *chilcuatomi*		Ac. *momatomi*	
Ab. *hunuotom*		Ab. *chilcuatom*		Ab. *momatom*	

SINGULAR EN *L* PLURAL *Q*

N. *quaàl*	gusano y tambien mosca	N. *jupul*	uno	N. *quaàlom*	
G. *quaàl*		G. *jupul*		G. *quaàlom*	
D. *quaàli*		D. *jupuli*		D. *quaàlomi*	
Ac. *quaàli*		Ac. *jupuli*		Ac. *quaàlomi*	
Ab. *quaàl*		Ab. *jupul*		Ab. *quaàlom*	

24r

en *h*

PLURAL

N. *Uch~~om~~*	dos	N. *Mahár*	cinco	N. *Pai*	tres
G. *Uchom*		G. *mahàrom*		G. *Pachom*	
D. *Uchmi*		D. *maharmi*		D. *Pachomi*	
Ac. *Uchmi*		Ac. *maharmi*		Ac. *Pachomi*	
Ab. *Uchom*		Ab. *maharom*		Ab. *Pachom*	

SINGULAR

N. *Om*	tu	N. *Uàis*	carne	N. *Muioc*	mucho
G. *O~~m~~*		G. *Uaiṡ*		G. *Muioc*	
D. ~~Oi~~ *Oi. o. oic*		D. *Uàis*		D. *Muioqui*	
Ac. *Oi. o oic*		Ac. *Uài*		Ac. *Muioqui*	
Ab. *Om*		Ab. *Uàiṡ*		Ab. *Muioc*	

SINGULAR

N. *hunuot* bear
G. *hunuot*
D. *hunuoti*
Ac. *hunuoti*
Ab. *hunuot*

N. *chilcuat* drinking glass
G. *chilcuat*
D. *chilcua*
Ac. *chilcuati*
Ab. *chilcuat*

N. *momat* sea
G. *momat*
D. *momati*
Ac. *momati*
Ab. *momat*

PLURAL

N. *hunuotom*
G. *hunuotom*
D. *hunuotomi*
Ac. *hunuotomi*
Ab. *hunuotom*

N. *chilcuatom*
G. *chilcuatom*
D. *chilcuatomi*
Ac. *chilcuatomi*
Ab. *chilcuatom*

N. *momatom*
G. *momatom*
D. *momatomi*
Ac. *momatomi*
Ab. *momatom*

SINGULAR IN *l* PLURAL *Q*

N. *quaàl* caterpillar and also fly
G. *quaàl*
D. *quaàli*
Ac. *quaàli*
Ab. *quaàl*

N. *jupul* one
G. *jupul*
D. *jupuli*
Ac. *jupuli*
Ab. *jupul*

N. *quaàlom*
G. *quaàlom*
D. *quaàlomi*
Ac. *quaàlomi*
Ab. *quaàlom*

24r

in *h*

PLURAL

N. *Uchom* two
G. *Uchom*
D. *Uchomi*
Ac. *Uchmi*
Ab. *Uchom*

N. *Mahár* five
G. *mahàrom*
D. *maharmi*
Ac. *maharmi*
Ab. *maharom*

N. *Pa* three
G. *Pachom*
D. *Pachomi*
Ac. *Pachomi*
Ab. *Pachom*

SINGULAR

N. *Om* you
G. *Om*
D. *Oi* Oi. o. oi
Ac. *Oi.* o oic
Ab. *Om*

N. *Uàis* meat *or* flesh
G. *uàis*
D. *Uàis*
Ac. *Uài*
Ab. *Uàiṡ*

N. *muioc* much
G. *muioc*
D. *muioqui*
Ac. *muioqui*
Ab. *muioc*

PLURAL

N. *Omom* vos	N. *Uàim*	N. *Muicom*
G. *Omom*	G. *Uàim*	G. *Muiocom*
D. *Omomi*	D. *Uàimi*	D. *Muiocomi*
Ac. *Omomi*	Ac. *Uáimis*	Ac. *Muiocomi*
Ab. *Omom*	Ab. *Uàim*	Ab. *Muiocom*

SINGULAR

N. *chaṅichṅiṡ* Dios

G. *chaṅichṅiṡ*

D. *chaṅichṅici*

Ac. *chaṅichṅici*

Ab. *chaṅichṅiṡ*

No hai generos Por ejemplo, si yo dijese un viejo valiente mató a un osso terrible. Se diría asi: *pnajanmalop mòcnac, souòjuochi hunuoti.*

En este pais no hay ninguna piedra que sea negra.

ivaqña quiña caiop mièc tota jubattajot.

Buscan un ciervo blanco, mas no le pueden hallar

haluonpom sucati jàiujoti pè pom cai tolòuiuon

Esta canoa es muy chica, y jàmas no podran entra[r] en ella cinco hombres.

ivip uejet pomminocopop quijut pè mo ivaña cai chulupajan majarom yàsichom.

24v

Conjugacion

Todos los verbos en el infinito terminan en *iṡ* [y] *uiṡ*, y en el presente, en vez dela *s* cogen la *ċ* y terminan en *iċ*. p. e. *majaniṡ*, dar, en el presente harà *majanic*, doi. ma[s] a quellos que terminan en el infinito en *aiṡ*, cortan *iṡ*, como p. e. *mocnaiṡ*, mattar, que hace *mocnaċ*, mato.

PLURAL

N. *Omom* you	N. *Uàim*	N. *Muicom*
G. *Omom*	G. *Uàim*	G. *Muiocom*
D. *Omomi*	D. *Uàimi*	D. *Muiocomi*
Ac. *Omomi*	Ac. *Uáimis*	Ac. *Muiocomi*
Ab. *Omom*	Ab. *Uàim*	Ab. *Muiocom*

SINGULAR

N. *chaṅichṅiṡ*   God

G. *chaṅichṅiṡ*

D. *chaṅichṅici*

Ac. *chaṅichṅici*

Ab. *chaṅichṅiṡ*

There are no genders. For example, if I were to say, "A brave old man killed a terrible bear," I would say: *pnajanmalop mòcnac, souòjuochi hunuoti.*

In this country, there is no stone that is black.

ivaqña quiña caiop mièc tota jubattajot.

They are looking for a white deer, but one cannot be found.

haluonpom sucati jàiujoti pè pom cai tolòuiuon.

This canoe is very small, and five men will never be able to get in it.

ivip uejet pomminocopop quijut pè mo ivaña cai chulupajan majarom yàsichom.

24v

Conjugation

All verbs in the infinitive end in *iṡ* and *uiṡ*, and in the present, instead of the *s*, they take *ċ* and end in *iċ*; for example, *majaniṡ*, "to give," in the present would make *majanic*, "I give." But for those that end in the infinitive with *aiṡ*, the *iṡ* cut off; for example, *mocnaiṡ*, "to kill," which makes *mocnaċ*, "I kill."

	SUPUL				SINGULAR	
N.	*Tota*	*Pala*		N.	Piedra	Agua
G.	*Tota*	*Pala*		G.	de la Piedra	del Agua
D.	*Totai*	*Palai*		D.	a la Piedra	al Agua
Ac.	*Totai*	*Palai*		Ac.	Piedra	Agua
V.	*Tota*	*Pala*		V.	Piedra	Agua
Ab.	*Tota*	*Pala*		Ab.	Piedra	Agua

	MUIOC			PLURAL	
N.	*Totam*	*Palam*		Piedras	Aguas
G.	*Totam*	*Palam*		De las Piedras	de las Aguas
D.	*Totami*	*Palami*		A las Piedras	a las Aguas
Ac.	*Totami*	*Palami*		Piedras	Aguas
Ab.	*Totam*	*Palam*		Piedras	Aguas

Todos los nombres en esta lengua son de genero comun.

	SUPUL			SINGULAR	
N.	*Màmajis*	*Lachis*		Amor	Ora
G.	*Màmajis*	*Lachis*		Del Amor	
D.	*Màmaji*	*Lachi*		al Amor	
Ac.	*Màmaji*	*Lachi*	Acc	Amor	
Ab.	*Màmajis*	*Lachis*		Amor	

Los nombres que nacen de los verbos no se usan en plural, como son estos

MUIOCOP CAI MIIC　　　No HAY PLURAL

	SUPUL			SINGULAR	
N.	*Not*	*chat*		Rey	lechuza
G.	*Not*	*chat*		del Rey	de la lechuza
D.	*Noti*	*chati*		al rey	a la lechuza
Ac.	*Noti*	*chati*		al rey	lechuza
Ab.	*Not*	*chat*		por el rey	lechuza

	MUIOC			PLURAL	
N.	*Notom*	*Chatom*		Reyes	Lechuzas
G.	*Notom*	*chatom*		De los Reyes	de las lechuzas

	SUPUL			SINGULAR	
N.	Tota	Pala	N.	Stone	Water
G.	Tota	Pala	G.	from the Stone	from the Water
D.	Totai	Palai	D.	to the Stone	to the Water
Ac.	Totai	Palai	Ac.	Stone	Water
V.	Tota	Pala	V.	Stone	Water
Ab.	Tota	Pala	Ab.	Stone	Water

	MUIOC		PLURAL	
N.	Totam	Palam	Stones	Waters
G.	Totam	Palam	from the Stones	from the Waters
D.	Totami	Palami	to the Stones	to the Waters
Ac.	Totami	Palami	Stones	Waters
Ab.	Totam	Palam	Stones	Waters

All of the nouns in this language have a common gender.

	SUPUL		SINGULAR	
N.	Màmajis	Lachis	Love	Prayer
G.	Màmajis	Lachis	Of love	
D.	Màmaji	Lachi	to love	
Ac.	Màmaji	Lachi	Acc. Love	
Ab.	Màmajis	Lachis	Love	

The nouns that come from verbs, such as these, are not used in the plural.

25v MUIOCOP CAI MIIC — THERE IS NO PLURAL

	SUPUL		SINGULAR	
N.	Not	chat	King	owl
G	Not	chat	of the king	of the owl
D.	Noti	hati	to the king	to the owl
Ac.	Noti	chati	the king	owl
Ab.	Not	chat	by the king	owl

	MUIOC		PLURAL	
N.	Notom	Chatom	Kings	Owls
G.	Notom	Chatom	of the Kings	of the owls

D.	*Notomi*	*chatomi*	A los Reyes	a las Lechuzas
Ac.	*Notomi*	*chatomi*	a los Reyes	Lechuzas
Ab.	*Notom*	*chatom*	Por los reyes	Lechuzas

26r *Pitoopauis*	Presente

UAUIS	Llamar
Supul	Singular
Non Uàuic	Yo llamo
Omop Uàuic	Tú llamas
Uonalop Uàuic	Aquel llama
MUIOC	PLURAL
Chaomcha Uàuiuon	Nosotros llamamos
Omomopom Uàuiuon	Vosotros llamais
Uonalompom Uàuiuon	Aquellos llaman
CHORÒAJOT	PERFECTO PRETÉRITO
Nonil Uàuaj	Yo llamè
Omopil Uàuaj	Tú llamaste
Uonálopil Uàuaj	Aquel llamò

27r Dejimos que si la palabra terminaba en consonante se le añadía solamente la silaba *op* y si terminaba en vocal se le añadía la sola letra *p*. mas que assi no sucedía, en las palabras de una silaba mas que cogían la silaba *op*. Aora digamos si [la] palabra es de una silaba en vez de añadirle la silaba *op*. se puede añadir, al verbo, no la silaba *op*. mas la letra *p*. por exemplo en vez [de] decir tu Padre viene o *Naop monà,* se puede decir, y se diría mejor, *monap o Nà.*

Hai otra manera para decir, o exprimir, lo que hemos hablado y son las voces *miċ. miċuas.* hai había. La primera voz se usa mucho para las cosas, la segunda voz para las cosa y personas. p.e. Que hai en tu cabeza? No se lo que sea. *Hichar o Yuño miċ, au-iċan.* Yo estoi y tambien me hallo en tus ojos; es verdad? *Nom o puṡño miċ, asunso?*

La segunda voz que mucho se usa, significa habia, era, etc. habia un hombre que siempre lloraba. *Niċuorapil supul ataj. pe apil mimchapan*

D.	*Notomi*	*Chatomi*	To the Kings	to the Owls
Ac.	*Notomi*	*Chatomi*	the Kings	Owls
Ab.	*Notom*	*Chatom*	by the Kings	Owls

26r   *Pitoopauis*   Present

Uauis   To call

   Supul   Singular

Non Uàuic   I call

Omop Uàuic   You call

Uonalop Uàuic   That one calls

Mᴜɪᴏᴄ   Pʟᴜʀᴀʟ

Chaomcha Uàuiuon   We call

Omomopom Uàuiuon   You call

Uonalompom Uàuiuon   Those call

Cʜᴏʀᴏ̀ᴀᴊᴏᴛ   Pᴇʀғᴇᴄᴛ ᴘʀᴇᴛᴇʀɪᴛ

Nonil Uàuaj   I called

Omopil Uàuaj   You called

Uonálopil Uàuaj   That one called

27r   We said that if a word ended in a consonant, one would add only the syllable *op,* and if it ended in a vowel, one added the single letter *p,* but that that did not happen in single-syllable words, which instead took the syllable *op.* Now let us say that if the word is one syllable long, instead of adding the syllable *op,* one can add to the verb, not the syllable *op,* but rather the letter *p.* For example: instead of saying "your father comes," *o Naop monà,* one can say, and it would be better said, *monap o Nà.*

There is another way of saying, or expressing, everything we have discussed, and that is through the words *mic̓, mic̓uas,* "there is, there was." The first word is used often for things, and the second word for things and persons. For example: "What is in your head? I don't know what it might be." *Hichar o Yuǹo mic̓, au-ic̓an.* "I am here, and I also find myself in your eyes, is that not true?" *Nom o puṡǹo mic̓, asunso?*

The second word that is often used means "had, was," etc. "There was a man who always cried." *Nic̓uorapil supul ataj. pe apil mimchapan*

ñaċuas. había otro que siempre reia *Auòpil micùas, pe apil mimchapan jimaċuas.*

Con todo esso, muchas vezes se deja la palabra ser, (como los latines que muchas veces dejan) y no se podría poner, porque sería un error, y no se podría entender. P.e. Quien es tu padre o chico, de quien eres hijo se dice en esta sola manera ni en otra se puede decir: *Nàtoso o Na.* quis pater tuus, quién tu padre, etc.

31r En el tiempo perfecto passado del verbo, quando se encuentran dos vocales la tilde se pone a la primera vocal, para que se [h]aga mas fuerza, como los Españoles ponen la tilde a la primera vocal, en la casi ultima sílaba del tiempo imperfecto de la tercera conjugacion, diciendo pedía, reñía, añadía, revivia. revestia, etc. assi nosotros *Quechñajuichom* en el perfecto passado hacemos *uocòa, hùnìaj, pàaj, cupùa, siquinìaj,* lleguè, enseñè, he bevido, durmiò, hize dar azotes, y los otros, esso sucede como dejimos quando dos vocales se encuentraban en la casi ultima sílaba del perfecto passado, lo que tambien sucede en el presente tiempo del verbo *uócòajis,* llegar. *non uocòaċ* yo llego, *omop uocòaċ,* tu llegas, *uonalop uocòaċ,* aquel llega, *chaomcha uocòajon,* nosotros llegamos, *omomom uocòajon,* vosotros llegais, *aenàlempem uocòajon,* aquellos llegan.

y tambien el verbo *hùnìis,* enseñar. *non hùnìiċ,* yo enseño, *omop hùnìiċ,* tú enseñas, *uonálop hùnìiċ, chaomcha, omomom, uonalempom hùníiuon.* nosotros enseñamos, vosotros enseñais, aquellos enseñan. Y este mismo verbo en todos los dichos tiempos tiene siempre sobre la primera [sílaba] la tilde. haciendo presente *hùnìiċ,* enseño. imperfecto. *hùnicuos* enseñaba, *hùnìaj,* perfecto enseñe. futuro *hùnìinepo* enseñarè, imperat[ivo] *hùnìi,* enseña tu. *hùnìyam* enseñad vosotros. Conjunt[ivo] *no hùnìipì,* para que yo enseñe. *o hùnìipi* para que tu enseñes. *po hùnìipi,* para que aquel enseñe. *cham hùnìipi,* para que enseñemos, *om hùnìipi* para que enseñeis, *pom hùnìipi* para que aquellos enseñen. imperfecto. *no hùnìicàla,* quando yo enseñaba. *o hùnìicàla,* quando enseñabas, *po hùnìicàla,* quando aquel enseñaba, *cham hùnìicala,*

ñacuas. "There was another who always laughed." *Auópil micùas, pe apil mimchapan jimacuas.*

With all that, often the word "to be" is left out (as the Latins often leave it out) and it cannot be put in, because it would be an error, and it could not be understood. For example: "Who is your father," or "Boy, whose son are you?" is said in this manner only, nor can it be said any other way: *Nàtoso o Na.* quis pater tuus, who [is] your father, etc.

31r   In the past perfect tense of a verb, when there are two vowels, the accent is placed on the first vowel, so as to give it more stress, as the Spanish put the accent on the first vowel in the penultimate syllable in the imperfect tense of the third conjugation, saying *pedía* (I used to ask), *reñía* (s/he used to quarrel), *añadía* (s/he used to add), *revivía* (s/he used to revive), *revestía* (s/he used to cover), etc. Thus in the past perfect we *Quechñajuichom* use *uocòa, hùniaj, pàaj, cupùa, siquiniaj:* "I arrived," "I taught," "I have drunk," "s/he slept," "I made one give lashes," and in other cases, this occurs, as we said, when two vowels [are]found in the penultimate syllable in the past perfect, which also occurs in the present tense of the verb *uócòajis,* "to arrive." *Non uocòac,* "I arrive"; *omop uocòac,* "you arrive"; *uonalop uocòac,* "that one arrives"; *chaomcha uocòajon,* "we arrive"; *omomom uocòajon,* "you [plural] arrive"; *uonàlempom uocòajon,* "those arrive."

And also the verb *hùniis,* to teach: *non hùniic,* "I teach"; *omop hùniic,* "you teach"; *uonálop hùniic,* * *chaomcha, omomom, uonàlempom hùniiuon:* "we teach, you [plural] teach, they teach. And this same verb, in all tenses mentioned, always has the accent over the first syllable, making present *húniic,* "I teach"; imperfect *hùnicuos,* "I used to teach"; perfect *hùniaj,* "I taught"; future *hùniinepo,* "I will teach"; imperative *hùnii,* "[you] teach" and *hùniyam* "[you (plural)] teach." Subjunctive *no hùniipi,* "so that I may teach"; *o hùniipi,* "so that you may teach"; *po hùniipi,* "so that that one may teach"; *cham hùniipi,* "so that we may teach"; *om hùniipi,* "so that you [plural] may teach; *pom hùniipi,* "so that those may teach." Imperfect: *no hùniicàla,* "when I used to teach"; *o hùniicàla,* "when you used to teach"; *po hùniicàla,* "when that one used to teach"; *cham hùniicala,* "when we

---

*Tac omits the Spanish translation for *uonálop hùniic,* which, based on the context, would be "that one teaches."

31v quando enseñabamos, *om hùnìicala,* quando quando enseñabaís, *pom hùnìicala,* quando enseñaban. Infinit. *hùnìiŝ,* enseñar. hay dos—ii y entonces quiere decir enseñar como es este *huniis,* y la tilde se pone sobre la primera segun dejimos mas arriba, si hay una i. y entonces quiere decir, casi transponer y es *hùn=iŝ.* Y todos los verbos que signi- fican accionque se hace muchas [veces] o se repite mas mandando como una vez deximos, y serían los que en *iniŝ* terminan, p.e. *tolou= uinìis,* hacer que se halle, nace del verbo *tolou=ìŝ,* hallar. *chaĉiuinìis:* hacer que se agarre, o mandar para que se agarre, y los demás.

Las palabras sirven para exprimir las actiones del cuerpo, por esso nosotros, quando queremos hacer la acción mas pronto, o mas tarde, si se quiere exprimir acción que se ha hecho con prontitud, entonces se pone la tilde, sobre la primera silaba, si la palabra es de dos, lo que muchas veces sucede, p.e. la palabra *jéchiŝ,* quiere decir dar bofetadas, mas quando se quiere exprimir la prontitud con que se dá, se pone sobre la primera silaba la tilde diciendo *poiope jèchiċ,* le dió bofetadas, *nùlo i cat,* lo empujó.

33r No me acuerdo de otro que del nombre o palabra, *Pajà,* que quiere decir, un animal casi como la culebra, que no daña, con sus dientes, mas da azotes, al que la quiere mattar, este nombre segun hemos dicho, siendo de la primera declinación de los nombres, que todos los nombres que terminaban en vocal debían solo coger una *m* en el plural, como *pala,* agua, que hacía *palam,* aguas, este nombre sigue, y se declina como los nombres de la segunda declinación, que todos terminan en vocal, cojiendo en el plural la silaba *om* como dejimos del nombre *Not.* capitan, que hacia *Notom.* capitanes, haciendo *Pajàom.* culebras.

Las voces de una silaba, como *Na* (1), Yo (2), tú (3), Padre (1), Madre (2), Madre dela Madre (3),* no son simples vocales, y mucho se distin- guen de las otras, porque con mas fuerza se dicen, se pronuncian que los Españoles con sus tildes, nos les pueden aun pronunciar porque la tilde de ellos no hace mucha fuerza en la pronuncia mas un poco le- vanta la voz. lo que en nuestras voces son casi dos tildes Españoles, puestos sobre las vocales de una sola silaba como *no. è,* mi *piè.* mi pié,

---

*In Tac's original, the numbers are written (without parentheses) immediately above the respective words, rather than following the word, as shown here.

31v   used to teach"; *om hùnìicala,* "when you [plural] used to teach": *pom hùnìicala,* "when they used to teach." Infinitive *hùnìis,* "to teach." There is a double *i,* and thus it means "to teach," as in *huniis,* and the accent is placed over the first one, as we said above; if there is one *i* and then it means "almost transfer," and it is *hùn=iś.* And all the verbs that signify frequently repeated actions, or frequently ordered actions, as we once said, would be those that end in *iniś.* For example, *tolou= uinìis,* "to make something be found," comes from the verb *tolou=ìs,* "to find"; *chaċiuinìis:* "to make something be gotten," or " to order that it be gotten," and so on.

Words are used to express actions of the body; that is why we—when we want to do an action promptly or [do it] later—if we want to express an action that has been done with promptness, then we put in the accent over the first syllable (if it's a two-syllable word, which often occurs. For example, the word *jéchiś* means "to strike blows," but when you want to express the promptness with which they are struck, the accent is placed over the first syllable, saying *poiope jèchiċ,* "he struck him with blows"; *nùlo i cat,* "he pushed him."

33r   I can't think of another besides the noun or word *Pajà,* which means an animal almost like a snake that does not harm with its teeth but lashes out at whomever tries to kill it. This noun, as we have said, being of the first declension of the nouns—in which all nouns ending in vowels should take only an *m* in the plural, like *pala,* "water," that became *palam,* "waters"—this noun follows and is declined like the nouns of the second declension, which all end in vowels, taking the syllable *om* in the plural—as we said of the noun *Not,* "captain," which became *Notom,* "captains"—becoming *pajàom,* "snakes."

One-syllable words, like *Na* (1), I (2), you (3), Father (1), Mother (2), Mother's mother (3), [do not have] simple vowels, and they are very distinct from the others, because they are said with a stronger stress. They are pronounced such that the Spaniards with their accents cannot pronounce them because their accent does not give much stress in pronunciation but only slightly raises the sound, which in our sounds are almost two Spanish accents, placed over the vowels of a single syllable like *no è,* "mi pié [Spanish for 'my foot']." "Mi pié" is softer in

33v en la pronuncia, es mas debil que *no. è,* palabra nuestra, que dejimos, casi se hallassen dos tildes Españoles, y no mas.

35r Las palabras de los Españoles para mi, para ti, para el para nosotros, para vosotros, para ellos explicamos con los dativos casos que serian *niiq. oiq. poiq. chamiq. omòmiq, pomòmiq.* Solos estos pronombres pueden hallarse en el caso dativo, mas los otros nombres se ponen en nominativo, y solo el pronombre *poiq.* queda en el caso dativo. p.e. para mi lo has hecho, y no para el. *Niiqṡo lovìaj pe cai poiq.* Para vosotros y no para ti cazò. *Omòmiq pè cai oiq muanàpil.* No compro para mi los sombreros mas para ellos. *Yumpiṡmin cai mìq, pomòmiqno samsaċ.*

Por mí, por ti, por el, por nosotros, por vosotros por ellos decimos, *no maṅai, o maṅai, po maṅai, cham maṅai pom maṅai, om maṅai.* y assi quando los Españoles dicen por amor o, bien, de mi, de ti de aquellos, de nosotros de vosotros, de ellos. decimos *no manài, o manai po manai, cham maṅai, om maṅai pom maṅai.* Por mi el aquí lo trajo. *No maṅai apil iuiq. hotajapil nomaṅai poi iuiq.* Por ti lloraba siempre, *o maṅai apil omimchapan ṅacuos.* Por ellos habló, *Pom maṅai apil tetelàa.* Por vosotros no queria venir, *om maṅaiapil cai hatiauichocuos.*

35v Por nosotros el hijo de Dios bajo de los Cielos, y tambien por nosotros muriò. *Cham maṅai apil Po Camar Chaṅiṅichṅis tupaṅai uòr-rà pé apil cham maṅài tacuài-ya.* Dice el demonio, no por mi, mas por vosotros murió el hijo de Dios *Sasquiyap yaċ. Cai apil nomaṅài, om maṅai apil Po cama Chaṅiṅichṅis tupàṅai uor-ra, tacùaiya.*

Todo por mi por mi bien hizo, y tambien por ti por el, por nosotros por vosotros, por ellos. *Chom apil nomaṅai lovi-aj. Pe apil omaṅai po maṅai cham maṅai pom maṅai.*

Con que nosotros ~~decimos~~, el para mi, para ti, el para el, etc. no tenemos, y en vez de esto, hacimos los pronombres de caso dativo todos sin otra voz, y los otros nombres es menester añadir la palabra *poiq,* que quiere decir para el y poner el nombre en nominativo.

33v pronunciation than *no è,* our word, as we have said, almost if there were two Spanish accents, and not more.

35r The Spanish words "for me," "for you," "for him," "for us," "for you [plural]," "for them," we explain with the dative case, which would be *niiq, oiq, poiq, chamiq, omòmiq, pomòmiq.* Only these pronouns can be in the dative case, but the other nouns are put in the nominative, and only the pronoun *poiq* remains in the dative case. For example: "For me you have done this, and not for him." *Niiqśo lovìaj pe cai poiq.* "For you [plural] and not for you [singular] did he hunt." *Omòmiq pè cai oiq muanàpil.* "I'm not buying the hats for myself, but for them." *Yumpiśmin cai mìq, pomòmiqno samsać.*

"For [the sake of] me," "for [the sake of] you," "for [the sake of] him," "for [the sake of] us," "for [the sake of] you [plural]," "for [the sake of] them," we say *no mañai, o mañai, po mañai, cham mañai, pom mañai, om mañai.* And thus, when the Spaniards say "out of love" or "for the good of me, of you, of them, of us, of you [plural], of them." we say *no manài, o manai, po manai, cham mañai, om mañai, pom mañai.* "For me [for my sake] he brought him here." *No mañai apil iuiq. hotajapil nomañai poi iuiq.* "For you [on your account] he always cried." *o mañai apil omimchapan nàcuos.* "For them [on their behalf] he spoke." *Pom mañai apil tetelàa.* "For you [because of you (plural)] he did not want to come," *om mañaiapil cai hatiauichocuos.*

35v "For us the son of God descended from the heavens, and also for us he died." *Cham mañai apil Po Camar Chañiñichñis tupañai uòr-rà pé apil cham mañài tacuài-ya.* "The devil says, 'Not for me, but for you the son of God died.'" *Sasquiyap yać. Cai apil nomañài, om mañai apil Po cama Chañiñichñis tupàñai uor-ra, tacùaiya.*

"He did everything for me, for my good, and also for you, for us, for you [plural], for them." *Chom apil nomañai lovi-aj. Pe apil omañai po mañai cham mañai pom mañai.*

So the "for me, for you," the "for him," etc., we do not have this, and instead we form all the pronouns of the dative case without another word, and [for] the other nouns it is necessary to add the word *poiq,* which means "for him, and to put the noun in the nominative.

37r   Cuando un *Quechnajuis* habla con una persona, sea amigo, o no, sea capitan u otra persona siempre le dice, tu, y no usted, como los Españoles, porque estos titulos no tenemos en nuestra lengua, ni tampoco hacemos la segunda persona del singular plural, hablando con una sola persona, como algunas veces usan los Españoles.

Pero cuando un padre habla a sus hijos, o un Capitan hace discurso a su Gente el puede hablar en numero plural, es decir, haciendo la primera persona del singular plural, como seria, yo mando, y nosotros mandamos. *Joṡnàcen, toṡnauoncha,* porque un Padre, o un Capitan, son personas de mucha autoridad o porque el padre hace toda su casa, y el capitan es la cabeza de su exercito, que debajo de si tiene toda la gente a quien puede mandar, y hacer conseguir su querer sin dificultad alguna.

Exemplos, Yo hablando contigo tiemblo. *Non oeṡ tetelacànoq gororserorac,́* se dice *oeṡ,* contigo, porque dejimos que no habiamos tantos titulos como los Españoles. Según las dignidades de la persona con que se hable exprimen, diciendo, su eccelencia, V.M., V.P., usted, vuestra reverencia, Tu eres Capitan de los Españoles? Si lo soy. *Omso Not Sosabitom? ohò notno.* Dejimos *omso,* tu, y tambien se podria decir, *Notso Sosabitom.* Eres capitan de los Españoles, sin decir tu. En esta manera tambien dejimos y explicamos la segunda persona del plural es decir, no diciendo ustedes, mas vosotros, *omom,* aunque se hable con personas grandes; p.e. ustedes, o vosotros, no aprendisteis

37v   esto? *Omomom cai ivi pilachàjom?* y tambien, *Caisom ivi pilàchaj.*

De estos exemplos se ~~en~~ conoce, que no tenemos titulos, mas la[s] mismas personas, o pronombres, diciendo *non. om, uonal, chaom, omom, uonalom.* yo, tu, aquel, nosotros, vosotros, aquellos. etc.

39r   El tiempo futuro de todos los verbos terminan en *in.* de esta regla se apartan los Neutros, que todos terminan en *jan.* v.e. el verbo *uocàl-ajaṡ* ir. yo iré, *nonopo uocàl-ajan;* yo me esconderé, *nonopo helèp-*

37r   When a *Quechnajuis* speaks with a person, whether a friend or not, whether a captain or other person, he always says *tú* [Spanish informal "you"] and not *usted* [formal "you"], (as the Spaniards would, because we do not have these titles in our language, nor do we make the second person of the singular plural when we are talking to a single person, as the Spaniards sometimes do.

But when a father speaks to his children, or a captain makes a speech to his people, he can speak in the plural, that is, making the first person of the singular plural, so it would be "I order" and "we order." *Joṡnàcen, toṡnauoncha*, because a father or a captain are persons of great authority, or because the father makes his household, and the captain is the head of his army, and beneath him he has all the people whom he can order, and make his will be done without any difficulty.

Examples: "I tremble when speaking with you." *Non oeṡ tetelacànoq goror-serorac̓,* using *oeṡ,* "*contigo* ['with you,' informal],", because, as we said, we do not have as many titles as the Spaniards. They express themselves depending on the status of the person to whom they speak, saying "your excellency," "V.M.," "V.P.," "*usted* [formal 'you']," "your reverence." "*Tú eres* ['You are,' informal] the captain of the Spaniards? Yes, I am." *Omso Not Sosabitom? ohò notno.* We say *omso,* "*tú* [informal 'you']," and one could also say *Notso Sosabitom,* "*Eres** the captain of the Spaniards?" without saying "*tú.*" In this manner, we also say and explain the second person of the plural, that is, not saying "*ustedes* [formal 'you' plural]," but "*vosotros* [informal 'you' plural]," *omom,* even when speaking with persons of authority: for example,

37v   "*Ustedes,* or *vosotros,* did you not learn this? *Omomom cai ivi pilachàjom?* And also, *Caisom ivi pilàchaj.*

From these examples, you can see that we do not have titles, but the same persons, or pronouns, saying *non, om, uonal, chaom, omom, uonalom.* I, you [informal singular], that one, we, you [informal plural], them, etc.

39r   In the future tense, all verbs end in *in.* The neuters do not follow this rule; they all end in *jan.* For example, the verb *uocàl-ajaṡ,* "to go." "I will go," *nonopo uocàl-ajan;* "I will hide," *nonopo helèp-pajan.* "I will

---

    *In Spanish the subject pronoun can be omitted, and Tac is saying that this can be done in Luiseño too.

pajan. yo lloraré *nonopo chaċajan* se hará, *lovíajanpo.* Y en esta manera el tiempo futuro de los neutros o Pasivos nuestros termina.

En el modo de quien manda, la primera persona del plural termina siempre en *uoncha,* como p.e. *yiyiuoncha* juguemos, *nauiuoncha.* escribamos, *cusan-ṁiuoncha,* tomemos *hùṁiuoncha, curàb-liuoncha, ċumì-iuoncha, hayàiuoncha. haluoncha.* enseñemos, desatemos, dejemos, ar[r]imemos, busquemos. Mas los neutros en *joncha* terminan en la primera persona haziendo, *helàp-pajoncha* escondamonos; *hèlajoncha,* cantemos *lovi-ajoncha* hagamonos. y assi los demas.

La segunda persona del plural termina en *yam* de todos los otros verbos haciendo *chiuiyam* venzèd *hùmiyam* enseñad. *càmiiyam* dejad, *tùchiyam* amarad, *moqnayam* matad, *chip-piyam* quebrad, *ràpiyam* sembrad, *choq-quiyam* cargad. *nattiyam* tirad, *haṅ-ṅiyam* colgad, *uòquiyam* cortad, *naiṁyam* quemad. Mas los neutros verbos, terminan en *jam,* p.e. *heleppajam,* escondeos, *hèlajam* contad. Y assi todos los verbos neutros.

39v El futuro del verbo *Ṅaṅiṡ* termina en *on,* p.e. yo llorarè *nonopo ṅaṅon,* tu lloraràs, *omopo ṅaṅon* aquel llorarà, *uonalpo ṅaṅon,* nosotros lloraremos, *chaomchapo ṅaṅon,* vosotros llorareis, *omomom ṅaṅon,* aquellos por fin lloraran, *umalomo ṅaṅon. ṅaṅ* llora, lloremos *nauoncha,* llorad *chacajam,* quando yo lloraba, *no ṅaċala,* etc. para que yo llore, *no ṅapi,* llorar, *ṅaṅiṡ,* llorando *naċanaq, ṅacat* el que llora, *ṅamocuiṡ,* el que ha llorado, *Ṅaṅiṡ* llanto.

41r Nosotros el Verbo ser de los Españoles explicamos por las mismas personas. *Non* yo. *Om* tu, *Uonal* aquel, *chaom* nos, *Omom* vos, *Uonàlom* aquellos, solamente añadiendo *op* a la tercera persona del singular, y a la segunda, *Cha* a la primera del Plural, *om* a la segunda, y por fin, *Pom,* a la tercera persona del Plural. Diciendo *Non, omop, uonalop, chaomcha, omomom, uonalompom.* yo soy, tu eres, aquel es. Nosotros somos, vosotros sois, aquellos son. Mas para solo para las personas, y en el solo tiempo presente, porque en los otros tiempos no hai. Exemplos: Yo soy tu hijo, tu eres mi padre, aquel es mi hermano, se dirà en esta manera. *Non o cama omop no Nà uonàlop no Pet.* Nosotros somos hombres, vosotros sois jovenes, aquellos son muchachos. *Chaomcha Yayichom, Omomom Auólom, Uonalompom Amayamalom.*

cry," *nonopo chaċajan;* "it will be done," *lovíajanpo.* And in this manner, the future tense of our neuters ends.

In the mode of commanding, the first person plural always ends with *uoncha,* for instance, *yiyiuoncha,* "let us play"; *nauiuoncha,* "let us write"; *cusan-ṁiuoncha,* "let us drink"; *hùṁiuoncha, curàb-liuoncha, ċumì-iuoncha, hayàiuoncha, haluoncha:* "let us teach," "let us untie," "let us leave," "let us move closer," "let us search." But the neuters in *joncha* end in the first person forming *helàp-pajoncha,* "let us hide"; *hèlajoncha,* "let us sing"; *lovi-ajoncha,* "let us do." And so the others.

The second person plural ends in *yam* in all the other verbs, making *chiuiyam,* "vanquish"; *hùmiyam,* "teach," *càmiiyam,* "leave"; *tùchiyam,* "tie"; *moqnayam,* "kill"; *chip-piyam,* "break"; *ràpiyam,* "sow"; *choq-quiyam,* "carry"; *nattiyam,* "throw"; *haṅ-ṅiyam,* "hang"; *uòquiyam,* "cut"; *naiṁyam,* "burn." But the neuter verbs end in *jam,* for example, *heleppajam,* "hide"; *hèlajam,* "count." And so it is for all neuter verbs.

39v The future tense of the verb *Ṅaṅiṡ* ends in *on;* for example, "I will cry," *nonopo ṅaṅon;* "you will cry," *omopo ṅaṅon;* "that one will cry," *uonalpo ṅaṅon;* "we will cry," *chaomchapo ṅaṅon;* "you [plural] will cry," *omomom ṅaṅon;* "those ones will finally cry," *umalomo ṅaṅon.* *ṅaṅ,* "cry, let us cry"; *nauoncha,* "cry"; *chacajam,* "when I used to cry"; *no ṅaċala,* etc.; "so that I cry"; *no ṅapi,* "to cry"; *ṅaṅis,* "crying"; *naċanaq, ṅacat,* "he who cries"; *ṅamocuiṡ,* "he who has cried"; *Ṅaṅiṡ,* "a cry."

41r The verb "to be" of the Spaniards we express with the same persons. *Non* [is] "I"; *om,* "you"; *Uonal,* "that one"; *chaom,* "we"; *Omom,* "you [plural]"; *Uonàlom,* "those." And we only add *op* to third person singular, and to the second; *Cha* to the first person plural; *om* to the second; and, finally, *Pom* to the third person plural. Saying *Non, omop, uonalop, chaomcha, omomom, uonalompom:* "I am," "you are," "that one is," "we are," "you [plural] are," "those ones are." But only for the persons, and only in the present tense, because in the other tenses they do not exist. Examples: "I am your son, you are my father, that one is my brother," would be said in this manner: *Non o cama omop no Nà uonàlop no Pet.* "We are men, you are youths, those are boys/girls." *Chaomcha Yayichom, Omomom Auólom, Uonalompom Amayamalom.*

Todos los nombres, si terminan en vocal, solamente se les añade, ~~la letra~~ P, si terminan en consonante se les añade, *op*. p.e. viene el Rey, el Capitan, el comandante, *Notop monà*. porque el nombre *Not*, o palabra termina en consonante. La flecha matò a tu Padre. *hulap*, o *Nai moqnaċ*. porque ~~ela~~ la palabra *hula* termina en vocal y por esso se le añade solamente la letra *p*. Las palabras de una silaba que terminan en vocal, que regladamente deben coger solamente la letra *.p.* todavia cogen la silaba *.op.* como serían *Nà. Yò, È, Cuà, Yù* y también *amù, ya.* que hacen *No Naop No Yoop. No Eop. No Cuaop. No Yùop.* es

41v   mi padre, es mi Madre es mi piè, es hermano mayor de mi avuela es mi cabeza.

43r   *má-maiṡ*

Segunda ~~declinacion~~ Conjugaciòn

m a-m-á-a

Los verbos de la segunda conjugación* terminan en el infinit. en *ajiis* y en *ais*, en el present[e] quitan la *jiṡ*, y añaden la *ċ* en el imperf. quitando la *c* ~~añadense~~ *ċuaṡ*. y en el perfect. quitando la *ċuaṡ*, anaden una otra *a*. y en el futuro, quitando la segunda *a* se añade una *n*. p.e. *màmaiṡ*, querer. yo quiero. *non màmaċ.* yo quería, *nonil màmaċuaṡ*, yo quise. *nonil màmaa.* Yo querè, *nónopo màman*, y así, los que terminan en *ajiṡ*, como *uitàajiṡ*, pararse, yo me paro. *Non uitàaċ*, yo me paraba. *nonil uitaaċuas*, yo me parè. *nonil uitàa.* yo me pararè, *nonopo uitáajan.* Los que terminan en *ajis* en el fut. terminan *ajan*, como el infinit. quitando *is* y haciendo *an*.

PRESENTE	IMPERFECTO		
Non uocàlaċ yo voi	*Nonil uocalaċuas* i[ba]	*Nonil uocàlaa* fui	*Nonopo uocàlajan* irè
omop uocalaċ	*omopil uocalacùas*	*omopil uocàlaa*	*omopo uocalajan*
uonalop uocàlacon	*uonàlopil uocalacuas*	*uonalopil uocàlaa*	*uonalpo uocalajan*
chaomcha uocàlajan	*chaomchamil uocalacuas*	*chaomchamil uocàlaa*	*chaomchapo uocalajan*
omomom uocàlajan	*omomomil uocalaċuas*	*omolomil uocàlaa*	*omomom uocalajàn*
uonalompo uocàlajan	*uonalomil uocalacuas*	*uonalomil uocàlaa*	*uonalomo uocalajàn*

---

*The word has *declinación* been overwritten by the *conjugación*.

All of the nouns, if they end in a vowel, have just ~~the letter~~ P added to them; if they end in a consonant, *op* is added. For example: "The king comes, the captain, the commander," *Notop monà*, because the noun *Not*, or the word, ends in a consonant. "The arrow killed your father" [is] *hulap, o Nai moqnać*, because the word *hula* ends in a vowel and for that reason just the letter *p* is added. The words with one syllable that end in a vowel, that by rule should take only the letter *p*, nonetheless take the syllable *op*, such as *Nà, Yò, È, Cuà, Yù* and also *amù, ya*, which become *No Naop, No Yoop, No Eop, No Cuaop, No Yùop.*

41v   "It is my father, it is my mother, it is my foot; he is the older brother of my grandmother; it is my head."

43r   *má-maiś*

Second ~~declension~~ Conjugation

m a-m-á-a

The verbs of the second declension end in the infinitive in *ajiis* and in *ais*. In the present tense *jiś* is removed, and *ć* is added. In the imperfect, removing the *ć, ćuaś* is added. And in the perfect, removing the *ćuaś*, they add another *a*; and in the future, removing the second *a*, an *n* is added. For example, *màmaiś*, "to want." "I want," *non màmać*; "I used to want," *nonil màmaćuaś*; "I wanted," *nonil màmaa*; "I will want," *nónopo màman*. And similarly [for] those that end in *ajiś*, like *uitàajiś*, "to stop"; "I stop," *non uitàać*; "I used to stop," *nonil uitaaćuas*; "I stopped," *nonil uitàa*; "I will stop," *nonopo uitáajan*. The [infinitives] that end in *ajis* end in *ajan* in the future tense, like the infinitive [but] removing *is* and adding *an*.

PRESENT	IMPERFECT		
Nom uocàlać I go	Nonil uocalaćuas [I used to go]	Nonil uocàlaa I went	Nonopo uocàlajan I will go
omop uocalać	omopil uocalacùas	omopil uocàlaa	omopo uocalajan
uonalop uocàlacon	uonàlopil uocalacuas	uonalopil uocàlaa	uonalpo uocalajan
chaomcha uocàlajan	chaomchamil uocalacuas	chaomchamil uocàlaa	chaomchapo uocalajan
omomom uocàlajan	omomomil uocalaćuas	omolomil uocàlaa	omomom uocalajàn
uonalompo uocàlajan	uonalomil uocalacuas	uonalomil uocàlaa	uonalomo uocalajàn

Los verbos de la primera conjugación* en el imperat. terminan en *i*, mas los de la segunda en *j*.

Uocalaj   vaia

Uocalajàncha cham   vamos

Uocalajam omom

El modo optat. se hace con una voz que es *pi* y se pone despues del verbo. p.e. yo quiciese que vosotros unáis† pronto. se dice: *nonopo màmaaj 'queleċ om hattajpi. queleċ, om uocalajpi.*

El modo conjunt. se hace con la voz *cala.* que en si no quiere decir alguna cosa, mas quando se pone despues del verbo significa quando, y tambien mientras. por ejemplo. quando yo me subi a caballo, entonces me siguieron. *no calaċalamil noi nononas.*

El modo Inf. termina en *iṡ, jis. ṅis.* y tiene un tiempo que es presente por e. matar, *mòcnaiṡ.*

El gerundio hai, y es *anoċ, inoc* que nada significa. mas quando se pone despues del presente del indicat. entonces es gerundio. por e. andando. bailando. cantando. se dice *uocalacanoc. tanninoċ, helecanoċ.*

Los Participios se componen con la voz *cat.* se pone ~~del~~ despues del presente del indicat. por e. amante o quien ama. se dice *màmacat*, quien hace, *loviicat,* mas estos se cogen como substantivos. p.e. el amador se dirá *màmàcat.*

Los participios de tiempo pasado se hacen con la voz *mocuiṡ* añadida, con el modo Infin. quitando la *s.* / p.e. ammarar *tùchiṡ* ammarado tu,
43v   *tuchimocuis,* yo fui el que ha vencido. *nomil po ciuui/mocuiṡ.*

~~Qua~~ tres suertes de verbos hai. Los primeros son activos, los segundos activos imperativos. Los terceros son activos que repiten el accion.‡ por ejemplo. el verbo activo *chippiṡ,* ~~el~~ quebrar, de donde nace el verbo activo *chippiniis.* hacer o mandar che se quiebre, el verbo que repite es este *chipchipiiṡ,* quebrar muchas veces, *chipinichipmiis.* participio *chippinichippimimoquis,* y el plural *chippinichippimimocuichom.* Los verbos pasivos derivan de los verbos activos, quitando el *is* del Infinit.

---

*Again, the word *declinación* has been overwritten by *conjugación.*

†This word is unclear in the original.

‡There follows the beginning of a sentence that is crossed out in the original; it is not included here.

The verbs of the first conjugation in the imperative end in *i*, but those of the second [end] in *j*.

Uocalaj   go

Uocalajàncha cham   let us go

Uocalajam omom

The optative mode is formed with the word *pi* and it is placed after the verb: for example: "I wish you may unite soon," is said: *nonopo màmaaj 'queleċ om hattajpi. Queleċ, om uocalajpi.*

The subjunctive mode is formed with the word *cala*, which in itself has no meaning, but when placed after the verb, it signifies "when" and also "during." For example: "When I got on the horse, then they pursued me," *no calaċalamil noi nononas.*

The infinitive mode ends in *iṡ, jis, ñis,* and it has one tense, which is the, for example, "to kill," *mòcnaiṡ.*

There exists the gerund, and it is *anoċ, inoc,* which means nothing. But when it is placed after the present indicative, then it is a gerund. For example, "walking, dancing, singing," are said *uocalacanoc, tanninoċ, helecanoċ.*

The participles are made with the word *cat,;* it is placed after the present indicative. For example "lover [*amante*]" or "one who loves" is said *màmacat;* "one who does," *loviicat,* but these are taken as nouns, for example, "the lover [*amador*]" would be *màmàcat.*

The past participles are formed with the word *mocuiṡ* added, with the infinitive mode, removing the *s*. For example "to tie," *tùchiṡ;* "you are tied," *tuchimocuis;* "I was the one who has vanquished," *nomil po ciuui/mocuiṡ*

There are three kinds of verbs. The first are active, the second are active imperatives. The third are active verbs that repeat the action. For example, the active verb *chippiṡ,* "to break," whence comes the active verb *chippiniis,* "to have or command that something be broken." The verb that repeats is *chipchipiis,* "to break many times;" *chipinichipmiis,* participle *chippinichippimimoquis,* and the plural *chippinichippimimocuichom.* The passive verbs derive from the active verbs, removing the *is* from the infinitive and adding *ajis.* For example, *chippis* is active; to make it passive it is necessary to remove the *is*

y añadiendo *ajis*. por e. *chippis* es activo para hacerlo pasivo es menester quitar la *is* del infinit. y añadir el *ajis, chippis* quebrar *chippajis* quebrarse. La costrucción de estos verbos no es como la de los Españoles. p.e. por mi fue vencido un osso, no se dirá así, mas yo he vencido un osso *nonil moxnaċ supuli hunuoti*.

Hai un modo de decir, y es, que en vez de usar dos verbos se usa uno solo, entreponendo la voz *vicho* y particularmente se entrepone, quando se quiere decir, el verbo /querer/ por e. yo ti quería dar mi espada, se dice /*nonioic majanṁ/vicho/cuasno uotquilai*. yo te quiero llevar siempre conmigo. /~~non oc oi hotti~~ *non oi mimohapan no iṡ hotti/vicho/c*

45r La concordancia es como aquella de los Españoles, es decir El porque de los Españoles primeramente es de quien pregunta; tambien y del preguntado que a quien pregunta responde; nosotros tambien tenemos el nuestro, *hiṅaiso*, porque. mas solo es de quien pregunta mas no de quien responde, mas contado esso, el preguntado puede usar y entonces es menester que el repita el mismo verbo de quien pregunta, o dejando el *hiṅais*, hacer el verbo un participio de tiempo presente: veamos con los exemplos.

Porque nosotros, no tocamos con las manos las estrellas, la Luna y el Sol? somos chicos de cuerpo. porque somos chicos de cuerpo. *Chaoomso hiṅai, cai cham matalom sùlami Mòivai, pe temèti milmiliuon? Quecatomcha cham milipi.* Porque no quieres escribir en este dia? Porque no quiero. *hinaiso ivina temeṅa cai nau-nauivichoċ? ċaino màmaċ; caino nàunauvichoc cai no nauicalaso tovyuṅ-niċ;* ~~por~~ *caino nàuivichocalaso tovyuṅ-ṅiċ* Porque yo les habia mandado no saben, y tu quieres saber! *Hiṅaiso pomomi no tośṅacalapom au-uiuon p̶ òmso ayal-livichoc.*

El segundo porque de los Españoles es, de quien no pregunta como seria, porque no duermo no se, o ~~de~~ no se la razon de despertarme. Y tambien nosotros no decimos *hiṅaiso!* porque *hiṅaiso* es voz de quien pregunta, mas decimos *hinai.* qual es la razon. qual sea, qual será, qual
45v fue. p.e. Aora te dirè la razon, porque no había querido ir contigo. *pitòonopo oic yajan hiṅai cai o eṡ no hatiacala. cai o eṡ no hatiavichocala.* No sabemos porque el te llame, mas te llama; y tu porque

from the infinitive and add *ajis: chippis*, "to break"; *chippajis* "to be broken." The construction of these verbs is not like the construction used by the Spaniards. For example, "The bear was vanquished by me" would not be said like that, but rather "I have vanquished a bear," *nonil moxnaċ supuli hunuoti.*

There is one way of saying it, and that is that instead of using two verbs, only one is used, interposing the word *vicho*, and it is particularly used when you want to say the verb "to want." For example, "I wanted to give you my sword" is said /*nonioic majanṁ/vicho/cuas no uotquilai.* "I want to take you with me always" /*non oc oi hotti non oi mimchapan no iṡ hotti/vicho/c.*

45r The agreement is like that of the Spaniards, which is to say: The "*porque* [why, because]" of the Spaniards is primarily for the one who asks, and also for the person being asked, who responds to the person who asks. We also have our own "*porque*," *hiṅaiso*, but it is only for the one who asks but not for the one who responds. Nonetheless, the person being asked can use it, and then it is necessary that he repeat the same verb as the one who asked, or dropping the *hiṅaiso*, convert the verb into a present participle of the present tense. We shall see this in these examples:

"Why are we unable to touch the stars, the moon, and the sun with our hands?" "We are small of body, because we are small of body." *Choomso hiṅai, cai cham matalom sùlami Mòivai, pe temèto milmiliuon? Quecatomcha cham milipi.* "Why do you not want to write this day?" "Because I don't want to." *hiṅaiso ivina temeṅa cai naunauivichoċ? ċaino màmaċ; caino nàunauvichoc cai no nauicalaso tovyuṅ-niċ; por caino nàuivichocalaso tovyuṅ-niċ.* "Why I had ordered them they don't know, and you want to know!" *Hiṅaiso pomomi no toṡṅacalapom au-uiuon p̶ òmso ayal-livichoc.*

The second "why" of the Spaniards is for one who does not actually ask, as in "Why I don't sleep I do not know," "I do not know the reason for waking up." And we also do not say *hiṅaiso!* because *hiṅaiso* is a word for the person asking, but we say *hiṅai*, "what is the reason,"
45v "what could it be," "what will it be," "what was it." For example, "Now I will tell you [the reason] why I didn't want to go with you," *pitòonopo oic yajan hiṅai cai o eṡ no hatiacala. cai o eṡ no hatiavichocala.* "We don't know [the reason] why he calls you, but he is

no quieres levantarte. *Au-uiuoncha hiṅai oi po uà-uiuacala, oi op ua-uiċ; hiṅaiso pe om caicuotavichoc.*

Hemos dicho que los Españoles tienen dos, porque, la primera es de quien pregunta, y del preguntado que al que pregunta da su respuesta, y decimos que nosotros deciamos. el porque de quien pregunta *hiṅaiso,* y tambien que el preguntado podìa responder con la misma voz repitiendo el verbo de quien pregunta y que el verbo del preguntado haciase con el participio de tiempo presente. Porque lo has castigato? ~~hiṅa~~ porque jugaba, y no escribia. *Hinàiso pei siċuiċ ~~siquiq~~ hinàison pei sicuiċ. po yi-yicala, pe cai po nàuicala.* Y por fin el segundo porque, que dejimos que era porque de quien quere la razon, y que nosotros la explicabamos con la palabra *hiṅai.* p.e. porque no trabajas no sabe. *hiṅai cai o tobjàcalapo au-iċ.* he aqui los dos porque para que mejor se conoscan que son *hiṅaiso.* y *hiṅai* el primero de quien pregunta y tambien del preguntado, el segundo de quien quiere saber la razon. como ya hemos dicho.

47r El Verbo *hatiajis* ir, en la primera persona del numero plural no termina regladamente y hace *hanicha* vamos. vamonos. Ay tambien el verbo *tosṅaiṡ* mandar, que no termina regladamente en el modo indicat. en el tiempo passado, mas repite la primera silaba sin la *s* haciendo *totoṡṅa* mandé. *Nonil totoṡna* yo mandè. *omopil totoṡṅa* tu mandaste. *uonalopil totoṡṅa,* aquel mandò, y ha mandado *chaomchamil totoṡṅa,* nosotros mandamos y hemos mandado. *omòmomil totoṡṅa* vosotros mandasteis, y haveys mandado, *uonalomil totoṡṅa,* aquellos mandaron y han mandado. ~~en el~~ solo en el tiempo passado del indic. porque todos los modos y tiempo[s] que siguen son regulares. como *tosṅan.* yo mandarè *tosṅanop.* tu mandaràs. *tosṅanpo,* aquel mandarà, *chaomchapo tosṅan,* u *tosṅanchapo,* nosotros mandaremos, *omoṁom tosṅan,* y tambien *tosṅanom* vosotros mandaràs, *uonalomo tosṅan,* u *tosṅanmo,* aquellos mandaràn. imperat. *tosṅa* manda tu, *tosṅauoncha* mandemos, *tosṅayam* mandad. *No tosṅacàla,* quando yo mandaba. *No tosṅapi* para que yo mande. *Tosṅais,* mandar, *tosṅais,* mandamiendo. *Tosṅacat* el que manda, *Tosṅamocuis* el que ha mandado. *tosṅacànoq.* mandando. exemplos. Vamonos a nuestra casa que ya es

calling, and [the reason] why you don't want to get up." *Au-uiuoncha hiñai oi po uà-uiuacala, oi op ua-uiċ; hiñaiso pe om caicuotavichoc.*

We have said that the Spaniards have two "*porque*"s. The first is for the one who asks, and for the one who is asked who responds to the questioner. And we said we would say *hiñaiso* for the "why" of the person who asks, and also that the person who is asked could respond with the same word, repeating the verb of the questioner, and that the verb of the person asked would be formed with the present participle. "Why have you punished him?" "Because he was playing and was not writing." *Hinàiso pei siċuiċ ~~siquiq~~ hinàison pei sicuiċ. po yi-yicala, pe cai po nàuicala.* And finally, the second "*porque*," which we said was the why of one who wants the reason, and which we explained with the word *hiñai.* For example, "[The reason] why you don't work he does not know." *Hiñai cai o tobjàcalapo au-iċ.* Here, then, are the two "*porque*"s, that they may be better known: that is, *hiñaiso* and *hiñai,* the first for the person who asks and also the person asked, and the second for the one who wants to know the reason, as we have said.

47r The verb *hatiajis,* "to go," in the first person plural does not end regularly, and it forms *hanicha,* "we go," "let us go." There is also the verb *tosñais,* "to command," which does not end regularly in the indicative mode of the past tense but repeats the first syllable without the *s,* forming *totosña,* "commanded": *Nonil totosña,* "I commanded"; *omopil totosña,* "you commanded"; *uonalopil totosña,* "that one commanded and has commanded"; *chaomchamil totosña,* "we commanded and have commanded"; *omòmomil totosña,* "you [plural] commanded and have commanded"; *uonalomil totosña,* "those commanded and have commanded." This is only in the past tense of the indicative, because all the modes and tenses that follow are regular, such as *tosñan,* "I will command"; *tosñanop,* "you will command"; *tosñanpo,* "that one will command"; *chaomchapo tosñan* or *tosñanchapo,* "we will command," *omoṁom tosñan,* and also *tosñanom,* "you [plural] will command, *uonalomo tosñan,* and *tosñanmo,* "those will command." In the imperative: *tosña* "you command;" *tosñauoncha* "let us command"; *tosñayam,* "you [plural] command." *No tosñacàla,* "when I used to command." *No tosñapi,* "that I may command." *Tosñais,* "to command"; *tosñais,* "command [noun]." *Tosñacat* "he who commands"; *Tosñamocuis,* "he who has commanded." *Tosñacànoq,* "commanding." Examples: "Let's go home, as it is already night," *haṁcha*

noche. *haṁcha chom quiq. namop yùbaċ.* Yo soy el que manda, y yo

47v siempre mandarè, en mi casa. *Nonpo tosṅacat, penopo mimchapan no quiniċ tosṅan.* Ya a todos he mandado para que se levanten. *Amùno choommi tosṅac, pom cuot-tajpi.* se levantaba quando yo le mandaba. *cuot-taċuosapil poi no tosṅaċala.* Mandando yo todo se calma. *chononop* taràtaráacat no tosṅaċala.* Mandando se murio, *tosṅàcanoqapil tacuay-a.* etc.

49r La voz para que de los Españoles explicamos, con la palabra *pi.* A que siempre se pone detras del verbo, y no se separa mas se añade al verbo y esta voz, es aquella misma, que en vez del infinito modo tenemos. baja del monte, para ~~que~~ levantarte, o para que te levante. se dice *càunàyop uonaċ oi po cuot-lipi.* llora, lloraba. llorò para que nos dejase. *nàċap, ṅaċuasapil ṅàṅapil, chami po ~~co~~ càmìipil.* uye para que no cojan, y te maten. *nàlaj, cai oi pom chaċiuipis pe momoqnapi.* uye y no te cogeran, y mataran, *nàlaj oimoca cai mocnan pe chaċcuin.*

Cuando los Españoles dicen escribe porque el maestro viene, nosotros decimos, y explicamos el Español como se no fuese el porque diciendo *naui hùniicatop monà.* escribe el maestro viene. corre, que el perro te muerde, *hiċcuaj. oi op aual còivichoċ.* llamalo pronto porque su padre lo quiere, y yo tambien, llamalo que su padre lo quiere y yo tambien.[†]

Los Españoles dicen en dos maneras, mas nosotros en una sola manera diciendo *Queleċ poi uà-ui, poi op po Nà poino pe no màemaċ.* Busca a mi cavallo, porque mañana me voi, irè o tambien, que mañana me voi, *Hal no asi, non ejṅa hati-auichoċ* y tambien *ejṅanopo hati-ajàn.*

49v Aunque; No tenemos, mas explicamos con el particípio de tiempo presente, Aunque el me despierte, yo no me levantaré, *Po ṅoi-icalanopo cai quet-tajàn.* y se explica, quando el me despierta, no me levantarè. Aunque tu no me lo digas yo lo sabre. *Cai miic o yà-cala ayàl-minopo.*

51r Hemos hablado de los nombres de los lugares, en que uno se halla, de donde sale, por donde saliendo pasa, y hasta donde llega, aora veremos los adverbios de los lugares, y son los que siguen, *ivà, ivàṅai, iviq/ uonà, uoṅai uoniq.* en este lugar, el segundo lo mismo, el tercero hasta este lugar hasta aquí allà, de alli, hasta allà *michà michai, michiq.*

---

*Unclear in the original.

[†]The phrase is repeated in the original.

chom quiq. namop yùbaċ. "I am the one who commands, and I will

47v always command, in my house," *Nonpo tosṅacat, penopo mimchapan no quiniċ tosṅan.* "I have already ordered everyone to get up," *Amùno choommi tosṅac, pom cuot-tajpi.* "He would get up when I ordered him to," *cuot-taċuosapil poi no tosṅacala.* "When I am commanding, everything is calm," *chononop taràtaráacat no tosṅacala.* "He was commanding when he died," *tosṅàcanoqapil tacuay-a,* etc.

49r The word[s] "so that" of the Spaniards we explain with the word *pi.* It is always placed after the verb, and it is not separated but rather added to the verb, and this word is the same one that we have instead of the infinitive form. "Come down from the hills, to pick you up," or "so that I may pick you up," is said *càuinàyop uonaċ oi po cuot-lipi.* "S/he cries, used to cry, cried so that you would leave us," *nàċap, ṅaċuasapil ṅaṅapil, chami po ~~eo~~ càmiipil.* "Flee so that they don't catch and kill you," *nàlaj, cai op pom chaċiuipis pe momoqnapi.* "Flee and they will not catch you and kill you," *nàlaj oimoca cai mocnan pe chaċcuin.*

When the Spaniards say, "Write because the teacher is coming," we say and we explain the Spanish as if there were no "why," saying *naui huniicatop monà,* "Write, the teacher is coming." "Run, the dog will bite you," *hiċcuaj. oi op aual còivichoċ.* "Call him right now, because his father wants him, and I do to." "Call him, his father wants him and I do too."

The Spaniards say it in two ways, but we in only one way, saying, *Queleċ poi uà-ui, poi op po Nà poino pe no màcmaċ.* "Go get my horse, because tomorrow I leave/will leave," or also "for tomorrow I leave." *Hal no asi, non ejṅa hati-auichoċ* and also *ejṅanopo hati-ajàn.*

49v We do not have "although," but we express it with the present participle. "Although he may wake me, I will not get up," *Po ṅoi-icalanopo cai quet-tajàn.* And this is explained, "When he wakes me, I will not get up." "Although you may not tell me, I will know it." *Cai miic o yà-cala ayàl-minopo.*

51r We have spoken about the names of places: where one is, from where one comes, through where one passes upon leaving, and the place to which one arrives. Now we shall see the adverbs of the places, and they are as follows: *ivà, ivàṅai, iviq/ uonà, uoṅai uoniq.* "In this place," the second is the same, the third "up to this place/up to here," "over there," "from there to that place over there," *michà, michai, michiq.*

Choonṅa, chooṅai, chooniq. en donde. de donde, a donde. *Pusunṅa, pusunṅai. pusùniq* en todo lugar. de todo lugar. a todos lugares. adentro, de dentro. a adentro. *uamcuṅa, uamcuṅai uàmiq.* exemplos. Que, tu en este lugar te hallas? *Omee ivà auc?* porque de qui salisteis, *hiṅaisom ivaṅai pulùchajon.* Aqui en este lugar quieres venir, *iviqso hatiavichoċ.* No hai allà ninguno, *uonà op cai ataj miċ.* de allí vino el fuego, *uinàṅàiopil cut uocòa.* allà vendremos *uoniq chapo hattiajan.* ~~de~~ en donde, en que lugar, estas? *michaso auc?* de donde vienes *michaiso monà,* adonde iremos? *michiqsom chaom hattiajàn?* Dios se halla en todo lugar. *Chaṅnichṅichop choonṅa auc.* de todos los lugares no sale. *Choonnaiop cai pulùpulùchaċ.* vienes de adentro, *pusunṅai so monà,* y los demas. Aqui de nuevo pondremos todos los adverbios juntos, para que mejor se conoscan.

Michà	Donde. en donde, en que lugar, y por donde.
Michai	de donde, de que lugar. o sitio.
Michiq	a donde hasta hasia, que lugar
Michaṅa	en que lugar. *micha* se usa mas que *michaṅa*
Michaṅai	a que sitio, *michai* se usa mas
Michiq	a donde
Ivà	aquí. en este lugar en que estoi, estas esta.
Ivài	de aquí, de este lugar
Iviq	acà, a este lugar.
Ivàṅa	en este lugar. *ivà* mejor se dice *ivà.*
Ivànai	de este lugar. *ivài.* mejor
Iviq	acà. a este sitio.

Uonà allá. en aquel
Uoṅai de alli. de aquel } lugar
Uoniq a alla. hasta aquel

Uonàṅa en aquel
Uonàṅai desde aquel] mejores son los primeros
Uonìq hasta, hasia

Uàmcuṅa en* lexos lugares. en lexana parte.
Uàmcuṅai de lexos lugares. desde lexanas partes.
Uàmiq a lexos lugares. hasia lexanas partes

---

*The word *en* has been written over the word *de.*

Choonṅa, chooṅai, chooniq, "where," "from where," "to where."
Pusunṅa, pusunṅai, pusùniq, "in all places," "from all places," "to all
places." "Within," "from within," "to within," *uamcuṅa, uamcuṅai
uàmiq.* Examples: "What, you, you're in this place?" *Omee ivà auc?*
"Why did you leave here?" *hiṅaisom ivaṅai pulùchajon.* "You want to
come here to this place," *iviqso hatiavichoc.* "There is no one over
there," *uonà op cai ataj mic.* "From there the fire came," *uinàṅàiopil
cut uocòa.* "We will come over there," *uoniq chapo hattiajan.* "Where,
in what place, are you?" *Michaso auc?* "Where do you come from?"
michaiso monà, "Where will we go?" *Michiqsom chaom hattiajàn?*
"God is in all places," *Chaṅnichṅichop choonṅa auc.* "He does not
come out from all places," *Choonnaiop cai pulùpulùchac.* "You come
from within," *pusunṅai so monà,* and so on. Here once again we will
put all the adverbs together, so they can be better known:

51v

Michà	where, in what place, and through where
Michai	from where, from what place or spot
Michiq	from which place to which place
Michaṅa	in what place; *micha* is used more than *michaṅa*
Michaṅai	to what spot; *michai* is used more
Michiq	to where
Ivà	here, in this place where I am, you are, he is
Ivài	from here, from this place
Iviq	over here, to this place
Ivàṅa	in this place; *ivà,* it is better to say *ivà*
Ivanai	from this place; *ivài* is better
Iviq	over here, to this spot
Uonà	over there, in that ⎫
Uoṅai	from there, from that ⎬ place
Uoniq	to there, up to that ⎭
Uonàṅa	in that ⎤
Uonàṅai	from that ⎥ (the first ones are better)
Uoniq	up to, toward ⎦

52r

Uàmcuṅa	in faraway places, in a distant part
Uàmcuṅai	from faraway places, from distant parts
Uàmiq	to distant places, toward distant parts

Choònṅa   en todos lugares. por do quiera que.

Choonṅai   de todos lugares. desde ~~hasta hacia~~.

Chooniq   a todos lugares. hasta. hasia

Pusunṅa   adentro. en medio.

Pusunṅai   de adentro. Desde el medio.

Pusuniq   a adentro. hasta hasia adentro

Auòṅa   en otro lugar. por otra parte. por otro sitio

Auònài   de otro lugar. de otra parte. desde otro sitio

Auòiq   a otro lugar. a otra parte. hasta hasia otro sitio

Cuìmcuṅa en el est	*Cuimcuṅai* de el est.
Payomcuṅa en el ouest.	*Payòmcuṅai* de el ouest.
Luichàmcuṅa, en el ~~nord~~ sud	*Luichàmcuṅai* de el sud
Tomàmcuṅa en el Nord.	*Tomàmcuṅai* de el Nord.

Cuimiq.   a, a la parte, hasta, hacia, el est.

Payomiq.   a, a la parte, hasta, hasia, el ouest.

Luichàmiq.   a, a la parte, hasta, hasia el Sud.

Tomàmiq.   a, a la parte, hasta, hasia el Nord.

53r   Los pronobres principales son tres, *non. om. po.* yo. tu aquel. principales, o primeros que no nacen de ninguna otra voz mas ellos dan ori-
gen a los pronobres que significan possesion, y estos son seis es decir
nomij. omij, pomij. mio, tuyo, suyo, los otros tres significan possesiòn
de muchos, y son *chammij, ommij pommij* nuestro vuestro. de aquellos.
estos seis pronobres son compuestos de los tres pronobres primeros,
quitando la *n.* al primero, y al segundo la *m.* p.e. a *non* se quita la *n.*
y al *om.* se quita *m.* y quedan *no. o. po.* de mi, de ti, de aquel: y de
la palabra *mijanis,* cosa, que se le tronca *anis* y queda *mij.* y entonces
nomij. omij. pomij ~~chom~~ quiere decir cosa que pertenece, a mi, a ti, a
aquel.

Los plurales de *non, om. po.* son *chaom omom, pomom,* nosotros
vosotros, y aquellos: quando se componen con la voz *mijànis,* o ~~para~~
quando se quiere decir, nuestro vuestro, de aquellos, de *chaom, omom,
pomom,* nosotros vosotros. aquellos. de *chaom* queda *cham.* de *omom*
om y de *pomom pom.* y añadienles la voz *mij.* forman las palabras
cham-mij, ommij. pom-mij: mío, tuyo, suyo. y se declinan assi

Choònna   in all places, everywhere that

Choonnai   from all places, from ~~up to, toward~~

Chooniq   to all places, up to, toward

Pusunna   within, in the middle

Pusunna   from within, from the middle

Pusuniq   to within, up to/toward the inside

Auòna   in another place, in another part, in another spot

Auòna   from another place, from another part, from another spot

Auòiq   to another place, to another part, up to/toward another spot

Cuìmcuna	in the east	*Cuìmcunai*	from the east
Payomcuna	in the west	*Payòmcunai*	from the west
Luichàmcuna	in the south	*Luichàmcunai*	from the south
Tomàmcuna	in the north	*Tomàmcunai*	from the north

Cuimiq,   to, to the part, up to, toward the east.

Payomiq.   to, to the part, up to, toward the west.

Luichàmiq.   to, to the part, up to, toward the south.

Tomàmiq.   to, to the part, up to, toward the north.

53r   There are three principal pronouns—*non, om, po:* "I," "you," and "that one." [They are] principal, or primary, ones that do not come from any other word but instead are the source of pronouns that signify possession, and these are six in number, that is: *nomij, omij, pomij;* "my," "your," "his/her"; the other three signify possession by many, and they are *chammij, ommij, pommij;* "our," "your," and "their." These six pronouns are composed from the three primary pronouns, removing the *n* from the first and from the second, the *m*. For example from *non* we remove the *n,* and from *om* we remove the *m,* and what remain are *no, o, po,* "my," "your," "that one's"; and from the word *mijanis,* "thing," *anis* is cut and what is left is *mij,* and so *nomij, omij, pomij* refers to the thing that belongs to me, to you, to that one.

The plurals of *non, om, po* are *chaom, omom, pomom,* "we," "you," and "those"; when they are combined with the word *mijànis*—or when one wishes to say "our," "your," "their" from *chaom, omom, pomom* ("we," "you," "those")—from *chaom* there remains *cham,* from *omom* [remains] *om,* and from *pomom* [remains] *pom.* And by adding the word *mij,* we form the words *cham-mij, ommij, pom-mij:* "mine," "yours," and "theirs." And they are declined thus:

N. *nomij. omij. pomij.* G. lo mismo. dat. *nomiji, omiji pomiji.* Ac. lo mismo. y assi tambien los otros tres, *chamij pommij. ommij* y en el plural *chammijòm ommijòm pommijòm,* Dat. *chammijmi ommijmi pommijmi.* jamas se usan con nombres substantivos, mas sirven solamente para decir mio, tuyo suyo segun. <u>mas quando</u> sin exprimir el nombre

53v substantivo, porque ia en la misma palabra se halla, quando se quiere exprimir el nombre, entonces se usan los genitivos de los pronobres *non. om, po.* que son *no o po.* p.e. se io dijesse mi animal. no podria decir *nomij aṡ,* mas solamente *no aṡ,* tu padre no quiere hablar contigo, no se diria, *omij Na cai op oeṡ tetelavichoċ,* mas, *Caiop o na o eṡ tetelavichoc.* todas mis gallinas ya se murieron: no se dice *choonampom càjàlom amù mijòm tacuayajòn,* mas *choomompom no càjalom amù tacuayajòn.*

55r Tenemos un otro tiempo futuro, mas exprime mas que el primero, y se puede explicar siempre por el verbo estar,* y se dirà, yo, tu, aquel, nos, vos, aquellos estaran y el verbo que sigue. y este tiempo futuro no se halla en todos los verbos. su terminacion es *majan* p.e. Aunque el llegue yo estarè jugando, con mis hermanos. *Po uocoaċalanopo yiyimajan.* Se hace la composicion con la voz, *majan.* y la segunda persona singular del modo imperativo. Si el Infinito del Verbo termina en *jiṡ.* el imperativo terminara en *i,* asi tambien el imperativo terminara en *i* vocal, añadiendo a esta terminacion la voz *majan.* P.E. *tolou-uimajan nopo.* yo estare hallando. *halmajanopo* estarè buscando, *toumajànnopo* estarè mirando. el Infinito di *tolou-uimajan* es *tolou-uiṡ* hallar. el imperat. hace *tolou-ui.* añadiendo *majan,* serà *tolou-uimajan,* estarè hallando. *Halmajan,* estare buscando el infinito hace *haliṡ,* buscar. el imperativo no termina en vocal porque no es regular, y hace *hal.* añadiendole *majan* quedarà *halmajan,* estarè hallando. *Làchimajan,* estarè rogando, *uauimajan,* estare llamando. *utimajan,*† estarè numerando.

55v El modo de quien manda, si el verbo en el modo infinito no termina en *ajis,* sale regladamente en vocal. y este vocal es *i.* p.e. *ñosiṡ. curabbiṡ. uyiṡ. queniṡ. choróiṡ. mommiṡ. uotis.* etc. morder, desatar. hacer la voz de los animales, o sea gritar. orar. medir. volver. remar. todos estos verbos haran en el modo de quien manda en *i. noṡi. curabbi. uyi. ̀queni.*

---

*The word *estar* is written over *estaba.*
†The word is not clear in the original.

Nominative *nomij, omij, pomij;* genitive, the same; dative *nomiji, omiji, pomiji;* accusative, the same. And thus too the other three: *chamij, pommij, ommij,* and in the plural *chammijòm, ommijòm, pommijòm;* dative *chammijmi, ommijmi, pommijmi.* Never are they used with substantive nouns, but they serve only to say "mine," "yours," "ours," as appropriate. <u>But when,</u> without expressing the substantive noun,

53v   because it is already found in the word itself, when one wishes to express the noun, then the genitive forms of the pronouns *non, om, po* are used, which are *no, o, po.* For example, if I were to say "my animal," I couldn't say *nomij aṡ* but only *no aṡ.* "Your father does not want to speak with you" would not be said *omij Na cai op oeṡ tetelavichoċ,* but *Caiop o na o eṡ tetelavichoc.* "All of my chickens have already died" is not said *choonampom càjàlom amù mijòm tacuayajòn,* but *choomompom no càjalom amù tacuayajòn.*

55r   We have another future tense, but it expresses more than the first tense, and it can always be explained by the verb "to be," and it would be said "I/you/that one/we/you [plural]/they will be" and the verb that follows. And this future tense is not found in all the verbs. Its ending is *majan.* For example, "Although he may come, I will be playing with my brothers," *Po uocoaċalanopo yiyimajan.* The construction is made with the word *majan* and the second person singular of the imperative mode. If the infinitive of the verb ends in *jiṡ,* the imperative will end in *i.* So too the imperative would end in the vowel *i,* adding to this ending the word *majan.* For example *tolou-uimajan nopo,* "I will be finding." *Halmajanopo,* "I will be searching"; *toumajànnopo,* "I will be looking." The infinitive of *tolou-uimajan* is *tolou-uiṡ,* "to find." The imperative makes *tolou-ui;* adding *majan,* it becomes *tolou-uimajan,* "I will be finding." [For] *halmajan,* "I will be searching," the infinitive [is] *haliṡ,* "to search." The imperative does not end in a vowel because it is not regular, and it forms *hal.* Adding *majan* leaves us with *halmajan,* "I will be finding." *Làchimajan,* "I will be pleading"; *uauimajan,* "I will be calling"; *utimajan,* "I will be enumerating."

55v   The mode in which one commands, if the verb in the infinitive does not end in *ajis,* regularly ends in a vowel, and this vowel is *i.* For example, *ñosiṡ, curabbiṡ, uyiṡ, queniṡ, choróiṡ, mommiṡ, uotiṡ,* etc. "To bite," "to untie," "to make animal sounds," or "to shout," "to pray," "to measure," "to return," "to row." All of these verbs in the mode of commanding would [end] in *i: ñosi, curabbi, uyi, ̇queni, choròi, mômi,*

choròi. mômi uòti. muerde desata. grita. ora. coje la medida. vuelve.
rema. los otros que terminan en *ajis.* en el Infinito modo, en el modo
de quien manda, queda la *j. mamajiś* amar. en el modo de quien manda
harà *mamaj.*se hallan pocos verbos que no terminen ni en *j.* ni *i.* y son
tou, mira, *hal.* busca ~~ete~~ y otros pocos.

57r Desde el principio dejimos que habian verbos activos, y neutros, es
decir verbos que exprimen que la persona hace una accion, mas la
accion no sale de la persona que hace esta accion, y que passivos pocos
se hallaban. Los verbos Neutros, casi todos en *jiś* terminan; como seria
taċuai-ajis. morir. De los verbos activos se hacen los passivos, mas
estos passivos no son perfectamente passivos, como los verbos de los
Españoles, mas casi como los neutros, porque explica la palabra, que
la accion se hace por la misma persona, mas que la accion que el hace,
de si no sale, como el verbo *heleppajis* esconderse. y el activo es
heleppiś. esconder, y se conjugan segun los verbos activos. el presente
hace, *non heleppaċ.* yo me escondo, *chaomcham heleppajon,* nosotros
nos escondemos yo me escondeba *nonil heleppacuas, chaomchamil
heleppacuas,* nosotros nos escondebamos, *nonil heleppa.* yo me
escondè. *chaomchamil heleppa.* nosotros nos escondimos. *nonopo
heleppajan* yo me esconderé, *chaomchapo heleppajan,* nosotros nos
esconderemos. *heleppaj* escondete tu, *heleppajoncha chaom,* escondamonos. *No heleppacala,* quando yo me escondeba *no heleppaċala.
po heleppacàla* quando aquel se escondeba. *cham heleppacàla,* quando
nos escondebamos. *om heleppacàla.* quando os escondebais. *pom
helippacala,* quando se escondeban aquellos *No heleppajpi.* para que
57v yo me esconda. *o heleppajpi po heleppajpi. cham heleppajpi.* Infinit
heleppajis. esconderse. *heleppajimocuis* quien se ha escondido.
heleppaċanoq, escondiendose.

57r

59r ## Conversion de los Sanl*

Dejemos los otros bayles, y tambien aquellos de las Mugeres, Aora
veamos los juegos, que aqui se sirven los San luiseños y digamos los
principales, y de que Mucho~~s~~ nos servimos. Hay el Juego llamado por
nosotros *(uauquiś),* es decir juego de la pelota con el palo, o mejor
garrote, empezemos por ellos.

---

*This is the first page of the history, which Tac will later give the general title "Con-
versión de los San Luiseños."

uòti: "bite," "untie," "shout," "pray," "take the measurement," "return," "row." The others that end in *ajis* in the infinitive retain the *j* in the mode of commanding: *mamajiś,* "to love," in the mode of commanding becomes *mamaj.* There are few verbs that do not end in *j* or *i,* and they are *tou,* "look," and *hal,* "search," and a few others.

57r   From the beginning we said there were active verbs and neutral verbs—which is to say, verbs that express that a person does an action, but the action does not come from the person who does the action—and that there are few passive verbs. The neutral verbs almost all end in *jiś,* as in the case of *taċuai-ajis,* "to die." From the active verbs are formed the passive verbs, but these passives are not perfectly passive, like the verbs of the Spaniards, but are almost more like the neutral verbs, because the word explains that the action is done by the same person, but that the action that he does does not come from him, as in the verb *heleppajis,* "to hide oneself"—the active is *heleppiś,* "to hide"—and they are conjugated according to the active verbs. The present makes *non heleppaċ,* "I hide myself;" *chaomcham heleppajon,* "we hide ourselves." "I used to hide myself," *nonil heleppacuas; chaomchamil heleppacuas,* "we used to hide ourselves." *Nonil heleppa,* "I hid myself"; *chaomchamil heleppa,* "we hid ourselves." *Nonopo heleppajan* "I will hide myself;" *chaomchapo heleppajan,* "we will hide ourselves." *Heleppaj,* "hide yourself"; *heleppajoncha chaom,* "let us hide ourselves." *No heleppacala,* "when I used to hide myself," *no heleppacala; po heleppacàla,* "when that one used to hide himself"; *cham heleppacàla,* "when we used to hide ourselves"; *om heleppacàla;* "when you used to hide yourselves"; *pom helippacala,* "when they used to hide themselves." *No heleppajpi,* "so that I can hide myself,"

57v   *o heleppajpi, po hepeppajpi, cham heleppajpi.* Infinitive: *heleppajis,* "to hide oneself." *Heleppajimocuis,* "one who has hidden himself." *Heleppaċanoq,* "hiding oneself."

59r   ## Conversion of the San L

Let us leave [aside] the other dances, and also those of the women. Now let us look at the games that here serve the San Luiseños, and tell of the principal ones, and of how well they serve us. There is the game we call *(uauquiś),* which means "the game of the ball and the stick," or better yet, "the club," let us begin with this.

Juego de la Pelota

El lugar en donde se juega es todo llano, largo un quarto y medio de hora, ancho lo mismo, los jugadores todos hombres de trenta hasta sesenta años, en todos pueden ser setenta, u ochenta, treynta u quarenta hombres de un lado, treynta u quarenta de el otro. dos caudillos se ponen, de este y de aquel lado, cada uno de los hombres tiene su garrote alto quatro palmos, gruesso cinco dedos juntos, de bajo arqueado, la pelota del juego es de madera, gruessa mas de que un huevo de [g]uajolote. hay dos señales donde ellos deben tirar la pelota, y quando el enemigo passa este señal el ha gañado.

La ley es que, no puedan llevar en mano por mucho rato, mas entierra con el garrote. En medio del juego entierran la pelota, y la deben sacar los dos caudillos con sus garrotes, cada uno quedandose hacia su señal, y de tras sus compañeros con los garrotes levantados esperando la pelota, y quando sale, cada uno quiere llevarla a su senal.

59v   Y aquí alborote, empuxones, fuerzas de hercules es menester, si uno por ventura saca la pelota y tirándola con toda fuerza a su señal, la echa en medio del señal los enemigos los siguen, otros detienen a otros, otros se tumban, quien cae corriendo resbalado, quien con igual carrera llega hasta la pelota, y de alli la lleva por otra parte corriendo, demiedo de que no se la quiten, y viendo de lejos a sus compañeros, les echa por el ayre la pelota, aquellos se la llevan corriendo a toda priessa a su señal, los enemigos los atajan, y aquí alborote, carrera de venado para huir, para que no los alcancen, o lleguen, y dura tres, o quatro horas este juego.

Tambien las Mugeres juegan, y esso cada Domingo, con permission

Los Sanluiseños saben bien jugar, hombres fuertes. Una vez salieron treynta Sanluiseños, y se fueron para S. Juan, otra Mission cercana a la Mission de S. Luis Rey de Francia nuestra Mission, alli llegaron, y fueron convidados a judar a pelota, ellos dejeron queremos, pero hagamos ley, que no se pueda la pelota llevarse en mano, aquellos si dijeron assi haremos, con toda justicia jugaremos. Al Domingo por la tarde, los Sanluiseños toman sus garrotes, y se van al lugar del juego. Aquellos los reciben y los llevaron al lugar del Juego. Empezaron a

The Ball Game

The place in which it is played is completely flat, in length a quarter and a half a league, and in width the same. The players, all men from thirty to sixty years of age, can be up to seventy or eighty in all: thirty or forty men on one side, thirty or forty on the other. Two team captains are put on this side and on that. Each of the men has his club, four palms in height, five fingers thick, arched at the bottom. The ball is wooden, thicker than a turkey egg. There are two marks to which they must throw the ball, and when the opponent passes the mark, he has won.

The rule is that they cannot have it in their hands for much time, but bury it with the club. In the middle of the game they bury the ball, and the two captains must get it out with their clubs, each one staying on the side of his mark, and behind him, his teammates with their clubs raised waiting for the ball, and when it comes out, each one tries to get it to his mark.

59v And in the commotion and pushing, the strength of Hercules is necessary If by luck one player gets the ball out and, hurling it with all his might at his goal, he throws it in the middle of the goal, the enemies give chase. Some hold others back; some knock each other over. One person slides and falls; another running just as fast gets all the way to the ball and from there runs with it to the other side, in fearing they might take it from him, and seeing at a distance his teammates, he throws the ball through the air at them, and they run with it as fast as they can to their mark. The opponents intercept them, and there is a great commotion, running like a deer to flee, so that they won't catch up to them, or reach them; and this game lasts three or four hours.

The women also play, and that takes place every Sunday, with permission.

The San Luiseños know how to play well; [they are] strong men. Once thirty San Luiseños came out, and they went to San Juan, another mission near Mission San Luis Rey de Francia, our Mission. They arrived there, and they were invited to play ball. They said "We'd like to, but let's make it a rule that you cannot take the ball in your hand." The others said, "We'll do it that way, and we will play with fairness." On Sunday in the afternoon the San Luiseños took their clubs and went to the place for the game. The others received them, and took them to the

judar con la misma ley como los Sanluiseños; y como ya hemos dicho adelante.

60r Toda la gente de este Pays estaba viendo el Juego, y el capitan tambien de aquel pays a cavallo estaba viendo. Todos treynta Sanluiseños bien jugaban, y a carrera vencian a los Sanjuaneños, quando un Sanjuaneño toma la pelota, y en mano la lleva, llega entonces un Sanluiseño, y agarrandolo por las cinturas, lo echa en alto, y lo hace caer, vino otro Sanjuaneño, para defender a su Paysano, van otros Sanluiseños a ayudar al primero, de tras de estos vino el capitan azotò a un Sanluiseño, entonces uno de los Sanluiseños, mas fuerte y de cuerpo gigante diò un brinco, tumbòlo, el cavallo lo pisò y arrastrado de bajo los pies levantarse no podia vino el pueblo por el alboroto con garotes en mano, las Mugeres siguieron un Sanluiseño, que no tenia garrote, mas se podìa bien defender, con brincos, aunque fuere torneado, y pordoquiera las Mugeres piedras le echaban pero no lo dañaron. Los Sanjuaneños huyen con sus rajadas cabezas, se quedan los solos Sanluiseños uno querìa dar golpe a otro creyendo que fuesse Sanjuaneño por tanto furor no conocianse, y de nada miedo tenìan. llegan los soldados Españoles ya que era acabado el alboroto porque ellos tambien tiemblaban y por palabras querian acabar el tumulto. El caudillo de los treynta Sanluiseños.

60v El caudillo de los Sanluiseños era indio y hablaba como los Españoles, el indio le decia levanta tu sable y entonces yo te comerè pero en su lengua, y despues no huvo novedad.

61r
Del Bayle

Los Bayles son de mucha[s] maneras segun los generos de Indios. Los Indios llamados Yumos, tienen sus Bayles, los Apaches otra gente tambien ella tiena su Bayle, los Dieguinos Christianos, tienen sus Bayles, los Sanluiseños que somos nosotros tenemos muchos los hombres, y otras maneras las Mugeres. Assi los Sanjuaneños Los Gabrileños, Los Fernandinos, y los de monte Rey tambien ellos tienen sus bayles diferentes los unos de los otros.

place for the game. They began to play with the same rules as the San Luiseños, the way we have already said.

60r All of the people of this region were watching the game, and the captain of that region was watching on horseback. All thirty of the San Luiseños were playing well, and they were outrunning the San Juaneños, when a San Juaneño took the ball and held it in his hand. Then a San Luiseño came and, grabbing him by the waist, threw him high and made him fall. Another San Juaneño came to defend his own, then other San Luiseños came to help the first one, and behind them the captain arrived and struck a San Luiseño with his whip. Then one of the San Luiseños, stronger and with a giant body, leaped up and knocked him down, and the horse stepped on him [the captain] and, swept under its feet, he couldn't get up. With all the commotion, the people of the village came with clubs in their hands. The women chased a San Luiseño who had no club, but he could defend himself well with leaps, even though he was surrounded, and from everywhere the women were throwing rocks at him, but they did not hurt him. The San Juaneños fled with their gashed heads, and the San Luiseños were left alone. One wanted to strike the other, thinking they were San Juaneño; for all the fury they didn't recognize each other, and they feared nothing. The Spanish soldiers arrived once the hubbub was over, because they too were trembling and wanted to end the tumult with their words. The captain of the thirty Luiseños.

60v The captain of the San Luiseños was an Indian, and he spoke like the Spaniards. The Indian told him, "Raise your saber and then I will eat you," but in his language, and thereafter nothing more happened.

61r On Dance

The dances are done in many different ways depending on the kind of Indians. The Indians called the Yuma have their dances; the Apache, another people, also has its dance; the Christian Diegueños have their dances; and we the San Luiseños have many for the men, and other ways for the women. So the San Luiseños, the Gabrileños, the Fernandinos, and those of Monterey, they too have their dances, each distinct from the others.

El Bayle en Europa es solo por alegria, Mas Nosotros por alegria, por llanto, por hacer guerra, por la buena cosecha. Aora que somos christianos solo baylamos por ceremonia, por recuerdo de nuestros Padres, Abuelos, porque murieron, u porque han sido vencidos en guerra. Tres maneras mejores ay de baylar para los hombres, uno es general, y nosotros llamamos *tanniś* baylar, o mejor dar patadas, Ninguno puede baylar sin la permission de los Viejos de aquella gente de donde el es, se enseñan a los Muchachos quando tienen diez, once, y mas años, y en cierto tiempo esso se hace, y se empieza a enseñar. Por la mañana estos bayladores se levantan y los Viejos les dan de beber Algo, y despues se dice que ellos son bayladores, y entonces pueden baylar sin que ninguno les pueda quitar del Bayle.

61v   Antes de Baylar empiezan a vestirse de plumas como los antiguos, y dos de ellos saliendo de la casa gritan queriendo decir que haga lugar, llevando dos espadas de madera, que llamamos *Uacatom*, y los hombres que van gritando.

63r   Conque el Missionero llega con poca gente: entonces el Capitan nuestro viendoles de lejos, y tambien los otros se espantan mas no uyen, ni cogen ~~las~~ armas para matarles, mas sentados las estaban viendo, mas quando aquellos mas se acercaron: entonces el Capitan se levanta, y les encuentra, el Fernandino le habla en Español, como en su lengua mas el Capitan no le entiende porque jamas havia visto hombres blancos, El Capitan le habla ni tampoco el Fernandino le podìa entender, el capitan quien sabe le havia dicho, que es lo que aquí buscais? mas por señales y en su lengua, *hichsom ivà hal-uon,* ~~hat~~ *palùchajam chamquiñai.* El P. Fernandino le dio regalos, y assi se amigaron. El Capitan viendo a esta gente tan liberal, volviendose a su gente y aquí (como es facil) habrà hablado a favor de los blancos, y por esso los Españoles no fueron Matados, porque aquel era el día en que dios sacàrnos de la Gentilidad querìa.

63v   Fue gran gracìa esta, que no mataron a los Españoles; y casi dificil a creerse, porque jamas han querido que otra gente con ellos habitase, que por esso hasta aquellos dias estaban guerreando. El Fernandino se

Dance in Europe is only for joy, but ours is for joy, for lament, to make war, for a good harvest. Now that we are Christians, we dance only for ceremonies, in remembrance of our Fathers, Grandfathers, because they died, or because they were vanquished in war. For men, there are three best ways to dance; one is general, and we call it *tanniś*, "to dance," or to put it better, "to kick." No one may dance without the permission of the Elders of the people to which he belongs. The boys are taught when they are ten, eleven, or older, and at a certain time that is done, and they begin to teach. In the morning these dancers get up, and the Elders give them something to drink. And after that it is said that they are dancers, and then they can dance without anyone removing them from the dance.

61v   Before dancing, they begin to dress themselves in feathers like the ancients, and two of them, emerging from the house, shout so as to tell everyone to make room, holding two wooden swords that we call *Uacatom*, and the men who go about shouting.

63r   So the missionary arrived with few people; then our captain, seeing them from afar, and also the others, became scared but they did not flee, nor did they take up arms to kill them, but seated they watched them. But when those men approached, then did our captain rise and meet them. The Fernandino* speaks to him in Spanish, as in his language, but our captain does not understand him because he had never seen white men. The captain speaks to him and the Fernandino could not understand him either. The captain somehow had asked him what he was seeking here, but through hand signals and in his language *hichsom ivà hal-uon,* ~~hat~~ *palùchajam chamquiñai.* The Fernandino father gave him gifts, and so they became friends. The captain, seeing these people so generous, turned to his people and here (since it is easy) must have spoken favorably of the whites, and that is why the Spaniards were not killed, because that was the day on which God wanted to release us from heathenism.

63v   This was a great blessing, that they did not kill the Spaniards, and almost difficult to believe, because they had never wanted other people to live with them, and for that reason, up to those days they were

---

*When Tac writes of P. Fernandino (the Fernandino father), he refers to the Franciscan Order. The Franciscans who came to California first received training at the Colegio de San Fernando in Mexico City.

queda en nuestro Pays, se hace un aduar, para aqui vivir, y decir Misa,
viviendo aquí y viendo las cosas como iban, teniendo por amigo el
capitan de nada tenìa miedo. Despues de havernos bautizado, Mandó,
y les dijo hagamos una casa grande para nosotros. Cortad los Arbores,
llevad piedras para los cimientos, haced ladrillos, texas, y lo necesario.
Los neofitos empiezan a trabajar, y entre pocos años, con los Maestros
que los ayudaron se cumpliò la obra. La casa fue echa, se hizo tambien
una Iglesia. Con sus campanas y ciminterio, quartel para los soldados.
casa para los mayordomos. La casa es quadrada tiene un gran patio,
en medio un relox de palo y a quatro lados, quatro plantas de naranjo
amargo.

con tres* ~~capillas,~~ altares, uno en medio, y los otros dos a los lados del
mismo. en el altar mayor ay estatuas de muchos santos, y en medio, la
de S. Luys Rey de Francia dorada. Mas abajo, la estatua de Maria
Virgen de palo, a mano derecha del altar mayor, ay el segundo altar, y

64r   las estatuas, que son las que siguen la estatua de S. Joaquin, de Santa
Ana. de Josè, el altar nuestro a mano isquierda es de S. Antonio de
Padua.

65r ## Conversion de los Saluiseños dela alt. Calif.

Los Alcaldes Volviendose a los Aduares cada uno dellos por donde
passa va gritando lo que el Missionero les habia dicho, en sus idiomas
y todo el pays està oyendo: Mañana, se empieza a siembrar y por esso
los gañanes vayan al gallinero y allì se junten; = y de nuevo estas
mismas palabras va diciendo hasta llegar a su mismo aduar para
tomar algo y despues acostarse, Y Mañana usted verrà a los gañanes
yrse para el gallinero, y aqui juntarse segun ayer noche habian oydo.

Con los gañanes se va un Mayordomo Español y otros Alcaldes Neofitos, para ver como se trabaja, si son flojos para apurarlos, que pronto
acaben lo mandado y castigar al culpable, o flojo, que dejando su arado,
se deja por el campo quedandose con su flogedad. Trabajan todo el
dia pero no siempre, a las doce se deja el trabajo, y entonces les trahen
(*Posole*) (*Posòle* dicen los Españoles de California el Mays cocido en

---

*The word *dos* has been written over in the original. In addition, Tac has made two
marks at the beginning of this sentence fragment suggesting that the remainder of the passage, through fol. 64r, was to be transposed to precede "Cortad los Arbores" (cut the trees),
above, on fol. 63v.

waging war. The Fernandino stayed in our country, and he made himself a hut to live here and to say Mass; living here and seeing how things went, having the captain as a friend, he feared nothing. After having baptized us, he ordered and he told them, "Let us make a great house for ourselves. Cut the trees, bring stones for the foundations, make bricks, roof tiles, and other necessary things." The neophytes set to work, and within a few years, with the master craftsmen who helped them, the building was completed. The house was done, and a church was also built, with its bells and cemetery, barracks for the soldiers, a house for the mayordomos. The house is square, and it has a large patio, in the middle wooden clock, and to the four sides, four bitter orange trees.

with three altars, one in the middle and the other two on either side. In the main altar there are statues of many saints, and in the middle the gilded statue of Saint Louis, King of France. Farther down, the wooden statue of the Virgin Mary; to the right-hand side of the main altar is 64r the second altar, and the statues, which are the following: the statue of Saint Joachim, of Saint Anne, of Joseph; and to the left-hand side, the altar of Saint Anthony of Padua.

65r ## Conversion of the San Luiseños of Alta California

The *alcaldes,* returning to the village, each one of them goes shouting out through every place he passes, [announcing] in their languages what the missionary had told them, and everyone hears: "Tomorrow we begin sowing, and so the workers must go to the henhouse and gather there." And they go repeating these same words until they get to their own hut, where they eat something and then go to bed. And the next day, you will see the workers leave for the henhouse, and gather there, as they had heard the night before.

A Spanish mayordomo and other neophyte alcaldes go with the workers to see how the work progresses, to hurry them if they are lazy so they can soon finish what was ordered, and to punish the guilty or the lazy person who, abandoning his plow, goes off into the fields, lingering in his laziness. They work all day long but not always; at noon they stop working and then they are brought *pozole* (the Spaniards of California call maize cooked in hot water *pozole*) and they eat with gusto,

agua caliente) y comen con gusto y se quedan artos hasta la tarde, quando se vuelven a sus aduares. Los Zapateros trabajan haciendo sillas, muchiles, riendas, zapatos, para los Vaqueros Neofitos, y Mayordomos y soldados Españoles, y quando han acabado llevan y entregan al Missionero para dar a los Vaqueros. Los herreros haciendo frenos, llaves, chapas, clavos para la Iglesia, y todos trabajan para todos.

65v Hemos dicho que *Quechla* era el primer de los Payses siendo esse el primer lugar del Padre Fernandino, y la misma Mission. Alrededor dello son puestos los otros Payses, y ranchos de la Mission de S. Luys Rey de Francia, hazia oriente hay, el rancho de S. Marcos, y el Pays llamado Pala, y otro rancho, azia setentrion ay Temeco, Uśva, y un rancho. En la Mission de S. Luys Rey de Francia està el Padre Fernandino como un Rey, tiene sus pages, Alcaldes, Mayordomos, Musicos, Soldados, huertos ranchos, ganados, caballos a millares, vacas toros a millares, Bueyes, mulos, asnos, corderos doce mil, cabras doscientas, etc. Pages para si y para los passageros Españoles y Mejicanos, Ingleses, y Anglos Americanos; Alcaldes para que le ayuden a gubernar, toda la gente de la Mission de S. Luys Rey de Francia, Mayordomos, se hallan en los payses lejanos, casi todos Españoles, Musicos dela Mission para los dias de Fiesta, y todos los Domingos y festividades del año con ellos los cantores, todos los Indios Neofitos. Soldados para que ninguno haga daño ni a Español, ni a Indio, que por todos don diez y van a caballo. huertos, que son por todos cinco y muy grandes; el Padre Fernandino poco toma, y como casi todos los huertos sacan vino, el que bien conoce las costumbres de los Neofitos, nada de vino quiere

66r dar a ninguno de ellos mas lo vende a los Ingleses, u a los Anglos Americanos, no por dinero, mas por ropa, para los Neofitos lienzo para la Iglesia, sombreros, fuciles, platos, cafè, tè, azucar, y otras cosas, La cosecha de la Mission es, Manteca de vaca, Cebo, Cueros, Gamuzas, pieles de osos, Vino, vino blanco, Aguardiente, Azeyte, Mays, Trigo, Frixol, y tambien cuernos de Toros, que los Ingleses se los llevan a millares a Boston.

Lo que se hace cada Dia

Quando el Sol sale y las estrellas y la Luna huyen, Entonces el viejo de casa despierta todos y empieza por el almuerzo, que es, tomar el *Juiuiś* calentado, y carne, y tortillas, que pan no tenemos, echo esto toma su Arco y flechas y sale de casa con sus perros valientes y ligeros, (esso es

and they remain sated until the afternoon when they return to their homes. The shoemakers work at making saddles, knapsacks, bridles, and shoes for the neophyte cowboys and Spanish mayordomos and soldiers, and when they have finished [their work], they bring it and hand it over to the missionary so that he can give it to the cowboys. The blacksmiths make bits, locks, keys nails for the church, and everyone works for all.

65v We have said that *Quechla* was the first of the countries, being the first place of Father Fernandino, and of the mission. All around it are located the other countries, and ranches of the Mission San Luis Rey de Francia, to the east is the San Marcos Ranch and the country called Pala, and another ranch; toward the north are Temeco, Uśva, and a ranch. At Mission San Luis Rey de Francia the Fernandino Father is like a king; he has servants, alcaldes, mayordomos, musicians, soldiers, orchards, livestock, horses by the thousands, cows and bulls by the thousands, oxen, donkeys, mules, twelve thousand lambs, two hundred goats, etc. Servants for himself and for the Spanish, Mexican, English, and Anglo-American travelers; alcaldes to help him govern all of the people of the Mission San Luis Rey de Francia; mayordomos are found in the far countries, almost all Spaniards; musicians of the Mission for feast days and for every Sunday and the yearly festivities with the singers, all of them neophyte Indians. Soldiers so that no one may harm either a Spaniard or an Indian; they are ten in all and go on horseback. Orchards number five in total, and very large. The father drinks little, and because almost all of the orchards produce wine, and he knows well the habits of the neophytes, he gives no wine to any of them, but

66r instead sells it to the English or to the Anglo Americans, not for money but for clothes for the neophytes, linens for the church, hats, guns, plates, coffee, tea, sugar, and other things. The products of the mission include lard from the cows, fodder, cowhides, suede, bearskins, wine, white wine, liquor, oil, maize, wheat, beans, and also bull horns, which the English take to Boston by the thousands.

What Is Done Each Day

When the sun comes out and the stars and the moon flee, then the elder of the house wakes everyone and begins breakfast, which consists of warmed *Juiuiś* with meat and tortillas, as we do not have bread. This done, he takes his bow and arrows, and he leaves the

si va al cazo y se lleva a los lejanos bosques llenos de osos, y liebres, venados, y millares de paxaros aquí està todo el dia mattando quantos puede, siguiendoles, escondiendose de tras los Arboles, subiendose por los mismos, y despues carcado de liebres se vuelve a casa Alegre; pero quando falta madera, el luego por la mañana sale de casa con su lazo a los hombros, y su acha, con compañeros, que se puedan ayudar, quando es muy cargado el cargo y por la tarde se vuelve a casa; Su vieja quedandose en casa hace la comida, el hijo si es hombre echo trabaja con los hombres, su hija con las Mugeres se queda haciendo

66v   camisas, y si estos tambien tienen hijos, y hijas, se quedan en la Mission, los hijos, a la escuela, a aprender el abecedario, y si ya saben, aprender el Catecismo, y si esso tambien, al coro de los Cantores, y si fue cantor, al trabajo, que ya todos los cantores musicos, el dia de trabajo trabajan, y al Domingo al coro a cantar, pero sin libro, porque ya antes el Maestros los ensegna a Memoria teniendo èl el libro. La hija se junta con las solteras que todas hilan para frazadas de los Sanluiseños, y para la tunica del P. Fernandino. A las doce comen juntos, y dejan su porcion al viejo, sus tazas de barro, sus vasos de yerba bien tejida que el agua no puede salir, sino quando es tenida ante la cara del sol, sus sartenes de barro, sus parillas de palo echas para aquel dia, y sus cantaros para el agua, tambien de barro, sentados alrededor del fuego estan hablando y comiendo, pobres de ellos si en aquel tiempo cierran la puerta, entonces el humo levantandose y siendo mucho, y siendo el aguxero pequeño que sirve de ventana, se vuelve abaxo queriendo salir por la puerta, queda en medio de la casa, y entonces se come hablando riendo y llorando sin quererlo. Acabada la comida se vuelven a sus trabajos, el Padre deja al hijo el hijo deja a la hermana, la hermana al hermano, el hermano a la Madre, la Madre a su Marido, con consuelo, hasta a la tarde, antes de acostarse de nuevo comen lo que la vieja y el Viejo han echo en aquel tiempo, y despues duermen.

house with his brave and agile dogs (if he is going hunting) and goes to the distant forests filled with bears, hares, deer, and thousands of birds, and there he spends the whole day killing as many as he can, tracking them, hiding behind trees and climbing them, and then laden with hares, he returns home happily. But when there is no firewood, he goes out in the morning with his lasso at his shoulders, and his ax, with companions who can help him when the load is very heavy, and in the afternoon he returns home. His woman, staying at home, makes the food; his son, if he is of age, works with the men; and his daughter stays with the women making shirts. And if they too have sons and daughters, they stay in the mission, the sons at school to learn the alphabet, and if they already know it, to learn the catechism, and if they know that too, to the choir with the singers, and if they have been singers, they go to work. For now the musician cantors work on workdays and sing in the choir on Sunday, but without a choral score, because the teacher has already taught them by memory, and he holds the score.* The daughter joins the unwed women, and they all spin to make blankets for the San Luiseños and the vestments of the Fernandino father. At twelve they eat together, and leave the elder his portion—their clay cups, and their glasses of aromatic plant fiber so tightly woven that water does not leak through them unless held before the face of the sun; their clay pans; their wooden grills made for that day; and their water pitchers, also made of clay. Seated around the fire they are talking and eating, and pity them should they close the door at that time; then the smoke, rising and being plentiful, and the opening that serves as a window being small, goes downward and, trying to get out through the door, gets trapped in the house, so that they eat while talking, laughing, and crying without meaning to. With the meal finished, they return to their work. The father leaves the son, the son leaves the sister, the sister the brother, the brother the mother, the mother her husband, contented, until evening. Before they go to sleep, they eat once again what the old woman and the old man have made in that time, and then they sleep.

66v

---

*These are usually elaborately painted books.

67r
De las Personas

Las Personas son tres que son *non, om, uonal,* yo, tu, aquel. y en
Plural *Chaom, Omom, Uonàlom.* Nos, vos, aquellos o mejor, Nosotros, Vosotros aquellos. Siendo las terminaciones de los verbos en
nuestra lengua, pocas, que se hallan especialmente en el presente del
Indicat., e Imperat., Mucho necessitamos de las personas para poder
distinguir quien de las personas pregunta, quien pida, quien repita,
p.e. la voz *naċmaċ* que significa oir, no se sabe quien oiga, porque falta
la persona que determine la significacion della. pero si yo pongo ante
aquella voz, *non,* entonces se podrà saber que yo oigo, si se pone, *om,*
tambien se sabrà, si pongo, *uonal,* lo mismo sucede. De aqui se vèe
que las personas es menester que se pongan, u se digan. Pero pregun-
tamos, ante el verbo u despues del mismo se pondran tales personas?
En donde los querreis poner. Pero con esta ley y regla, que quando
querreis poner ante el verbo la primera persona que es, *Non,* yo, se
deje como està no añadiendo ni nada quitandole, p.e. yo amo, yo
quiero, se dice, *Non Màmaċ.* La segunda y tercera persona que son
om tu, *uonal* aquel, quieren despues de si esta voz, *op,* que por si

67v
nada significa Como seria *om op* tu, *uonalop* aquel, y ninguna pala-
brita se ponga en medio que ya es error, ni tampoco se deje porque
tambien hai error. p.e. tu escrives, se dice *omop nauiċ,* aquel sabe,
uonalop ayal-liċ. Vamos adelante . . . La Primera Persona del Plural
que es *Chaom* requiere tambien despues, esta voz, *cha,* y unida queda
Chaomcha, no se puede dejar. p.e. Nosotros sabemos *Chaomcha ayal-
liuon,* Nosotros aprendemos *Chaomcha pilàchiuon.* La segunda
quiere, *om,* conque se dirà *omom om* vosotros, p.e. vosotros comeis,
omom om hilàiuon. La tercera del Plural quiere *pom,* que unida se
pone ante el verbo en esta manera p.e. aquellos huyen. *uonalom pom
Nàlajon,* Assi se pondran Ante el verbo; veamos aora ~~quando~~ como se
ponen despues del verbo. La Primera Persona que es *non* se muda en
an, unida con el verbo, p.e. yo sé, *ayal-lican,* yo tomo, *p curan-niċan.*
La Segunda que es *om,* se muda en *ap,* y tambien a la tercera se añade,
mas añada usted a la segunda *om.* P.e. tu lloras, *ñacap om.* aquel

On Persons

There are three persons, which are *non, om, uonal,* "I," "you," "that
one"; and in the plural *Chaom, Omom, Uonàlom,* "we *[nos],*" "you
[vos]," "those ones," or, better said, "we *[nosotros],*" "you *[vosotros],*"
"those ones." As verb endings in our language are few, and they are
especially found in the present indicative and in the imperative, we
have a great need for the persons to distinguish who is asking, who is
requesting, who is repeating. For example, in the word *nacmac,* which
means "to hear," we cannot know who is hearing, because what is
missing is the person [i.e., the personal pronoun], which determines
the meaning of the word. But if I put *non* before that word, then one
will know that I hear; if one puts *om,* it will also be known; if I add
uonal, the same thing happens. From this we can see that it is necessary to put in or say the person. But, we ask, should the persons be
added before the verb or after it? Wherever you want to put them. But
with this rule, when you want to put before the verb the first person,
which is *non,* "I," it should be left as is, neither adding nor taking away
anything. For example, "I love," or "I want," is said *Non Màmac.* The
second and third persons, which are *om,* "you," and *uonal,* "that one,"
need after them this word *op,* which by itself means nothing. So it
would be *omop,* "you," and *uonalop,* "that one," and no word should
be put in the middle, as that is an error, nor should it remain [alone]
because that is also an error. For example, "you write" is said *omop
nauic;* "that one knows," *uonalop ayal-lic.* Let us go on . . . The first
person plural, which is *Chaom,* also requires the word *cha* after it, and
once joined, it becomes *Chaomcha,* which cannot remain [alone]. For
example, "we know," *Chaomcha ayal-liuon;* "we learn," *Chaomcha
pilàchiuon.* The second [person] takes *om,* so that one will say *omom
om* "you," for example, "you eat," *omom om hilàiuon.* The third [per-
son] of the plural requires *pom,* which when joined is placed before
the verb in this manner, for example: "Those people run," *uonalom
pom Nàlajon.* Thus would it be placed before the verb; now we will
see how it is placed after the verb. The first person, which is *non,* becomes *an,* joined with the verb; for example, "I know," *ayal-lican;* "I
take," *curan-nican.* The second [person], which is *om,* becomes *ap,* and
it is also added to the third [person], but you add to the second *om;*

duerme *cupċap*, y tambien *cupċap uonal*. A la Primera Persona del Plural sigue la voz, *Cha*, y se añade al verbo, p.e. Nosotros hablamos, *tete lauoncha*, y tambien *tetelauonchachaom*. A la Segunda sigue *Om*. Conque se dira p.e. vosotros ganais *chiùiuon om*, por fin la tercera despues de si quiere *pom*, con que se dirà aquellos llegan, *Uocòajonpom*. Vienen aquellos, *MonuonPom*, aquellos hacen *LojauonPom*. Y assi todos . . . .

69r El Verbo *Ṅaṅiṡ*, llorar, en el modo de quien manda ni termina en *j*. ni en *i*. como dejimos, y como todos los otros verbos hacen, y terminan, y toman una de estas dos letras, que entonces la *j*. toman quando en el infinit. terminan en *jis*. como p.e. *helep-pajiṡ* esconderse hace *helep-paj*. escondete tu. y en la *.i.* quando en el infinit modo terminan en todas las otras silabas, y vocales, como *nubliṡ* empujar. imperat. hace *nubli*. empuja. Este de ellos se aparta y en *ṅ* termina haciendo *ṅaṅ*, llora, y en el indicat. se conjuga diciendo, *non ṅaċ*, yo lloro, *om op ṅaċ* tu lloras, *uenalop ṅaċ*, aquel llora, plural. *chaomcha nauon*, nosotros lloramos, *omomom ṅauom*, vosotros llorais, *uenàlompom ṅauon*, aquellos lloran.

El verbo *ṅaṅiṡ*, llorar, se dice mejor para significar el llanto de los hombres, o personas grandes, porque tenemos otro verbo para significar el llanto delos niños, muchachos, y de todos los pequeños. p.e. Mi madre llora por mi hermano Mayor. se dice *No yò ṅaċ, po maṅai no pàas*. El hombre llora, *Yaàṡ op ṅaċ*, la avuela llora, *o tù op ṅaċ*.

Chacajiṡ se dice quando un muchacho llora, y casi quiere decir llorar gritando, segun los niños y muchachitos lloran gritando,

69v El muchachito jugando llora, *Amàyamalop yiyiċanoq-chàc chaċaċ*. con todo esso aora no se hace mucho caso de estos dos verbos, ~~porque~~ mas no se toma el uno por el otro, p.e. Mi padre llora, no se diria bien *no nàop chaċaċ*, y no se dice mas *ṅaċap*. y si yo quisiere decir mi hermano minor llora podria decir, *no petop ṅaċ*, sin error. De aqui se ve que el llanto o llorar del niño se puede decir, y exprimir por los dos verbos *chacajiṡ* y *ṅaṅiṡ*, mas el del hombre por el solo verbo *Ṅaṅiṡ*, porque assi el hombre llora, y no como el muchacho por sus trabesuras llora gritando, y quejandose de lo mal echo. Y bien se dice *Yaaṡ op Ṅaċ*, el hombre llora, *Amàyamalop chàċaċ*, el muchacho llora.

for example, "you cry," *ñacap om;* "that one sleeps," *cupċap,* and also *cupċap uonal.* In the first person plural the word *Cha,* and it is added to the verb; for example, "we spoke," *tete lauoncha,* and also *tete-lauonchachaom.* The second is followed by *Om.* So one will say, for example, "you win," *chiùiuon om.* And finally, the third requires *pom* after it, so that one will say "those ones arrive," *Uocòajonpom;* "those ones are coming," *MonuonPom;* "those ones are doing," *LojauonPom.* And thus for all . . .

69r   The verb *Ňañiś,* "to cry," in the command mode does not end in *j* or in *i,* as we have said, and as all the other verbs do and end taking one of these two letters. Thus they take the *j* when the infinitive ends in *jis,* so, for example, *helep-pajiś,* "to hide oneself," makes *helep-paj,* "hide yourself,"; and the *i* when the infinitive ends in all the other syllables, and vowels, such as *nubliś,* "to push," [whose] imperative makes *nubli,* "push." This [verb] departs from the others and ends in *ñ,* making *ñañ,* "cry," and in the indicative it is conjugated by saying *non ñać,* "I cry"; *om op ñać,* "you cry"; *uenalop ñać,* "that one cries"; plural *chaomcha ñauon,* "we cry"; *omomom ñauom,* "you cry"; *uenàlompom ñauon,* "those ones cry."

The verb *ñaniś,* "to cry," is said rather to signify the crying of men or adults, because we have another verb to signify the crying of infants, children, and all the little ones. For example: "My mother cries for my older brother," is said *No yò ñać, po mañai no pàas.* "The man cries," *Yaàś op ñać.* "The grandmother cries," *o tù op ñać.*

Chacajiś is used when a child cries, and it almost means to cry out screaming, as infants and children do.

69v   "The little boy cries while playing," *Amàyamalop yiyiċanoq-chàc chaċać.* With all that, we won't pay much attention to these two verbs now, but we should not mistake one for the other. For example, "My father cries" would not be said *no nàop chaċać,* and it is not said [in any way] but *ñaċap.* If I wanted to say "my younger brother cries," I could say *no petop ñać* with no error. From this we can see the cry or weeping of a child can be said and expressed by both the verbs *chacajiś* and *ñañiś,* but a man's weeping only by the verb *Ňañiś,* because that is how a man cries, and not the way a child cries out screaming on account of his mischief, complaining of the bad deed. And to speak correctly, one says, *Yaaś op Ňać,* "the man cries"; *Amàyamalop chàċać,* "the boy cries."

71r *Ṅai,* aunque esta palabra en sì nada signifique; todavìa quando es
puesta de tras de la palabra que le sigue, (para decir mejor, es como
la palabra *ṅa,* en, que sola no puede hallarse) significa *de,* y tambien
desde. p.e. Bajò de el monte, o desde el monte, se dira: *Uórapil ċauiṅai,
ċauinaropil uòra.*

La voz, *hasta,* de los Españoles no tenemos, mas se exprime añadiendo
una *q* al nominat. del nombre, o lugar, ~~en~~ hasta que se va. p.e. tus hijos
corren hasta tu casa: *o camayompom hiccuajom o quiq.* desde el riyo,
corrió hasta el mar: *uaniṅaiopil hiccuà momaiq.* te ~~esperaremos~~
llevaremos hasta tu tierra, *oichapo hatin o quiq.*

Y tambien en esta manera, explicamos la vos azia. de los mismos, es
decir añadiendo la *q.* al nominat. del nombre o lugar, azia que se va.
p.e. Voy asia el rio, y despues me volvere a casa mya. *Non uaniq, monc,
pe nopo ip. no quiq hatiajan hatialajàn.* esta piedra caerà azia el poniente. *ivipo tota hulucajan payomiq.* el viento sopla de el poniente
hasia el levante. *Huṅlap jòyiċ payomcanai cuimiq.* el rio baja desde
el Nord hasta el Sud. *Uóracap uaniṡ tomamcoṅai quichamiq.*

72r *Pe hélhelajòn, hajso ivi ohonvaċ.*

De estos exemplos se conoce, que ~~la~~ nuestra palabra *conà.* indica cosa
que por cierto no se sabe, mas según a uno parece el dice, porque tambien nosotros el Verbo decir lo exprimimos. p.e. te digo que no hables
fuerte, *cai pomminoq o tetelapin oic yaċ.* quien te dijo, o muchacho,
que tu padre vendria, en esta noche, con tu madres y hermanos, de tu
pais? *Amayamal hajso oic yà, o Nà pom eṡ o Yo, pè o petom, ìvaṅa
tucbaṅa, o quiṅai po uocoacapi po uocòapi?* Dicen. decìan. se dice, se
decìa. quando significan quasi ignorantia explicamos con la palabra
conà, esta palabra misma queda assi con la personas, o cosas, de numero singular, mas quando son plurales coge ella tambien la *m**
como si fuesse un nombre y no adverbio. se dice que venian tres
Reyes de lejos payses del Oriente. Se dirà: *Moncuasconam pachom
Notom, uamcunai ejnài cuimcuṅai.* jamas se antepone, y si se

---

*There is a letter crossed out before *m.*

71r   *Ṅai*, although this word has no meaning on its own, nonetheless, when it is placed after the word that goes with (or to put it better, it is like the word *ṅa*, "in," which cannot be on its own), means "from [*de*, and also *desde*]." For example, "He came down from the hills," or "all the way from the hills," would be said, *Uórapil ċauiṅai, ċauinaropil uòra.*

The word "*hasta* [to, up to]" of the Spaniards we do not have, but it is expressed by adding a *q* to the nominative noun, or place, to which one goes. For example: "Your children run up to your house," *o camayampom hiccuajom o quiq.* "From the river, he ran up to the sea," *uaninaiopil hiccuà momaiq.* "We will take you to your land," *oichapo hatin o quiq.*

And in this manner, we also express the word "*hacia* [to, toward]." In the same [ways], which is to say, adding the *q* to the nominative of the noun or the place toward which it goes. For example: "I am going to the river, and afterward I will return to my house"; *Non uaniq, monc, pe nopo ip no quiq hatiajan hatialajan.* "This rock will fall toward the west"; *Ivipo tota hulucajan payomiq.* "The wind blows from the west toward the east"; *Hunlap joyii payomcanas cuimiq.* "The river descends from the North to the South"; *Uóracap uanis tomamconai quichamiq.*

72r   *Pe hélhelajòn, hajso ivi ohonvaċ.**

From these examples we can see that our word *conà* indicates a thing that is not known for certain, but as it appears to one, he says it, because we also express the verb "to say." For example; "I tell you not to speak loudly," *cai pomminoq o tetelapin oic yaċ.* "Who told you, boy, that your father would come tonight with your mother and brothers, from your region?" *Amayamal hajso oic yà, o Nà pom eṡ o Yo, pè o petom, ìvaṅa tucbaṅa, o quíṅai po uocoacapi po uocòapi?* "They say," "they used to say," "it is said," "it used to be said," when they signify almost ignorance, we use the word *conà*. This word remains as is with persons, or things, that are singular in number, but when they are plural, it too takes the *m,* as if it were a noun and not an adverb. "It is said that three Kings came from faraway countries of the Orient" would be said, *Moncuasconam pachom Notom, uamcunai ejṅài cuimcuṅai.* It is never placed in front, and if it were placed in front, it would not be

---

*Fols. 72r and 72v appear to be in reverse order. We have followed the order of the manuscript as found in the archive. (The same occurs with fols. 74r and 74v below.)

anteponesse, no se podria entender. mas se pospone a una, o dos palabras y es como el *quoque* de los Latines.

72v La voz nuestra, *conà*, no se como bien explicarla en la de los Españoles, todavìa con los exemplos que siguen, y con los que podremos decir, se podrà algo explicar, y entenderse, conque empezemos. La voz .*conà*. nuestra indica, una cosa que no se sabe por cierto, e indica ignorancia, y los Españoles la pueden explicar, con las voces del Verbo decir: como serìan, dice que, decìa que, dijo que. y en otras muchas maneras. p.e. dice que ha aprendido todo, y ~~Au~~ que no quiere mas apprender. se explica. *choon conà pilàchaj, pe con cai pilàchivichoċ:* el dice mas no sabemos la verdad de su sabiduria: dijo, que queria matar a todos los extanjeros cercandose a su pais: *Choonmi conà atajmi po quiq hayàacajoq mocnavichocùos.* el dijo, mas no se sabe por cierto se el llegando matò segun abìa dicho antes que se fuese. Dicen, que aquel quando guerea siempre vence con su fuerza a todos. *Uonalcona po pumlotal necpicnaq, mimchapan choonmi yayismi chùichsùiċ necpicanoċ,* dicen, mas con todo eso no dicen por cierto, dicen segun les parece, mas verdaderamente no saben: Se dice que allà en aquel lugar se hallan lobos, y que estos muy bien pintan escriben, y cantan. tambien cantan, quien lo cree: *Ysuotom conà uonà a-uon, àvimconà pè pomminoq ayalinoq, naunauiuon.*

73r
Dialogo

S U I S

Cuottaj Oula no pet uamop juaiac, omop cai najamnal auólop, pe hamicha muancatom.

Cuottaj teopca cupmajan oinopo chilchilin patal, pe nopo iviajanminoc quottin oi.

Puluchaċan, peno ~~naiċ~~ cai tiuiċ mesmalmi, amuop yauaiuaiṡ pulùchaċ temet, poloiṡ cham muanpi.

O U L A

Tusjo nii ñoii, non ayalinoc cupċ:

Non cuottavichoc, pe op tamet hilavichoċ.

Niic o uiymí pè o sauacmi majanmi nonopo queleq cuottajan.

understood. But it is placed after one or two words, and it is like the *quoque* of the Latin.

72v Our word *conà*, I don't know how to explain it well in [words] of the Spanish, but with the examples that follow, and with what we are able to say, it can be explained somewhat and understood, so let's begin. Our word *conà* indicates a thing that is not known for certain, and it indicates ignorance, and the Spaniards can explain it with the forms of the verb "to say," which would be "he says that," "he used to say that," "he said that," and in many other ways. For example, "He says that he has learned everything and that he does not want to learn any more" is explained: *choon conà pilàchaj, pe con cai pilàchivichoċ*—he says so, but we do not know the veracity of his wisdom. "He said he wanted to kill all the foreigners approaching his country," *Choonmi conà atajmi po quiq hayàacajoq mocnavichocùos*—he said so, but it is not known for sure if he killed when he arrived, as he said he would when he left. "They say that when that one goes to war, he always vanquishes everyone with his strength," *Uonalcona po pumlotal necpicnaq, mimchapan choonmi yayismi chùichsùiċ necpicanoċ*—they say so, but despite all that they cannot say for certain; they say as it appears to them, but in truth they don't know. "They say that over there in that place there are wolves, and that they paint, write, and sing very well; they even sing, who believes it?" *Ysuotom conà uonà a-uon, àvimconà pè pomminoq ayalinoq, naunauiuon.*

73r   Dialogue

SUIS

Cuottaj Oula no pet uamop juaiac, omop cai najamnal auólop, pe hamicha muancatom.

Cuottaj teopca cupmajan oinopo chilchilin patal, pe nopo ivia-janminoc quottin oi.

Puluchaċan, peno ~~naie~~ cai tiuiċ mesmalmi, amuop yauaiuaiṡ pulù-chaċ temet, poloiṡ cham muanpi.

OULA

Tusjo nii ṅoii, non ayalinoc cupċ:

Non cuottavichoc, pe op tamet hilavi-choċ.

Niic o uiymí pè o sauacmi majanmi nonopo queleq cuottajan.

Cuottajansis no majannicala oic. Olaò pe qùeliq.

Uuanmi no uiui, pe ayanni no sauac- Caino.
mi hichso auoi mámaċ, non opo oic
choon o lachicala majannin, màmanoc
no eś o hatiajpi.

Hanicha muancotom. Hamicha.

Temet po chulúpacala, cham quinachape Tiuinchapo o tetelacala.
uocóajan cham Naichapo sucatmi ma-
jannic pe mo cham muanni pomom
hilàin.

73v *Oula ayáli o Catapi, chaomcha* omca ayáli
uam uamina auon.

Oula oula séi úi suiś hajiyś, oiso no seppi mámac.

Non so suis. No tuñop, pe no ohó ata ivip o tusi.
cai asun suiś.

Hanicha cham quiq, chaomcha oi nil amu yaċ.
cai his polovi loviium, choonña
iviña temeña tetelatalomcha
nenecpiuon.

Omañai oula cai sucati mocnacan Omopil cai suiśi mámaac no
moconopi

74r Sangre, compone a tu arco, che ya y tu tambien.
nosotros nos hallamos en el bosco

Sangre, Sangre, mata a este conejo. A quien, a ti quieres que mate?

Que yo soy conejo. mi nombre es, Si este es tu nombre.
mas yo no soy un verdadero conejo.

Vamos a casa, no hemos hecho algo Ya te dije.
de bueno, nosotros en este dia
peleamos con las palabras.

Por ti o Sangre, no mate al venado. Tu no quisiste que matase al conejo.

Cuottajansis no majannicala oic.   Olaò pe qùeliq.

Uuanmi no uiui, pe ayanni no sauac-   Caino.
mi hichso auoi mámaċ, non opo oic
choon o lachicala majannin, màmanoc
no eṡ o hatiajpi.

Hanicha muancotom.   Hamicha.

Temet po chulúpacala, cham quinachape Tiuinchapo o tetelacala.
uocóajan cham Naichapo sucatmi ma-
jannic pe mo cham muanni pomom
hilàin.

73v   Oula ayáli o Catapi, chaomcha   omca ayáli
uam uamina auon.

Oula oula séi úi suiṡ   hajiyṡ, oiso no seppi mámac.

Non so suis. No tuṅop, pe no   ohó ata ivip o tusi.
cai asun suiṡ.

Hanicha cham quiq, chaomcha   oi nil amu yaċ.
cai his polovi loviium, choonṅa
iviṅa temeṅa tetelatalomcha
nenecpiuon.

Omaṅai oula cai sucati mocnacan   Omopil cai suiṡi mámaac no
moconopi

74r   Blood, prepare your bow,   And you also.
for we are now in the forest.

Blood, Blood, kill this rabbit.   Who do you want me to kill, you?

I am rabbit, my name is, but I am not   If that is your name.
a true rabbit.

Let us go home, we have not done   I told you so.
anyhing good, this day we have
battled with words.

For you, O Blood, I did not kill   You didn't want me to kill the rabbit.
the deer.

74v

Dialogo

CONEJO	SANGRE
Levantate mi hermano Sangre que ya hace dia, tu no eres viejo mas joven, y vamonos a cazar.	No me despiertes, que yo duermo muy bien.
Levantate, si ~~dae~~ te quedaras, te echarè agua a la cara, y asi te levantarè.	~~No me~~ Yo me quiero levantar, mas el dia no es bueno.
Sali a fuera, y no vi ninguna* nube ya el sol lindo saliò, bueno para el cazo.	Dadme tu atole, y tu pan, que yo pronto me levantarè.
Te levantaras, quando te darè?	Si y muy pronto.
Toma mi atole, y pan, lo que quieras y me pediras todo te lo darè, queriendo que vaias conmigo.	No quiero mas.
Vamos a cazar.	Vamosnos.
Quando el sol cayra en el occidente entonces llegaremos a la casa nuestra y daremos al Padre nuestro los venados y ellos comeran ~~a~~ la que hemos cazado.	Veremos lo que hablas.

75r   Mas Dios quiso hacernos Christianos, el capitán empieza a hacerse amigo del Fernandino, y le deja que se quede en nuestro Pays, y como casas de piedra no habían porque todas eran aduares, también el Fernandino dormiò, con sus ciete soldados que llevaba con sigo. Assi estubo muchos dias; aqui decia Misa, hasta que se hizo una casa que el, y los cinco mil podian habitar. Sigue . . . Nuestro Pays antes que el Fernandino llegase era un bosque, el mandò que se cortassen los arbores para hacer en esta manera una llanura, se cortaron los Arbores, Mandò a traher piedras desde el mar, (que no es lejos) para los cimientos, se hicieron ladrillos, mescla, bigas, texas, y lo que ne-cesitaba. En pocos años acabaron la obra, la casa fué echa con su

---

*The word *alguna* is written over.

74v

Dialogue*

RABBIT	BLOOD
Rise up, my brother Blood, the day has dawned, you are not old but young, and let us go hunting.	Do not wake me, as I am sleeping so well.
Rise, for if you stay, I will throw water in your face, and so wake you.	I want to wake up, but the day is not good.
I went out, and I saw no cloud and the sun came out beautifully, perfect for hunting.	Give me your corn porridge and your bread, as I shall rise soon,
You will rise, when will I give it you?	Yes, and very soon.
Take my corn porridge, my bread, whatever you want and ask of me I shall give you, wishing that you come with me.	I want nothing more.
Let us go hunting.	Let us go.
When the sun drops in the west, then we shall arrive at our home and give our father the deer and they shall eat what we have hunted.	We shall see what you speak of.

75r   But God chose to make us Christians. The Captain begins to become friends with the Fernandino [the Franciscan] and he lets him stay in our country, and as there were no stone houses because they were all simple huts, the Fernandino too slept [here], with the seven soldiers he brought with him. It was like that for many days, he said Mass here, until he made a house that he and the five thousand could inhabit. Continue . . . † Our country before the Fernandino arrived was a forest, he ordered that the trees be cut down so as to make in this way a flat expanse of land. The trees were cut; he ordered stones to be brought from the sea (which is not far) for the foundations. They made bricks, mortar, rafters, roof tiles, and anything else that was needed. In a few years they finished the building, the house was

---

*Fols. 74r and 74v appear to be in reverse order. We have followed the order of the manuscript as found in the archive.

†Tac usually gives an indication to "continue" at the page break.

Iglesia, y otras dos chicas casas, la primera para los soldados, la segunda para los Mayordomos. Officinas de Zapatería, Carpintería, telar, Herrería, Jabonería y más Almazenes, torres, quartos, La casa es cuadrada, ay pilares adentro y tambien afuera mas solo antes las puertas del Padre Fernandino.

76r *yulam.* cabellos.

yù. cabeza.

ċma. frente.

Puṡ. ojo.

muoil. nariz.

tamát. diente

tamat. boca.

ueijiṡ. lengua. *ueiiṡ*

musiṡ. barba *musiṡ*

nacmaiṡ. oreja.

sàrat. gula.

sacat. pescuezo.

al. pecho.

cùalmal.

màt. brazo *mat*

nà. mano.

Sulàt, uña. *súlat tudùṡ.*

Aè. piè.

Sulatom. uñas *súlatom*

~~*Tajauiṡ*~~

cuajmaṡ

tajauiṡ. cuerpo. *tajauiṡ*

Ataj. hombre. *atáj*

77v Tal. con, de estrument.

La prep. *tal.* en sí non significa alguna cosa, mas quando se pone despues del nombre, coge la fuerza dela palabra con, p.e. matà, con su flecha, a la tigre, *mocnacpil po hulatal tucati.*

made with its church, and two other small houses: the first for the soldiers, the second for the mayordomos. Workshops for shoemaking, carpentry, looms, blacksmiths, soapmaking, and more storage ware-houses, towers, and rooms. The house is square; there are pillars inside and also outside, but only in front of Fernandino Father's doors.

76r   *yulam*   hair

yù   head

ċma   forehead

Puṡ   eye

muoil   nose

tamát   tooth

tamat   mouth

ueijiṡ   tongue   *ueiiṡ*

musiṡ   chin   *musiṡ*

nacmaiṡ   ear

sàrat   gullet

sacat   neck

al   chest

cùalmal

màt   arm   *mat*

nà   hand

Sulàt   nail   *súlat tudùṡ*

Aè   foot

Sulatom   nails   *súlatom*

~~*Tajauiṡ*~~

cuajmaṡ

tajauiṡ   body   *tajauiṡ*

Ataj   man   *atáj*

77v   *Tal*, "with," instrumental

The preposition *tal* in itself has no meaning, but when it is placed after the noun, it takes the meaning of the word "with." For example: "He kills, with his arrow, the tiger," *mocnacpil po hulatal tucati.*

Mañai. por.

La prep; *mañai,* queria decir, de mi mano, mas se usa como adverbio
o prep. de causa. p.e. por mi se murió mi padre, *no manai op. no Nà
tacuayac.* por nosotros murió el Hijo de Dios. *cham mañai op po
camai Chañichñiš tacuayac,* y ~~jama~~ nunca se mete adelante, y quien
haria en este manera no le entenderían. p.e. Si huviese dicho *mañai op
po camai chañichñiš tacuayac.* mas se mete una palabra, y entonces se
puede entender.

So.

So. voz, ~~este~~ que sirbe para preguntar, y se pone despues de̶l cualquie[r]
palabra, ni jamas adelante p.e. para donde vas con tus hermanos?
Michic só monà po os o potom? y en plural, se añade una *.m.* p.e. para
donde vais, en este dia, tan lluvioso? *michic som monà ivina temeña,
po jilacala.* quieres venir conmigo, a jugar? *No eiš sò hati ivichoc o
yiyipi?* Porque no quieres amarlo? *Hiñai so poi cai màmàvichoc.*

Hiñai. porque

Hinai, adverbio. ~~este~~ que ~~indica~~ significa, porque, quando se pregunta,
y se pone adelante, y después, p.e. porque no hiciste lo que te dije.
hiñai so cai loviiqoer os no yòjpi.* mas no se usa quando se quiere
responder.

Conversion de los SanLuiseños de la Alta California.

Despues que quitaron las Missiones a los Padres Jesuitas de la
California, vinieron los Padres de la Religion de S. Francisco, y de S.
Domingo, los primeros para la Alta California, los segundos para la
baja California, California es una, dividida en dos partes es decir Baja
California, y alta California assi llamada por el Señor Don Cortez, que
fue el primero que la hallò. La Baja California empieza desde la
Mission de S. Lucas, hasta la Mission de S. Diego, desde la Mission de
S. Diego la Alta California, hasta mas arriba de Monte Rey.

---

*Unclear word in the original.

Mañai, "for"

The preposition *mañai* would mean "of my hand," but it is used as a causal adverb or preposition. For example: "For me my father died," *No manai op. no Nà tacuayac.* "For us the son of God died," *cham mañai op po camai Chañichñis tacuayac.* And never is it placed in front; if someone should do it in that manner, they would not understand him. For example: if one said *mañai op po camai chañichñis tacuayac* but put one more word in, then it can be understood.

So.

So: Word used to ask a question, and it is placed after any word, never in front. For example: "Where are you going with your brothers?" *Michic só monà po os o potom?* And in the plural, you add an *m,* for example: "Where are you going, on such a rainy day as this?" *Michic som monà ivina temeña, po jilacala.* "Do you want to come with me to play?" *No eiṡ sò hati ivichoc o yiyipi?* "Why don't you want to love him?" *Hiñai so poi cai màmàvichoc.*

Hiñai, "why"

Hiñai: adverb that signifies "why" when asking a question, and it is placed in front and after. For example: "Why did you not do what I told you?" *Hiñai so cai loviiqoer os no yòjpi.* But it is not used when one wants to respond.

^{78r}
Conversion of the San Luiseños of Alta California

After they took the missions from the Jesuits of California, the priests of the orders of Saint Francis and Saint Dominic, the former to Alta California, the latter to Baja California. California is one, divided in two parts, which is to say Baja California and Alta California, as they were named by Lord Don Cortez, who was the first one to discover them. Baja California begins at Mission San Lucas* and goes up to Mission San Diego. From Mission San Diego up to just above Monterey is Alta California.

---

*Mission San José del Cabo, the southernmost Jesuit mission, was located about twenty miles up the coast from Cabo San Lucas.

Se sabe de la historia que los primeros que se fueron para la California de los Missioneros, fueron los P. Jesuitas, y el primer entre ellos el Padre Salvaterra, Juan renombrado en la historia de la California por sus obras de Piedad. llegaron los Padres de la Religión de S. Domingo en la baja California, y los Padres de la Religion de S. Francisco en la Alta. Los Padres Franciscanos de los que yo aqui hablo en Mexico se llaman, Padres Fernandinos, porque el Colegio u convento en que se hallan se llama el convento de S. Fernando Rey de España. llegaron estos Padres a la alta California y uno de ellos llegò en nuestro Pays que lo llamamos *(quechla)* y nosotros por esso nos llamamos *quechna-juichom* es decir habitantes de Quechla; quando estabamos en paz: porque siempre huvo guerra, siempre pleyto dia y noche con los que en otra lengua hablaban. Parece que nuestro[s] enemigos fueron los que aora se llaman Dieguinos, ~~y de~~ por los Españoles, y *quicham-cauichom* por nosotros, que quiere decir los de Sud.

78v

Antes de ir á guerra se pintaban para ser terribles a los enemigos, y se cojia al enemigo o quando estaba durmiendo, o quando los hombres salian de casa, quedando solo las Mugeres, y mataban Mujeres, Viejos y Niños, echo esto, se quemaban los aduares uyendose ellos a sus casas, las armas eran Arcos flechas y ciertas Espadas de leño, lanzas de leño. por nuestra lengua llamados, *uacatom*. los Arcos eran echos de palo fuerte que facilmente no podia romperse, largo que llegaba hasta los hombros. del hombre, gruesos en medio un dedo y medio, anchos tres dedos. las flechas eran de carizo. gruesos al tamaño de un dedo, largos quatro palmas, en la punta un palito encajado largo una palma y media, los ojos de la flecha eran tres de pluma de qualquier sea paxaro. La Espada era larga quatro palmas ancha tres dedos, y de la tercera palma empezaba a arquear. La lanza era larga ocho palmas grueso quatro dedos y la punta tenia aguda, para llevar las flechas tenian atràs de las espaldas un cuero de coyote u otro animal, las espadas se echaban al enemigo, o tenièndolas se rajaba la cabeza del enemigo, las espadas quando se tiraban corrian mas que quinientos pasos de hombre gigante.

79r

Con estas armas iban a guerra, que tambien aora los tenemos. era muy miserable la vida de entonces, porque siempre habia pleytos. El Dios a que entonces se adoraba era el Sol, y el Fuego, Asi se vivia entre los bosques, hasta que Dios Misericordioso nos sacó de estas miserias.

It is known from history that the first missionaries to go to California were the Jesuits, and the first among them was Father Juan Salvatierra, renowned in the history of California for his acts of piety. The Dominican Fathers arrived in Baja California and the Franciscan Fathers in

78v Alta California. The Franciscan Fathers of whom I speak here in Mexico are called the Fernandino Fathers, because the college or monastery where they are found is called the Convent of San Fernando King of Spain. These Fathers arrived in Alta California, and one of them arrived in our region, which we call *Quechla*—which is why we call ourselves *quechnajuichom,* which is to say "inhabitants of Quechla"— when we were at peace; because there was always war, always conflict day and night with those who spoke other languages. It appears that our enemies were those who today are called Diegueños by the Spanish and *quichamcauichom* by us, which means "those of the south."

Before going to battle, they painted themselves to be fearsome to their enemies, and they captured their enemies either when they were sleeping or when the men were away from home, the women remaining alone, and they killed women, elders, and children. This done, they then burned the huts, fleeing back to their homes. Their weapons were bows and arrows, and certain wooden swords, wooden lances that in our language are called *uacatom.* The bows were made of strong wood that could not be easily broken, and were so long that

79r they reached all the way to the shoulders of the men; they were one and a half fingers thick at the midpoint and three fingers broad. The arrows were made of reeds, one finger thick and four palms long. At the point, a small piece of wood, a palm and a half in length, was set. The fletching of the arrow was made of three feathers of any bird. The sword was four palms in length and three fingers broad, and from the third palm, it took on an arched shape. The lance was eight palms long and four fingers thick and the point was sharp. To transport the arrows they had on their backs the skin of a coyote or other animal. The swords were thrown at the enemy, or holding them, slashed the head of the enemy. The swords, when thrown, would go farther than five hundred paces of a giant man.

With these arms they went to war, which we still have today. Life then was miserable, because there were always conflicts. The God that was worshipped then was the Sun, and Fire. Thus we lived in the forests, until God All Merciful released us from these miseries, through Father

Por el P. Antonio Peyri Catalan que llegò en nuestro Pays a la tarde
con siete soldados Españoles.

Sigue la Conversion . . . . primer papel . . .

80r   Llegando el Missionero con poca gente en nuestro Pays; el Capitán
nuestro viendoles de lejos, y tambien los otros se espantan, mas no
uyen ni cojen armas para matarles, mas sentados los estaban viendo,
mas quando aquellos se acercaron: entonces el Capitan se levanta
(porque estaba sentado con los otros) y los encuentra, aquellos se
paran, y al Missionero entonces empieza à hablar el Capitan diciendo
quizà en su lengua, *hichsom ivà haluon, pulùchajam chom quiñai*,
Que es lo que aqui buscais, salid de nuestro pays, mas aquellos no
le entendian, tambien ellos en español le respondian, y el capitan
empezo por señales, y el Fernandino entendiendole, le dio regalos,
y en esta manera se hizo su amigo. El Capitán volviendose a su gente,
(como creo) habrá [h]ablado bien de los blancos, y por esso les de-
jaron, aqui dormir, No habia entonces casa de piedra, mas todas eran
aduares (como se dice). Este fue aquel feliz dia en que vimos Gente
Blanca; por nosotros llamada (*Sosabitom*), O Dios misericordioso
porque nos dejaste por muchos Siglos, años, Meses, y días en las
tinieblas, despues que veniste al Mundo, Bendito seas desde este dia
hasta los siglos futuros.

80v   El P. Fernandino se queda en nuestro Pays con su poca gente que llevaba, se hace un aduar, y aqui viviò por muchos dias, por la mañana
decia su Misa, y despues discurria entre sì mismo, como les bautizarìa,
en dónde pondrìa su Casa la Iglesia, y como harìa con cinco mil almas
(que eran todos los Indios) como les sustentarìa, y viendo como se
podia hacer; teniendo por amigo al capitan de nada tenia miedo. Fue
gran gracia esta, que no mataron a los Españoles los Indios quando
llegaron; y muy admirable, porque nunca han querido, que otra gente
con ellos habitase, por lo que hasta aquellos dias estaban guerreando.
Mas assì ha querido el que solo puede querer. No se si los Bautizò
antes de hacer la Iglesia u despues de haverla echo, mas creo que les
Bautisaze antes de hacerla.

Ya era muy amigo del Capitan, y tambien querido por los Neofitos,
Algo le podian entender, quando el como Padre de ellos les mandò
que llevasen piedras desde el Mar para los cimientos (que no es lejos)
hiciesen ladrillos, texas, cortasen bigas, carrizos, y lo necessario. Lo

Antonio Peyri, [the] Catalan who arrived in our country in the afternoon with seven Spanish soldiers.

> The Conversion continues . . . . first paper . . .

80r   As the missionary was arriving with a few people to our country, our
captain, seeing them from afar, and also the others, became scared,
but they did not flee, nor did they take up arms to kill them, but seated
they watched them. But when those men approached, then did our
captain rise (because he had been seated with the others) and meet
them. They stop, and then the captain begins to speak to the missionary, perhaps saying in his language *hichsom ivà haluon, pulùchajam
chom quiñai,* "What is it that you seek here? Leave our country!"
But they did not understand him, and they also responded in Spanish.
And the captain began using hand signals, and the Fernandino, understanding him, gave him gifts, and in this manner, he became his friend.
The captain, turning to his people, must have spoken well of the whites
(I believe), and for this reason they let them sleep here. There were no
stone houses then but only huts (it is said). That was the happy day
we saw white people, called by us *Sosabitom.* O merciful God, why
did you leave us for so many centuries, years, months, and days in
darkness, after you'd come to the world, blessed may you be from
this day for centuries to come.

80v   The Fernandino Father stayed in our country with the small entourage
he brought, and he made himself a hut, and here he lived for many days.
In the mornings he would say his Mass, and afterward, he would ru-
minate on how he would baptize them, and where he would put his
House the Church, and how he would manage with five thousand souls
(which were all the Indians), how he would provide for them, and seeing how all this could be done. Having the captain as his friend, he
feared nothing. This was a great blessing, that the Indians did not kill
the Spaniards when they arrived, and very admirable, because they had
never wanted other people to live with them, which is why up to those
days they were waging war. That is how he wished it, he who can only
love. I don't know if he baptized them before building the church or
after having done it, but I believe he baptized them before building it.

He was now great friends with the captain, and also loved by the neophytes. They could understand him some, when he as their father ordered them to bring stones from the sea (which was not far) for the
foundations, make bricks, roof tiles, cut rafters, reeds, and other

81r hicieron, con los Maestros que los que les ayudaban, y entre pocos años acabaron de trabajar,

Sigue. Conversion . . . papel segundo.

82r

Nauiŝ	Señalar	Pintar	Escribir
Nauiŝ	Señal	Pintura	Escritura
Nauicat	Señalador	Pintor	Escritor
Nauimocuiŝ	quien señalò	quien pintò	quien Escriviò
Nauinoq	señalando	pintando	escriviendo
Nauiniiŝ	hacer señalar	hacer pintar	hacer escrivir
Nauiniiŝ	el hacer señalar	el hacer pintar	el hacer escrivir*
Nauimicat	quien hace señalar	quien [hace] pintar	quien hace escrivir†
Nauimimocuiŝ	quien hizo señalar	quien hizo pintar	quien hizo escrivir
Nauiminoq	haciendo señalar	haciendo pintar . . .	haciendo escrivir
Nau-nauiŝ	señalar muchas veces	pintar m. v.	escrivir m. v.
Nau-nauiŝ	el señalar muchas vezes	el pintar m. v.	el escrivir m. v.
Nau-nauicat	quien señala muchas veces	quien pinta m. v.	quien escrive m. v.
Nau-nauimocuiŝ	quien ha señalado m. v.	[quien] ha pintado m. v.	quien ha escrito m. v.
Nau-nauinoq	señalando muchas vezes	Pintando m. v.	escribiendo m. v.
Nauininauiiniŝ	hacer señalar muchas. v.	hacer pintar m. v.	hacer escrivir m. v.
Nauininauiiniŝ	el hacer señalar m. v.	el hacer pintar m. v.	el hacer escrivir m. v.
Nauininauiniicat	quien hace señalar m. v.	quien hace pintar m. v.	quien hace escrivir m. v.
Nauininauiimocuiŝ . . .	quien ha [hecho] señalado m. v.	quie[n] ha hecho pintar m.v.	quien ha hecho escrivir m. v.
Nauininauiniinoq	haciendo señalar m. v.	haciendo pintar m. v.	haciendo escrivir m. v.

---

*It appears that Tac originally wrote *pintar* here and then wrote *escrivir* over it.

†Here Tac again appears to have written *pintar* and then written *escrivir* over it. In the line immediately below, he begins to write *pi* and then writes *escrivir* over it.

81r necessary things. They did it, with the master artisans who helped them, and within a few years they finished working.

Conversion continues . . . second paper.

82r			
Nauiš	to sign, signal, mark, indicate	to paint	to write
Nauiš	sign (n.)	painting (n.)	writing (n.)
Nauicat	signer	painter	writer
Nauimocuiš	person who signed	person who painted	person who wrote
Nauinoq	signing	painting	writing
Nauiniiš	to make one sign	to make one paint	to make one write
Nauiniiš	the act of making one sign	the act of making one paint	making one write
Nauimicat	person who makes one sign	person who [makes one] paint	person who makes one write
Nauimimocuiš	person who made one sign	person who made one paint	person who made one write
Nauiminoq	making one sign	making one paint	making one write
Nau-nauiš	to sign many times	to paint m. t.	to write m. t.
Nau-nauiš	the act of signing m. t.	the act of painting m. t.	the act of writing m. t.
Nau-nauicat	person who signs m.t.	person who paints m. t.	person who writes m. t.
Nau-nauimocuiš	person who has signed m. t.	[person who] has painted m. t.	person who has written m. t.
Nau-nauinoq	signing m. t.	painting m. t.	writing m. t.
Nauininauiiniš	to make one sign many t.	to make one paint m. t.	to make one write m. t.
Nauininauiiniš	the act of making one sign m. t.	the act of making one paint m. t.	the act of making one write m. t.
Nauininauiniicat	person who makes one sign m. t.	person who makes one paint m. t.	person who makes one write m. t.
Nauininauiimocuiš	person who [made one] sign m. t.	person who made one paint m. t.	person who made one write m. t.
Nauininauiniinoq	making one sign m. t.	making one paint m. t.	making one write m. t.

84r Hicieron una Iglesia bastante para todos los Neofitos, con tres altares; el altar mayor es todo casi dorado, dos capillas, dos sacristias, dos coros, un jardin de flores para la Iglesia, una torre alta, con cinco campanas dos chicas y tres grandes. el cimenterio para todos los que aqui mueren y en medio una cruz clavada. Empezemos por la torre. La torre es puesta a lado derecho de la Iglesia con cinco campanas dos chicas y tres grandes la voz o sonido se oye de lejos, y algunas vezes de Ušva quatro, o cinco leguas de la Mission de S. Luis Rey de Francia distante. de la Iglesia ya se dijo. Despues de la Iglesia sigue el lugar de los albañiles, aqui dejan la mescla, cal. etc. Despues de esto sigue el almazen de vino adentro hay docientos pipas, de vino, aguardiente, y vino blanco, quatrocientos bariles, para la Misa, para vender a los Españoles, y para passageros Ingleses, A que muchas veces vienen a la Mission para vender ropa, lienzo manta, y lo que ellos trahen de Boston, y nò para los Neofitos lo que es prohibido a ellos porque facilmente se ven borrachados; 5. sigue el lugar en donde se hace el vino. 7. ventana del apossento del General de la California, quando llega en la Mission. 8. Puerta del P. Fernandino, hay quatro apossentos para los pasageros.

84v en medio hay la sala Mayor, tres retratos, uno de S. Luis Rey de Francia, el Segundo de la Divina Pastora, el tercero de la Virgen de Guadalupe. en un rincon un Relox. y mas adelante el comedor. 9. Ventanas del Missionero de vidrio. 10. puertecita para el Missionero en tiempo de los temblores para huyr facilmente. 11. Aposento del Siervo del Missionero. 12. casa para los passageros. 13. Puerta que se llama la Mayor de todas, por aqui entran y salen los Neofitos para trabajar. 14.15.16.17.18.19 casas para los Mayordomos Españoles de la Mission. 20. apossento grande para los Muchachos Neofitos. con su patio y dos plantas, 21. Xaboneria. 22. Apossento para las Muchachas. 23. corral para los ganados. 24. Mulín. 25. corral de los corderos. 26. casa del Pastor. 27. corral. 28. 28. Trox 29. Trox, 30. Lugar para los caballos del Missionero, y de los passageros y tambien para los costales de cebo. 31. Enfermería para las Mugeres. 32. Enfermería para los hombres. 33. Cimenterio. 34. lugar endonde se hace el posole y atole. 34. Apossentos para los Mayordomos. 35. Quartel. 36. Almazen Tapanco. 37. Trox. 38. Trox. 39. Lugar para el panadero. 40. Relox. 41. Cocina. 42 camaras para los passageros. 43. Almazen. 44. jardín. 45 Almazen de frazadas. Almazen de [h]arina. 46. Molin. 47. telar minor. 48. telar Mayor. 49. Lugar en donde se hace el azeyte.

84r They made a church sufficient for all the neophytes, with three altars. The main altar is almost entirely gilded, two chapels, two sacristies, two choirs, a garden of flowers for the church, a tall tower with five bells, two large and three small. A cemetery for everyone who dies here and in the middle, a nailed cross. Let us begin with the tower. The tower is placed to the right side of the church with five bells, two small and three large, and the voice, or sound, can be heard from afar, and sometimes from Usva, four or five leagues away from Mission Saint Louis King of France. The church has been spoken of. After the church comes the place of the builders, here they leave the mortar, lime, etc. After this comes the wine storehouse in which there are two hundred casks of wine, brandy, and white wine, four hundred barrels for the Mass, to sell to the Spaniards, and for English travelers who often come to the mission to sell clothes, linen, blankets, and what they bring from Boston, but not for the neophytes, since it is forbidden to them because they get drunk easily. 5. Next is the place where the wine is made. 7. The window of the General of California's room, when he comes to the mission. 8. The Fernandino Father's door; there are four guestrooms for travelers.

84v In the middle is the main room, [with] three paintings: one of Saint Louis King of France, the second of the Divine Shepherdess, and the third of the Virgin of Guadalupe. In one corner [is] a clock, and farther down, the dining room. 9. Glass windows of the missionary. 10. Small door for the missionary, so as to flee easily in case of an earthquake. 11. Room of the missionary's servant. 12. House for travelers. 13. Door that is called the main door; the neophytes enter and exit through here to work. 14. 15. 16. 17. 18. 19. Houses for the Spanish mayordomos of the mission. 20. Large room for the many neophytes, with a patio and two plants. 21. Soapmaking facility. 22. Room for the girls. 23. Corral for the livestock. 24. Mill. 25. Corral for the lambs. 26. The shepherd's home. 27. Corral. 28. 28. Granary. 29. Granary. 30. A place for the missionary's horses and [those] of travelers, and also for the sacks of fodder. 31. Infirmary for the women. 32. Infirmary for the men. 33. Cemetery. 34. Place where *pozole* and *atole* are made. 34. Rooms for the mayordomos. 35. Barracks. 36. Storage loft. 37. Granary. 38. Granary. 39. Place for the baker. 40. Clock. 41. Kitchen. 42. Traveler's chambers. 43. Storehouse. 44. Garden. 45. Storage for blankets. Storage for the flour. 46. Mill. 47. Small loom. 48. Large loom. 49. Place where oil is made.

85r 50. herreria. 51. ~~Zapateria. 52 Ap~~ Trox 52. Zapateria. 53. Lugar de los
arrieros. 54. puerta segunda Mayor. 55. Apossento del mayordomo de
Pala. 56. Carpinteria. 57. Lugar de las vigas. 59.* lugar de los cueros.
en pocos años se hizo todo.

Conversion. Sigue . . .   papel : tercero.

86r Hazia Sud hay un huerto muy grande con su potrero á lado; dejimos
que la Mission era puesta sobre un montecillo, Conque debajo de este
montecillo hay una fuente perenne de donde trahen los Neofitos y el
Missionero, el agua para beber. Hicieron dos fuentes ante la puerta
del huerto, en medio de ellas una escalera para bajar y subir por lo
que es echa. toda de ladrillos. La puerta para entrar en medio tiene
tres gruessos palos, uno de ellos encajado en la† tierra llega arriba
a la pared, los dos casi lo fajan haciendo una cruz. de todas partes si se
quiera ver, y el aguador queriendo passar, empuja un palo, y los dos se
vueltan y en esto el passa con comodidad llevando la cantara sobre sus
cargadores espaldas mas fuertes que de los mismos Asnos. La escalera
es muy alta, ~~y~~ que en un mismo viage no se pueda subir por ella, y es
menestar descansarse en medio de la misma. Sucede muchas veces que
se cansen en balde (como se dice) porque llegando a la puerta
queriendo passar por ella de priessa se quiebra la cantara, y se vuelven
a casa sin agua, y cantara bañados de agua.

Se pusieron los palos para no dejar entrar a los toros, caballos, bravos,
quando ay el torèo, aunque ellos entraron muchas veces y hirieron a
las vi[e]jas que aqui se hallaban lavando sus ropas.

86v Mas adelante de las dos fuentes ay la puerta del huerto que de las
fuentes se passa por un puentecito, de bajo passa el agua de las dos
fuentes corriendo hacia el ouest como una zanja y baña otro huerto
casi una legua distante de la Mission. El huerto es espacioso, lleno de
arboles de frutos de Peras. Manzanas, o Perones (como dicen los
Mexicanos), duraznos, Membrillos, Peras dulces, Granadas, higos,
Sandias, Melones, Legumbres Coles, Lechugas Chiles, Rabanos, yervas
buenas, peregiles, y otros de los que no me acuerdo.

Las Peras, Manzanas, duraznos, membrillos, Granadas, Sandias, Melones Para los Neofitos los de mas que quedan para el Missionero,

---

*Item 58 is missing in the original.
†In the original the words *en* and *la* have been overwritten.

85r 50. Forge. 51. Granary. 52. Shoemaking workshop. 53. Place for the muleteers. 54. Second largest door. 55. Mayordomo of Pala's room. 56. Carpentry workshop. 57. Place for the beams. 59. Place for the leather skins. In a few years, it was all completed.

Conversion. Continues . . . paper: third.

86r To the south there is a very large orchard, with a pasture next to it. We said the mission was located on a little hill, so at the base of the little hill there is a perennially full spring from which the neophytes and missionaries bring the drinking water. They made two such springs at the entrance of the orchard, and in the middle of them a stairway to go up and down, made entirely of bricks. The door to enter in the middle has three thick pieces of lumber; one of them, buried in the ground, goes up above the wall, the [other] two almost sashing it to form a cross of all the parts if one might see it. And the water carrier, wishing to pass through, pushes one piece of lumber, and the two turn, whereupon he passes easily while carrying the pitcher on his weight-bearing back, stronger than even an ass. The stairway is very high, so you cannot ascend it in one go, and it is necessary to rest in the middle of it. Often they get tired in vain (as they say) because on arriving at the door, trying to pass through in a hurry, the pitcher gets broken, and they return home without water or pitcher, soaked in water.

They put the crossbeams in place to keep out the bulls and horses, which become wild when there is a bullfight, although they have gotten in many times and injured the matrons who were washing their clothes here.

86v Beyond the two springs is the orchard gate that you arrive at by crossing over a little bridge. Beneath it passes the water of the two springs flowing to the west like a gully, and it waters a second orchard almost a league in distance from the Mission. The orchard is expansive, full of fruit trees like pears, apples or *perones* (as the Mexicans say), peaches, quinces, sweet pears, pomegranates, figs, watermelons, melons, [and] vegetables [like] cabbages, lettuce, chilies, radishes, mint, parsley, and other that I can't recall.

The pears, apples, peaches, quinces, pomegranates, watermelons, and melons are for the neophytes. The rest is for the missionary, and must

Alque cada dia debe llevar el hortelano. Ninguno de los Neofitos puede ir al huerto o entrar para cortarse los frutos, Mas si el quiere pida al Missionero que prontamente le darà lo que pide porque el Missionero es padre de ellos. Pobre alque encontrare el hortelano andando y cortando los frutos, que luego lo sigue para castigarlo, hasta que se salga de las paredes del huerto Brincando como ellos muy bien saben (que parecen venados por los montes).

87r Una vez un Neofito entrò en el huerto sin que lo supiese el hortelano, y como tenìa mucha hambre, se subio a un higo, aqui empezò a comer a toda priessa, un higo maduro y grande, no a pedazos, mas entero se lo dejò caer por la Garganta, y el higo se atorò por ella, el entonces empezò a torcerse hasta que gritò como un cuervo y se lo tragò. El hortelano oyendo la voz del cuervo, y con ~~circunspec~~ Indios ojos luego hallo al cuervo que de miedo no comía y mas lo estaban viendo, el le dixo, ya te veo cuervo sin alas, aora te herire con mis flechas, entonces el Neofito a toda priessa se huye lejos del huerto . . .

hacia est del huerto ay el Potrero para los caballos del P. Fernandino, y para de los Passageros Anglo Americanos, es espacioso como el huerto, por debajo lleno de agua, y por eso verdes yervas tiene, ay muchos árboles, muchos paxaros, muchissimos cuervosvos* llegan a la tarde para dormir, y se dejan caer desde el alto haciendo maromas hasta llegar sobre los Arboles. Aqui también los trabajadores hallaron un Leon Californes, que es igual al gato de Europa, pero más valiente de un tigre, no por sus fuerzas, mas por su agilidad, que ~~por~~ es muy

87v difficil a matarse, el mata a los caballos con un brinco, ~~casi~~ agarran-dolos, luego los degolla, y por esso el es temido. Los trabajadores lo hallaron, y porque eran ellos muchos el leon de ellos tenia miedo, y tambien por los gritos que echaban siguiendole, corria brincando allende y aquende al rededor del Potrero, los Indios escondidos de tras de los Arboles lo tiraban con piedras hasta que uno le tirò en medio de la frente y pronto desmayado cayendo luego murio.

Aqui se hacen ladrillos, y texas para la Mission, No se hallan venados.

Mas allá del huerto sigue el camino hacia el presidio de S. Diego, en donde està el General de la California.

---

*Sic.

be brought to him every day by the gardener. None of the neophytes may enter the orchard or go in to pick fruit. But if he wants some, he asks the missionary, who will promptly give him what he asks for, as the missionary is their father. Woe betide anyone whom the gardener finds wandering and picking fruit, for he will chase him to punish him, until he goes out from the orchard walls, leaping as they well know how to (like deer leaping through the woodlands).

87r One time, a neophyte entered the orchard without the gardener noticing, and as he was very hungry, he climbed a fig tree, and there he began to eat in a great hurry a large ripe fig, not in pieces, but instead dropping it whole down his throat, and the fig got stuck in his throat. He began to writhe until he croaked like a crow and swallowed it. The gardener, hearing the cry of the crow, used his Indian eyes to spot the crow, who out of fear was not eating, but they were watching him, and he said, "I see you, crow without wings. Now I'm going to wound you with my arrows," and then the neophyte, in a great hurry, fled far from the orchard . . .

Due east from the orchard is the pasture for the horses of the Fernandino Father, and for [those] of the Anglo-American travelers. It is as broad as the orchard, with plenty of water below. That is why it has green grass and many trees. Multitudes of crows come in the evenings to sleep, and they drop from the sky, tumbling down until they reach the trees. Here the workers also came upon a California lion, which is the same as the cat of Europe, but braver than a tiger, not for its strength, but for its agility, so it is very difficult to kill them. It kills

87v horses with one leap, ~~practically~~ grabbing them, then it slashes their throats, and that is why it is feared. The workers found it, and because there were many of them, the lion was afraid of them, and also because of the way they shouted as they chased it, it ran leaping hither and thither all around the pasture. The Indians, hidden behind trees, were throwing stones at it, until one man threw a stone that hit the middle of its forehead, and suddenly falling in a faint, it then died.

Here is where the bricks are made, and roof tiles for the mission. There are no deer.

Beyond the orchard continues the road to the fort in San Diego, where the General of California is.

88r   Los lugares principales quando uno se mueve, o quando uno camina
son tres, el primero es. quando de donde uno sale, el segundo por
donde caminando passa, y el tercero hasta donde llega caminando:
nosotros explicamos la primera voz, con la voz *ṅai* como ya dejimos
de la misma. la segunda explicamos con la palabra *ṅa* que significa en,
y tambien por donde se passa, y la tercera que se explica con la
palabra, y mejor digamos con la letra *q* como ya tambien
explicamos . . .

Primeramente el lugar en que uno se halla, se exprime con la palabra
ṅa como dejimos que significaba en. p.e. yo estaba sentado en tierra
al lado de mi padre hablando con él. *Ejṅanil auċuas po chejṅa no
Na po es tetelaċanoq.* exemplos para las otras tres, para la primera.
Saliendo de mi casa hallè a mi Padre, que estaba sentado en la puerta:
No quiṅainil puhichacanoq, tolounajnil no nai po pucṅa po auċala.
Quando el saliò de la Iglesia, llegando un perverso hombre al punto
lo dejò muerto con su cuchillo. *Chaṅichṅis po quiṅai po pulúchacala
hichacat apil yaaṡ, uocòacanoc, poi uenàṅapo notbatal mòmocan.*
Alque aqui passò le pidiò lo que en su cabeza llevaba porque tenia
hambre. *Haċmauiṡapil ivaṅa not-lacati po puticala làchoj.* Por aqui
passan los Españoles, *ivàpom Sosabitom not-nolajin.*

88v   Hasta donde se llega caminando, como tambien dejimos, que se anade
la letra *q* al nombre del lugar. p.e. mañana llegaremos a casa nuestra,
Ejṅa chapo uocoajan cham quiq. assi no decimos, mas *Ejṅa chapo
cham quiṅa uocoajan.* quieres ir al Cielo se dice regladamente *tupaiqso
hatiavichoċ.*

Ya se van acercando al monte, *uampom cauiq hayàajon.*

92r   Por no hablar mucho de los huertos de la Mission de S. Luis Rey de
Francia, de la alta California, el P. Fernandino hizo cinco huertos
grandes (es decir) tres en la misma mission, uno en el pays llamado
por nosotros *(Pala)* el quinto en otro pays (que aora no me acuerdo
el nombre), todos uberrimos ~~todos~~ de lo que se siembra. Quattro
Payses, la Mission, Pala, Temeco, y Uṡva, tres ranchos. La Mission
de S. Luys Rey de Francia assi nombròla el Padre Fernandino despues
de haber cumplida toda la casa, porque el patron nuestro es el Rey
S. Luys. Mas nosotros en nuestra lengua la llamamos *(Quechla)* assi

Conversion Continues . . . . Fifth Paper

88r When one moves or walks, there are three principal places. The first is <u>when</u> and from where one goes forth; the second is where one passes as one walks; and the third is where one arrives by walking. We explain the first with the word *ñai,* as we already said of it. The second we explain with the word *ña,* which means *en* ["in" or "on"] and also *por donde se passa* ["through where one passes"]. The third is explained with the word, or rather we should say the letter, *q,* as we have also already explained.

First of all, the place in which one finds oneself is expressed with the word *ña,* which we said means *en.* For example: "I was sitting on the ground next to my father, talking with him." *Ejñanil auċuas po chejña no Na po es telelaċanoq.* Examples for the other three, taking the first: "Leaving my house, I found my father, who was sitting in the doorway" *No quiñainil puhichacanoq, tolounajnil no nai po pucña po auċala.* "When he left the church, a wicked man arriving right then left him dead with his knife," *Chañichñis po quiñai po pulúchacala hichacat apil yaaṡ, uocòacanoc, poi uenàñapo notbatal mòmocan.* "He asked the one who passed by here for that which he was carrying on his head, because he was hungry," *Haċmauiṡapil ivaña not-lacati po puticala làchoj.* "Through here pass the Spaniards," *ivàpom Sosabitom not-nolajin.*

88v The destination to which one arrives by walking, as we also said, has the letter *q* added to the place name. For example: "Tomorrow we will arrive at our house." We do not say *Ejña chapo uocoajan cham quiq,* but rather *Ejña chapo cham quiña uocoajan.* "Do you want to go to heaven?" we say, following the rules, *tupaiqso hatiavichoċ.*

"They are nearing the mountain," *uampom cauiq hayàajon.*

92r Not to speak much about the orchards in Alta California's Mission San Luis Rey: the Fernandino Father had five large orchards planted; that is to say, three at the mission, one in the country called by us *Pala* and the fifth in another country, whose name now eludes me, all very fertile with whatever is sown. That is four countries: the Mission and the three ranches Pala, Temeco, and Uṡva. Mission San Luis Rey de Francia was so named by the Fernandino Father after he had completed the house entirely, because our patron saint is Saint Louis the King. But we call it *Quechla* in our language. Thus did our grandfathers

nuestro[s] avuelos la llamaron porque en este pays habia una calidad de piedras que se llamaban *quechlam* en plural, y en singular, *quechla,* y nosotros habitadores de *Quechla,* nos nombramos *Quechñajuichom* en plural, *Quechnajuis* en Singular quiere decir habitadores de *quechla.* En *Quechla* no mucho a, habia cinco mil almas, con todos sus payses cercanos, ya por un mal que vino a California dos mil almas murieron, y tres mil se quedaron. El Padre Fernandino como el era solo, y muy solito con sus Españoles Soldados, viendo que seria muy difícil que el solo pudiesse mandar a aquella gente, y mas, gente que pocos años ante[s] dejado habia los bosques, puso Alcaldes, puso por esso Alcaldes de la misma gente, que sabian mas que los otros hablar Español.

92v Y que por costumbres mejores eran de los otros, estos Alcaldes fueron siete con sus bastones por señal que ellos podian juzgar a los demas. El Capitan se vestiò como los Españoles, quedando siempre Capitan pero no mandando a su gente, como en antiguo, quando eran todavia Gentiles. El Mayor de los Alcaldes se llamaba el General sabia el nombre de cada uno, y quando se tomaba algo en general el entonces ~~llamaba~~ nombraba cada sujeto por su nombre. Los Alcaldes por la tarde se juntan a la casa del Missionero llevando novedades de aquel dia, y si el Missionero les dice Algo, que toda la Gente del Pays debe saberlo, ellos volviendose a los aduares van gritando; Mañana por la mana*

94r *Te = ca.*   si

Tènopca	*téopca*	*tépoca*	*techamca*	*téomca*	*témoca*
si yo	si tu	si aquel	si nosotros	si vosotros	si aquellos

Esta voz *te/ca* nada significa, mas quando se le añade la persona. entonces coge la fuerza de la palabra Si. si yo me moriria, que harias sin Padre, ni Madre?

Te~~jo~~nopca no tacuuyaj hichsocma om loviaj, pom yauacala, o Ná, pè Oyò?

Si tu me mandaras que yo aga esto, no lo harè.

Teopca om, nii no loviipi tosñan, cainopo loviin.

---

*Incomplete word in the original; the narrative breaks off midline here, with half the folio left blank.

name it because in this country there was a kind of stone called *quechlam* in the plural, and *quechla* in the singular. And we inhabitants of *Quechla* called ourselves *Quechnajuichom* in the plural, *Quechnajuiŝ* in the singular, which means "inhabitants of *Quechla.*" In *Quechla* not long ago there were five thousand souls, with all the countries nearby; due to a sickness that came to California, two thousand souls died, and three thousand remained. As the Fernandino Father was alone, and very accustomed to his Spanish soldiers, seeing that it would be very difficult to take charge of these people on his own—especially people who only a few years before had come out of the woods—he appointed alcaldes, chosen from the people themselves, [those] who knew how to speak Spanish more than the others.

92v   These alcaldes, who because of their behavior were better than the others, were seven, with staffs (or canes) that signaled that they could cast judgment on the others. The Captain dressed like the Spaniards, still remaining a Captain but not ordering his people, as in older times, when they were still heathens. The chief alcalde was called the General and knew everyone by name, and when meals were taken together, he would name each of the subjects by their names. In the evening the alcaldes gather in the missionary's house, bringing the news of the day, and if the missionary tells them anything that all the people of the country must know, they, returning to the mission villages, go about shouting: "Tomorrow in the morn . . ."

94r   *Te = ca.*   if

Tènopca	*téopca*	*tépoca*	*techamca*	*téomca*	*témoca*
if I	if you	if that one	if we	if you	if those ones

This word *te/ca* means nothing, but when a person is added as a subject, then it takes on the import of the word "if." "If I should die, what would you do without a father or mother?"

Tenopca no tacuuyaj hichsocma em loviaj, pom yauacala, o Ná, pè Oyò?

"If you ordered me to do this, I would not do it."

Teopca om, nii no loviipi toŝnan, cainopo loviin.

Si aquel se agacha, entrarà muy bien en la casa.

Tepoca uonal lòcajan, ayalinocpo, quiṅa chulúpajan.

Si cantaras bien, os pagaré, muchos dineros.

Teomca omom ayalinoc hélajan omomi nopo, siquinabolmi muyocmiṅechin.

Si aquellos me venceran, yo me nascondere.

Temoca uonalom, nii chiuin, nonopo helépajan.

Uajamcuna. Uajacuonai.   a la tarde.

Los cuervos en la tarde, siempre van a sus casas.

Aluotompom uajamcunà, pom quiq <u>minchapan</u> butihatiajan.

Amùejṅa   mañana por la mañana

Me quiero alzar mañana por la mañana.

~~Non~~ *amuejṅanocuot-tivichoc.*

96r Todo a su Eccelencia lo que yo se, he enseñado de esta lengua; y si falta algo, como yo creo que falta, lo que sucede muchas veces quando se escribe, en otro tiempo se podrà acabar.

Le havria mas enseñado, mas quien puede enseñar a otros lo que el no sabe? Asi yo lo que sabia enseñè lo que no sabia he dejado, mejor es callarse, que hablando decir mentiras.

Aora es menester que juntemos todos los papeles y de nuevo escrivirles regladamente como podremos . . . .

97r   De las reglas

Los verbos activos tienen sus reglas y estas se pueden dividir en dos, la primera es de los verbos que reciven el caso acusat. la segunda es de los que reciven el dat.

"If that one stoops, he will enter the house just fine."

Tepoca uonal lòcajan, ayalinocpo, quiña chulúpajan.

"If you would sing well, I will pay you much money."

Teomca omom ayalinoc hélajan omomi nopo, siquinabolmi muyocmiñechin.

"If they defeat me, I will hide myself."

Temoca uonalom, nii chiuin, nonopo helépajan.

Uajamcuna. Uajacuonai.   in the evening

The crows always return to their homes in the evening.

Aluotompom uajamcunà, pom quiq <u>minchapan</u> butihatiajan.

Amùejña   tomorrow in the morning

I want to rise tomorrow in the morning.

~~Non~~ *amuejñanocuot-tivichoc.*

96r   I have taught Your Excellency all that I know about this language; and if something is missing, as I believe it is, which happens many times when one writes, at another time it can be finished.

I would have liked to teach you more, but who can teach others what they don't know? So, what I knew, I taught, what I didn't know, I've left out. It is better to be quiet than in speaking to tell lies.

Now it is necessary to collect all the papers and once again begin to write the rules as we are able . . . .

97r   On the Rules

The active verbs have their rules, and these can be divided in two. The first relates to the verbs that take the accusative case. The second is about those that take the dative.

1.

La primera regla de los activos recive el caso acusat.; sea de persona o cosa. p.e. Dios creo, el Cielo. *Chaṅichṅisapil tupai loviaj.* yo te mando que no [h]agas *oi notoṡṅac cai o lovíipi.*

Verbos pasivos no se hallan, mas solamente activos y Neutros. Jamas en esta lengua se oie al modo infinit. hablando.

2.

La segunda regla de los activos recive el caso dat. y el verbo de esta regla es el solo dar, p.e. yo te quiero dar toto mi mismo. *Non oic chooni no tajaui majàṅṅivichoc.*

Tambien se pone en dat. quando el verbo significa, hacer una cosa a favor de alguno. p.e. para mi lo has hecho. *Nicso loviiċ.*

EXEMPLOS

I

Porque lloras, lloro por mi padre que fue comido por los lobos.

Hiṅaiso naċ, ṅaċan no nai, poi pom hilàicala isuotom.

Corre a tu casa, y llamame tus hermanos.

Hiccuaj o quiq, po opetmi uáui.

De los participios

99r

Los participios presentes se distinguen con las voces, *no. o. po.* yo. tu. aquel, o para decir mejor, quando en español se halla la voz quando de tiempo, entonces se usan uno de estas voces *no. o. po.* por e. Quando yo cantaba de bajo de un arbol, vino una aguila: *No helacala, po eṅa supulṅa calautṅa uocòapil supul aṡuot.* en esta manera se hacen todos los participios. Y jamas se puede dejar alguna de aquellas voces que dejimos, porche entonces no se podria ente[nde]r qual de las personas hablase, y por eso siempre se ponen.

Los modos infinitos, y estos no son muchos, que segun se pronuncian tienen su significaciòn, p.e. ladrar se dice *uáiṡ,* poniendo el acento en el

1.

The first rule of active verbs takes the accusative case, whether [the object is] a person or a thing. For example: "God created heaven," *Chaṅichṅisapil tupai loviaj.* "I order you not to do [it]," *oi notosṅac cai o lovíipi.*

There are no passive verbs, only active and neutral. Never in this language is the infinitive mode heard in speaking.

2.

The second rule of active verbs takes the dative case, and the verb for this rule is the only "to give." For example: "I want to give all to you myself," *Non oic chooni no tajaui majàṅṅivichoc.*

The dative is also used when the verb signifies doing something on behalf of someone. For example: "For me you have done it." *Nicso loviiċ.*

EXAMPLES

I

Why do you cry, I cry for my father who was eaten by the wolves.

Hiṅaiso naċ, ṅaċan no nai, poi pom hilàicala isuotom.

Run to your house, and call your brothers for me.

Hiccuaj o quiq, po opetmi uáui.

On Participles

The present participles are distinguished by the words *no, o,* and *po*. "I," "you," "that one"; or to put it better, when in Spanish there is the word "when" for time, then you use the one of these words: *no, o,* or *po*. For example: "When I was singing beneath a tree, an eagle came," *No helacala, po eṅa supulṅa calautṅa uocòapil supul aṡuot.* All the participles are made in this way. And one can never leave out any of those words we mentioned, because then one could not understand which person speaks, and that is why they must always be used.

The infinitive modes, which are few, get their meaning from the way they are pronounced. For example: "to bark" is *uáiṡ*, putting an accent

á. para distinguir el nombre *uaiŝ*, que quiere decir, carne, y asi el verbo *móliŝ*, recordarse, y *mol-iŝ*, tragar.

de la Concordancia

Las concordancias en esta lengua son de dos suertes, es decir, el adjetivo, con el substantivo el verbo con el nombre: el nombre adjetivo se concorda con su substantivo, en numero y caso: mas no en genero, porque dejimos que no habian: al verbo con el nombre en número: p.e. yo tomo siempre el agua que es limpia. *Mimchapano pàapaiċ, palai téfajoti tefajot,* limpia, o limpio, es el adjetivo, que se concorda con el substantivo *pala.* agua. como se vee en el exemplo que hemos hecho. ‖ en la noche oscura, los hombres no pueden veer = *túcbaṅa yùbajotṅa, caipom atájom tiù-tiuiuon:* | el hombre fuerte vence = *pumlop ataj chiùchiuiċap.* mis compañeros son buenos, *no pevso-ṅompom polovim,* etc. El verbo con el nombre en numero y nada mas, nosotros mañana moriremos y nos enterraran los otros: *ejṅaichapo chaom taċuayajan, pè mo auom chami napiṅ.*

ayer he visto tu hermano, que estaba jugando con un otro muchacho.

Uajamnil o pasi tiùaj po ès a uò amaiamal po yìyiċala.

El perro de mi padre es tan lijero, que corriendo arriba hasta los ligeros venados.

Po aŝap no Nà pomminocop sataŝtaŝ, pe op hiċċuinoc sucatmi sataŝaŝmi haiàhaiàiċ.

Coge al hombre que viene de tras de mi para mattarme, y ammaralo.

Chàcui ataji no cuasmaṅa monċati, nii mocnavichacati, pè poi tuchi.

Dice a tu Padre que yo mañana le daré todos mis perros.

Yaj o Nai, ejṅai poic no majamnipi, chonmi no aualmi.

Vaia, que yo te cargarè tu fucil, y te darè carne, para que puedas comer.

Hatiaj nonopo chòquin o patquilai, pè nopo, oic uaiŝ mojamnin o hilaipi.

La tercera manera de concordancia, que tienen los Españoles es el relativo con el antecedente. en esta lengua no se añade nada, quando

on the "a" to distinguish it from the noun *uaiś*, which means "meat." So too the verb *móliś*, "to remember," and *mol-iś*, "to swallow."

On Agreement

Agreement in this language is of two kinds; that is to say, the adjective with the noun, [and] the verb with the noun. The adjective agrees with its noun in number and case, but not in gender, because as we said, there is none. The verb [agrees]with the noun in number. For example: "I always drink water that is clean," *Mimchapano pàapaiċ, palai téfa-joti; tefajot.* "Clean" ([in Spanish] *limpia*, [masculine] *limpio*) is the adjective, and it agrees with the noun *pala* ("water"), as can be seen in the example we have made. "In the dark of night, men cannot see" = *túcbaṅa yùbajotṅa caipom atajom tiù-tiuiuon.* "The strong man wins" = *pumlop ataj chiùchiuiċap.* "My companions are good," *No pevsoṅompom polovim*, etc. The verb [agrees] with the noun in number and nothing more. "Tomorrow we will die and the others will bury us," *ejṅaichapo chaom taċuayajan, pè mo auom chami napiṅ.*

"Yesterday I saw your brother, who was playing with another lad."

Uajamnil o pasi tiùaj po ès a uò amaiamal po yìyiċala.

"My father's dog is so swift, that when running, it reaches the swift deer."

Po aśap no Nà pomminocop sataśtaś, pe op hiċċuinoc sucatmi sataśaśmi haiàhaiàiċ.

"Get the man who comes after me to kill me, and tie him up."

Chàcui ataji no cuasmaṅa monċati, nii mocnavichacati, pè poi tuchi.

"Tell your father that tomorrow I will give him all my dogs."

Yaj o Nai, ejṅai poic no majamnipi, chonmi no aualmi.

"Go, and I shall carry your rifle, and I will give you meat, so that you can eat."

Hatiaj nonopo chòquin o patquilai, pè nopo, oic uaiś mojamnin o hilaipi.

The third form of agreement that the Spanish have is that relative to the antecedent. In this language, you add nothing when the tense is

es presente el tiempo, y se entiende muy bien, p.e. yo, que te quiero |
non oi màmacat | explicando a palabra queria decir, yo que soi ama-
dor de ti. Mas quando es de tiempo passado, se hace con los partici-
pios de tiempo passado. yo soi el que te creò | *non oi loviimocuiŝ* |
explicando a palabra quiere decir | yo soi, quien te ha creado.

La persona ~~casi siempre~~ se pone adelante y despues del Verbo p.e. Mi
Padre cogió una aguila con la flecha. *No Nàapil chàcuaj. sapuli asuoti
po. hulatal.* y asi tambien se puede decir *Chàċuicap No Nà sapuli
asuoti sèinoc.*

Non, yo, si quisiese anteponer, se deja como esta, mas quando se
quisiera poner despues del verbo menester es que sea unido con el
verbo, y de *non* se hace *an* en el tiempo presente, y en el passado se
hace *nil.* p.e. yo me muero | *non tacùayaċ* | metiendo despues el verbo
se dice | *tacùayaċlan* || yo me morì, | *nonil tacuayaa* | *tacùaianil* | yo
me morirè | *non opo tacùaiajan,* | *tacùaiajanopo* y asi en todos los
verbos.

de los ~~preposiciones~~ Adverbios

Los adverbios son estos,   *mimchapon*   siempre

Amù.   Ya, adelante, hace tiempo.

Pítov.   Aora.

Yp.   después

Ohò.   Sí, es verdad.

Cai.   No, no es así.

Uam.   yà

Ayalinoc.   bien.

Ejnai.   mañana.

mùiŝc.   mucho

uohmal.   poco

queleċ.   pronto.

mahati.   . . . . lento.

pomminoċ.   muy. mucho.

present, and it is well understood. For example: "I who love you" | *non oi màmacat* | explaining literally it means, "I who am the lover of you." But when it is in the past tense, it is formed with past participles. "I am he who created you" | *non oi loviimocuiṡ* | explaining literally it means, "I am the one who has created you."

The subject is ~~almost always~~ placed in front, and the verb comes after. For example: "My father shot an eagle with his arrow." *No Nàapil chàcuaj. sapuli asuoti po. hulatal.* And we can also say, *Chàcuicap No Nà sapuli asuoti sèinoc.*

Non, "I," if one wishes to put it in front, is left as it is, but when one wishes to place it after the verb, it is necessary that it be linked to the verb. And from *non,* you make *an* in the present tense, and in the past tense, *nil.* For example: "I am dying" | *non tacùayaċ* | Putting the verb after, one says | *tacùayaċlan* || "I died," *nonil tacuayaa* | *tacùaianil* | "I will die" | *non opo tacùaiajan,* | *tacùaiajanopo,* and so on with all the verbs.

On ~~Prepositions~~ Adverbs

These are the Adverbs,   *mimchapon*   always

Amù.	already, ahead, some time ago
Pítov.	now
Yp.	after
Ohò.	yes, it is true
Cai.	no, it is not so
Uam.	already
Ayalinoc.	well
Ejnai.	tomorrow*
mùiṡc.	much
uohmal.	little
queleċ.	quickly
mahati.	.... slowly
pomminoċ.	very, much

---

*Both the Spanish word *mañana* and the Luiseño word *ejnai* can mean either "tomorrow" or "morning," but "tomorrow" is given here as the adverb.

Numeros

Supul.   Uno

Ueh.   dos

Pài.   tres

Uasà.   quatro.

Mahàr.   Cinco.

Mahàr pè supùl.   Seis

Mahàr pe Ueh.   Ciete.

Mahàr pè pai.   ocho.

Mahàr pe uasà.   nueve.

Ueh con Mahàr.   dies.

Ueh con Mahar pè supul.   once

Ueh con Mahar pè Ueh.   doce

Ueh con Mahar pé pai.   trece.

Ueh con Mahar pè uasà

Pai con   Mahar.   Venti.

Uasà con Mahar.   Tre[i]nta.

Conversion de los Sanluiseños
Del Bayle de los Indios.

Cada gente de Indios tiene sus Bayles, deferentes de los otros Bayles.
En Europa se bayla por alegría, por festín, por alguna novedad fausta.
Pero los Indios de California no solo por festín baylan, mas también
antes de empezar la Guerra, por llanto, porque han perdido la Vic-
toria, por recuerdo de los avuelos, tíos, Padres, ya muertos. Aora
que somos nosotros Christianos baylamos por ceremonia. El Bayle
de los Yumos es casi siempre triste, y assi el canto, lo mismo es el de
los Dieguinos. Pero nosotros Sanluiseños tenemos tres maneras principales solo de los hombres, porque las Mugeres tienen otros, y que
~~nunca~~ jamas pueden baylar con los hombres. tres principales, dos
para muchos, y el otro para uno, el que es más diffícil. De estos dos
en muchos baylar se puede, y en una manera se puede baylar dia, y
noche, y en otro, solo por la noche.

102r   Numbers

Supul.   one

Ueh.   two

Pài.   three

Uasà.   four

Mahàr.   five

Mahàr pè supùl.   six

Mahàr pe Ueh.   seven

Mahàr pè pai.   eight

mahàr pe uasà.   nine

Ueh con Mahàr.   ten

Ueh con Mahar pè supul.   eleven

Ueh con Mahar pè Ueh.   twelve

Ueh con Mahar pé pai.   thirteen

Ueh con Mahar pè uasà

Pai con Mahar.   twenty

Uasà con Mahar.   thirty

104r   **Conversion of the San Luiseños**

          On the Dance of the Indians

All Indian peoples have their own dances, distinct from each other.
In Europe they dance for joy, for festivals, or for some piece of good
news. But the California Indians do not dance just for festivals but
also before starting a war; in grief, because they have been defeated;
in remembrance of the grandparents, uncles and aunts, and parents
now dead. Now that we are Christians, we dance ceremonially. The
dance of the Yuma is almost always sad, as is their chanting, and that
of the Dieguiños is as well. But we San Luiseños have three principal
ways only for males, because the women have other dances, which
they can never dance with men. Three principal dances, two for groups
of dancers, one for an individual, which is the most difficult. In the
first two many can dance; one kind can be danced day and night, and
the other only at night.

Primer bayle

Qualquiera no puede Baylar sin la permissión de los Viejos, y debe ser de la misma gente, joven de diez y más años. Los Viejos antes de hacerlos Baylar publicamente, los enseñan el canto y los hacen aprender perfectamente, porque el bayle consiste en saber el canto, porque segun el canto se hagacha, según el canto da tantas patadas quantos saltillos hacen los cantores, que son los viejos, las Viejas y otros, mas de la misma gente.

104v Quando han aprendido, entonces les pueden hacer baylar, ~~los vestidos~~ pero antes de esso les dan algo de beber, y entonces aquel es baylador, puede baylar y no quedarse, quando los otros baylan. Entonces los vestidos son de plumas de varios colores, y el cuerpo pintado, el pecho es abierto, y desde la cintura ~~cuelgan plumas~~ hasta las rodillas se cubren, los brazos sin vestido, en la mano derecha llevan una madera echa para quitarse el sudor, la cara pintada, la cabeza fajada con faja de cabellos tejida, para poder encajar los *cheyatom,* nuestra palabra, este *cheyat* es echo de plumas, de cualquier paxaro, y casi siempre del cuervo, y del gabilan. y en medio un palito agudo para poder encajar. Assi están en la casa, quando al instante salen dos hombres llevando cada uno dellos dos espadas de palo y gritando, sin decir alguna palabra, y después parándose ante el lugar en donde se bayla estan mirando al cielo un rato, la gente se calla, y ellos se vuelven y entonces salen los bayladores. // Estos dos hombres se llaman por nosotros *Pajaom,* quiere decir serpientes vermejos; en California hay serpientes vermejos largos, estos no muerden, mas se dan azotes a quien se arrima a ellos: // Los bayladores en este bayle pueden llegar hasta treinta, o menos o mas, saliendo de casa, vueltan la cara a los cantores y empiezan a dar patadas, pero no fuerte, porque no es tiempo, y quando se acaba el canto el capitán de los bayladores, tocando sus pies grita *hù* y todos se callan, él de nuevo viene a los cantores, y canta, y todos baylan, y al fin grita, *hù,* y se callan los cantores, y ellos hacen la voz del caballo

106r que busca a su hijo. La voz *hù* nada significa en nuestra lengua; pero los bayladores entienden que signifique callaos. Quando el capitán no dice *hù,* no pueden callarse los cantores y repiten, y repiten el canto hasta el alvedrio del capitán. Después van ante los cantores y toda la gente que los está viendo, y el capitán de los bayladores canta y bayla, y los otros lo siguen, baylan en circo dando patadas, y quien

First Dance

No one may dance without the permission of the elders, and they must be from the same people, youths ten years of age or older. The elders, before having them dance publicly, teach them the song and make them learn it perfectly, because the dance consists of knowing the song. For it is following the song that one bows, and following the song one gives as many kicks as the little leaps made by the singers, who are the elder men, and women, and others from the same people.

104v When they have learned, then they can make them dance, but before that, they give them something to drink, and then that one is a dancer, and can dance and not stay behind when the others dance. Now the clothes are of feathers of various colors, and the body is painted. The chest is exposed, and from the waist ~~hang feathers~~ down to the knees they are covered. The arms are unclad. In the right hand, they have a wooden piece made to wipe the sweat. The face is painted, the head girded with a band of hair woven so that the *cheyatom*, as we call it, can go in. This *cheyat* is made of feathers of any bird, and almost always from crows and from hawks, and in the middle a sharp little stick that allows it to go in. Thus they are in the house, when suddenly two men go out, each of them bearing two wooden swords and shouting, without saying any word. And then, stopping in front of the place where one dances, they stand looking skyward for a while. The people go quiet, and the men return, and then out come the dancers. // We call these two men *Pajaom,* which means red snakes. In California there are long red snakes. They do not bite, but instead whip anyone who comes near them. // The number of dancers in this dance can grow to thirty, more or less. Emerging from the house, they turn to face the chanters and begin kicking, but not strongly, because it is not time yet, and when the chant is completed the captain of the dancers, stamping his feet, shouts *hù,* and they all go silent. He approaches the chanters anew, and he sings, and everyone dances; and at the end he shouts *hù,* and the singers go silent, and they make the sound of a horse in

106r search of its colt. The word *hù* signifies nothing in our language, but the dancers understand that it means "be quiet." If the captain does not say *hù,* the singers cannot be silent, but they repeat and repeat the song as long as the captain wishes. Then they go before the singers and all the people who are watching them, and the captain of the dancers sings and dances, and the others follow him. They dance in a circle,

se cansa, queda en medio del circo y después sigue a los otros, ninguno puede reír en este bayle, y todos con la cabeza agachada, los ojos hazia la tierra siguen a los primeros; quando está para acabarse el bayle todos se quitan el *cheyat*, y teniéndolo en mano derecha, lo levantan al cielo sopplando a cada patada que dan a la tierra, y el capitán con un *hù* acaba el bayle. y todos se vuelven a la casa de los vestidos, y en esto los Viejos empiezan a chupar, o fumar, y todo el humo echan al Cielo, tres veces antes de acabar el Bayle. echo esto se acaba, el Viejo se vuelve a su Casa canzado Porque el Bayle dura tres horas, y es menester cantar por tres horas, se bayla en medio día, quando el sol quema más, y entonces las Espaldas de los Bayladores parecen fuentes de agua, por tanto sudor que les cae. Este bayle es diffícil, y entre dos mil hombres había uno que sabía bien baylar.

Segundo Bayle

El Bayle segundo jamàs me plegue porque quien mas puede gritar grite, quien brincar brinque pero siempre según el canto, y mucho se assemeja al Bayle Español. hay un viejo cantor que tiene un galapago muerto, en medio un palito, y las manos y pies, la cabeza, y la cola son tapados y se ponen dentro piedritas, y assi moviéndole da su sonido.

106v Y siempre se bayla por la noche, pueden baylar entre muchos, quando baylan los Viejos les echan trigo y mays, y aqui también pueden baylar las Mugeres.

Tercero

El Tercero es el mas diffícil, y por esso pocos son sus bayladores desta manera. En este bayle uno bayla, antes que el baylador salga, salen dos hombres que llamanse serpientes vermejos (como hemos dicho). El Baylador lleva su *pàla* de las cinturas hasta las rodillas, echa de plumas, por los hombros passa un cordoncito y endonde son colgadas muchas plumas. En la cabezza lleva una larga pluma de un águila, y en las manos dos palitos bien hechos, gruesos como un carrizo, y largos una palma y media, y todo el cuerpo pintado. El círculo endonde Bayla es su circunferencia de ochenta pasos, mas o menos según el lugar; y a quattro a siete passos, hay un viejo que cuida

kicking, and whoever gets tired remains in the middle of the circle, and afterwards follows the others. No one may laugh in this dance, and everyone, head bowed and eyes turned toward the earth, follows those ahead. When the dance is almost finished, everyone removes their *cheyat*, and holding it in their right hand, they lift it skyward, blowing out air with each kick they deliver to the earth, and the captain with one call of *hù* ends the dance. And everyone returns to the house where the dance regalia is kept, and then the elders begin to suck, or smoke, and they puff all the smoke skyward three times before finishing the dance. Once this is done, it is over. The elder returns to his house tired because the dance lasts three hours, and it is necessary to sing for the three hours. It is danced in the middle of the day, when the sun burns the most, and then the backs of the dancers look like water fountains with all the sweat that falls from them. This dance is difficult, and among two thousand men there was one who knew how to dance well.

Second Dance

The second dance I never took pleasure in, because whoever can shout the most should shout, whoever can leap should leap, but always in keeping with the song, and it much resembles Spanish dancing. There is an old singer who has a dead tortoise with a little stick in the middle; the hands and feet, the head, and the tail are sealed, and they put little pebbles inside, and thus by moving it, it gives its sound.

106v And it is always danced at night. Many can dance, and when they dance, the elders throw wheat and maize at them, and here women can also dance.

Third

The third is the most difficult, and that is why few are dancers of this style. In this dance one person dances. Before the dancer comes out, two men come out who are called the red serpents (as we have said). The dancer wears his *pàla* made of feathers, from the waist to the knees; across his shoulders runs a string hung with many feathers. On his head he has a long eagle feather, and in his hands two well-formed sticks, thick as a reed, and a palm and a half in length, and his whole body is painted. The circle in which he dances is eighty paces in circumference, more or less, depending on the site. Every four to seven

para que el Baylador no pueda caer, lo que es muy fácil, porque debe mirar al cielo, un pié empinado, el otro en terra, un brazzo por el ayre, y el otro hacia la terra, y assi debe caminar alrededor de aquel círculo, este circulo es hecho de gente que quiere ver el bayle.

Empezemos; Salen los serpientes, y la gente se calla, y entonces dos cantores empiezan a cantar con el *cheyat* por la bocca diciendo *hù* . . . . por tres veces, dejimos que nada significan. Sale después el baylador y empieza a correr por el círculo, los cantores cantan, el bayla según el canto como hemos dicho, y quando baylando se arrima a un Viejo, él le dice, *hù* y levanta sus manos, y el baylador sigue su camino, él no puede ni reír, ni hablar. se acaba, los Viejos fuman, y se vuelven a sus Aduares.

8. Papel.

. . .

[n.p.] Que oygo!
Oygo una voz, que assi canta;
Paraos o Pastores paraos
hoy con vosotros nació el hijo de Dios
Sí: el Creador de todas las cosas
se hizo como uno de ellos;
id pronto, id a su casa,
Allí vereis al niño Rey
que duerme en la cuna;
Vereis en un lado a su Madre
que adora a su Hijo,
en el otro a un pío viejo
que vee a todas estas cosas.
Vereis la bella corona de aquellos
celestiales y también los vereis
ariba quando assi cantan
Gloria, Gloria a Dios, y paz a los hombres,
Vereis al poderoso que tiembla;
Y por fin a los animales que le
calientan. Paraos, o Pastores Paraos.

paces, there is an elder who ensures that the dancer does not fall, which can easily happen, since he must look up at the sky, with one foot raised and the other on the ground, and with one arm in the air and the other toward the earth. So must he walk around that circle, which is made of people who want to see the dance.

Let us begin. The serpents come out, and the people go quiet, and then the singers begin singing with the *cheyat* and they say *hù* . . . . three times; we said that it signifies nothing. Then the dancer emerges and begins to run around the circle. The singers sing; he dances according to the song, as we have said, and when while dancing he comes near an elder, he tells him *hù* and raises his hands, and the dancer continues on his way, he can neither laugh nor speak. It is over; the elders smoke, and they return to their huts.

8th Paper*

. . .

[n.p.] What do I hear?
I hear a voice that so does sing:
"Stop, O Shepherds, stop!
Today the Son of God was born unto you
Yes: The Creator of all things
Made himself as one of them;
Go quickly, go to your homes,
There you shall behold the infant King
Who sleeps in the crib;
At one side you will see his Mother
Who adores her Son,
At the other, a pious old man
Who sees all these things.
You shall see the beautiful crown of those
Celestial beings, and you will also see them
On high as they so do sing:
'Glory, Glory to God, and peace to mankind,'
You shall see the powerful one who trembles;
And finally, the animals who
warm him. Stop, O Shepherds, stop."

---

*The dictionary, written in three separate booklets, was numbered fols. 107r–142v. It appears on pp. 215–61 of the present edition.

144v La palabra *michá* quiere decir endonde, en que lugar, o sitio, por e. endonde esta tu padre, en que lugar se halla, en que sitio; se dice; *micháso o Ná auċ.* y assi, endonde está Dios? *micháso Chaṅmichṅiṡ auċ.* También significa, como: en que manera, quando se le añade la voz *ajanninoq.* p.e. en que manera lo haré? *Micháson ajanninoc loviin.* De aquí nace el nombre adjetivo, *Michaiuiṡ,* de donde, de que lugar, p.e. Vosotros de donde ~~de~~ sois? *Michaiuichomsom omom?* Somos del oriente, se diría *Cuimcuṅaiuichomcha.* Y de aquí también nacen los dos adverbios, y estos son, *Michai,* y el otro *Michiq.* el primero significa de donde, el segundo, para donde: p.e. De donde vienen estos águilas? se dice: *Michaisom ivim asuotom uoċònocoajan.* Para donde vas quando es noche? *Michiċsom hatihatiajon omom po yubacala.*

Los nombres adjetivos quando se quieren hacer del grado supremo se les antepone la palabra o adverbio *pomminoq,* que significa muy. por e. para decir grandìssimo, como también los Españoles dicen muy grande, assi nosotros decimos, *pomminoq yot,* assi muy malo *pomminoq hichacat;* muy bueno, *pomminoq polov.* muy largo: *pomminoq tabulbuṡ.* mas el adjetivo muchissimo no se dice *pomminoq muioq,* mas solamente se dice *muioq,* y nada mas.

145r *Ejlapil amù hichacat*
Po toṡnaċala mìmchapan
Touiṡ ṅaċuaṡ tùchaċanoq.
Mimchapanchamil nèċpiċuaṡ
Amù cham jùlamil àbbaċuaṡ
Oulam pom màṅai Atájom.
Cham sunàquimil nàlaċuaṡ
Cham yàuacala pe nàċuaṡ
~~Pe nama~~ hálcanoq cham càmayom.
O màṅai Palòv Chaṅmichṅiṡ
O uomaċala tùpaṅai
Poi o camiicala jimapil.
Sùcamil o maṅai Angelom
Uonai iviq o mònċala
Oi YA Chaṅmichṅiṡ toùċanoq
O maṅàiamil Surquiyam
Seròramilpe queù queuaj

144v The word *michà* means "where, in what place or spot?" For example: "Where is your father? In which place is he? In what spot?" This is translated as: *michaso o Nà auċ*. And thus, "Where is God?": *michàso Chaṅṅichṅiṡ auċ*. It also means "how," "in what manner," when one adds the word *ajanninoq*. For example: "In what manner shall I do it?" *Michàson ajanninoc loviin*. From here comes the adjective *Michaiuiṡ*, "from where, from which place," for example: "Where are you [plural] from?" *Michaiuichomsom omom?* "We are from the East," would be said *Cuimcuṅaiuichomcha*. And from here also come the two adverbs, and they are *Michai* and *Michiq*. The first means "from where," and the second means "to where." For example: "Where do these eagles come from?" is translated as *Michaisom ivim asuotom uoċònocoajan*. "Where do you go when night falls?" is translated as *Michiċsom hatihatiajon omom po yubacala*.

When you want to form the superlative of an adjective, the word or adverb *pomminoq* is placed before, which means "very." For example, to say "*grandísimo* [extremely large]," as the Spaniards too say "very large," thus we say *pomminoq yot*; or very bad, *pomminoq hichacat*; or very good, *pomminoq polov*. Very long: *pomminoq tabulbuṡ*. But the adjective "*muchísimo* [very many]" is not said *pomminoq muioq;* one just says *muioq,* and nothing more.

145r *Ejlapil amù hichacat*
Po toṡṅaċala mìmchapan
Touiṡ ṅaċuaṡ tùchaċanoq.
Mimchapanchamil nèċpiċuaṡ
Amù cham jùlamil àbbaċuaṡ
Oulam pom màṅai Atájom.
Cham sunàquimil nàlaċuaṡ
Cham yàuacala pe nàċuaṡ
~~*Pe nama*~~ *hàlcanoq cham càmayom.*
O màṅai Palòv Chaṅṅichṅiṡ
O uomaċala tùpaṅai
Poi o camiicala jimapil.
Sùcamil o maṅai Angelom
Uonai iviq o mònċala
Oi YA Chaṅṅichṅiṡ toùċanoq
O maṅàiamil Surquiyam
Seròramilpe queù queuaj

O maṅai chami Caminoq.
Ejlapil o uòrracàla jima,
Timamil Atajòm o màṅai
Choonomilpè taràa
Oicha pitòo yejiuon
Oiq cham sunmi majàniuon
Oipe Supùli Ohòvauon
Chaṅṅichṅiṡ . . . . .

147r La tierra ante gemia
Atada siempre Luzbel
El soberbio mandando.
Siempre guerras habia
y vermejas las armas se vían
Por el nemigo sangre.
Nuestras Mugeres huían
Nosotros faltando, nuestros
y lloraban hijos buscando.
Por ti Dios clemente
Porque bajabas del Cielo
Porque lo dejaste riò
Por ti los Angeles se espantan
de allí acà bajar
viendote, Gran Dios.
Por ti los Demonios ~~tiemblaron~~
tiemblaron y gritaron
dejandonos por ti.
Rió por ti la tierra
Rieron por ti los hombres
Todo se quedò en paz.
Te ~~Dios~~ Alabamos, aora
A ti damos corazones nuestros
Y en ti uno creemos,
Dios.

148r *CALIFORNESE.*

Hichson nacmaċ!
   Nacmaċan supúli járai ivàajanninoċ
   po hélaċala; hatiajam Ċuavchocatom hatiajam
   pitóop om eṡ

O mañai chami Caminoq.
Ejlapil o uòrracàla jima,
Timamil Atajòm o màñai
Choonomilpè taràa
Oicha pitòo yejiuon
Oiq cham sunmi majàniuon
Oipe Supùli Ohòvauon
Chañnichñiṡ . . . ..

147r   Before, the earth used to wail
Ever bound to Luzbel
The arrogant one commanding.
There were always wars
And the weapons were seen reddened
By enemy blood.
Our women were fleeing
We being absent, our
And children were weeping, searching.
Because of you, merciful God
Because you descended from heaven
Because you left it, it laughed.
Because of you the angels are frightened
Seeing you, Great God,
Descend here from up there.
Because of you the demons
Trembled and cried out
Leaving us because of you.
The earth laughed because of you;
Mankind laughed because of you.
Everything remained in peace.
We praise you ~~God,~~ now
To you we give our hearts
And in you as one we believe,
God.

148r   *CALIFORNESE.*

Hichson nacmaċ!
   Nacmaċan supúli járai ivàajanninoċ
   po hélaċala; hatiajam Ċuavchocatom hatiajam
   pitóop om eṡ

huluccaċ Chaṅichṅiṡ
Ohó, po op loviiċat choonmi
Po tajauip loviiċ, loviimocuiṡ anquiṡ;
hatiajam queleq,
hatiajam po quiq.
Uonámo tiuin Noti ammáyamali
po houaċala pácoṅa anquiṅa.
Tiuinom po chejṅa supulṅa
po Yoi, po làchiċala po Cámai.
Auiṅamo tiuin polovi najanmali
po touċala choonmi ivimi mijanmi.
Tiuinom yauaiuai pom punni ounalom
Tupaṅauichom, pomomim tiuin echṅa pom hélacala;
Yéjiṡ, Yéjiṡ Chaṅichṅichi, pé taráajis Atajmi.
Pumloiom tiuin po seróraċala, pé omca tiuin aṡmi.
poi pom saquicala; hatiajam Cuavchocutom hatiajam.

[n.p.] EXPLICACION.

Que oygo!
Oygo una voz que assì canta
paraos o Pastores paraos
hoy con vosotros nació el hijo de Dios;
Sí, el Creador de todas las cosas
se hizo como uno de ellos
id pronto, id a su casa.
Allí vereis al niño Rey
~~en la~~ que duerme en la cuna;
Vereis en un lado a su Madre
que adora a su hijo,
en el otro a un pío viejo
que vee todas estas cosas.
Vereis la bella corona de aquellos
Celestes, y tambien les vereis ariba
que assi cantan. Gloria, Gloria
a Dios, y Paz a los hombres.
Vereis al poderoso que tiembla,
y porfin a los animales que
le calientan, Paraos o Pastores, Paraos.

huluccaċ Chańichńiṡ
Ohó, po op loviiċat choonmi
Po tajauip loviiċ, loviimocuiṡ anquiṡ;
hatiajam queleq,
hatiajam po quiq.
Uonámo tiuin Noti ammáyamali
po houaċala pácoṅa anquiṅa.
Tiuinom po chejṅa supulṅa
po Yoi, po làchiċala po Cámai.
Auiṅamo tiuin polovi najanmali
po touċala choonmi ivimi mijanmi.
Tiuinom yauaiuai pom punni ounalom
Tupaṅauichom, pomomim tiuin echṅa pom hélacala;
Yéjiṡ, Yéjiṡ Chańichńichi, pé taráajis Atajmi.
Pumloiom tiuin po seróraċala, pé omca tiuin aṡmi.
poi pom saquicala; hatiajam Cuavchocutom hatiajam.

[n.p.] EXPLANATION.

What do I hear?
I hear a voice that so does sing:
"Stop, O Shepherds, stop!
Today the Son of God was born unto you
Yes, the Creator of all things
Made himself as one of them;
Go quickly, go to your homes.
There you shall behold the infant King
Who sleeps in the crib;
At one side you will see his Mother
Who adores her son,
At the other, a pious old man
Who sees all these things.
You shall see the beautiful crown of those
Celestial beings, and you will also see them
On high as they do sing: 'Glory, Glory
To God, and Peace to mankind.'
See the powerful one who trembles
And finally, the animals
Who warm him. Stand, O Shepherds, stand.

Fernandini.

Mihi animo atque hilari saltando celeres atque hoc ludorum genere reliquis multum per usque praestiterunt, celeriter ludum, spectantibus jucundiorum efficient, Catholicam dicunt se profiteri fidem.

Barbareñi.

Eadem religione, animoque sunt Barbareñi praediti insigniores, quam Gabrileñi, et capillatiores,

Pauca de animo californiensibus atque indole dixi, nunc aliquid de linguarum differentia inquam, quoad mihi delata est.

Linguarum affinitas et differentia

1. Omittendo Apaches quos nullo pacto unquam loquentes audire potui, inititer mihi de Yumis ducere liceat, hisque affirmabam, Yumi et Diegueñi affini lingua utentur, ut galli et itali, quibus interest affirmes, Yumi ut ipse percepi, leniter verba proterunt, et armoniam quandam emantumque in dicendo adhibent, Diegueñi contra absone et aspere, sunt utrique sunt peculiares voces, sed affinitate quadam.

2. Sanluiseñi et Sanjuaneñi eadem utuntur, interfere pronunciatione differunt, quid majore isti vehementique spiritu, hos ut quondam ullo querer ad calcem sermonis protuli. *Temet po yobbacàla,* sol scilicet, cum occideret cachinum opere tellere, quie causam quaerenti quae nam est videndi ne respondere quidem impediente achinno potherunt. Sensii tamen (neque enim erat difficile) me non adhihuste spiritum illis praecipue gratissimum, ut non latine dicere.

Ario videbatur is, qui, h, vocalibus non praeponeret, cum ille homo horribilis, maxime tum, cum quantum posiet, diceret hinsidiar, laetaretur; hi vocalem detrahunt aliquando et geminant spiritus, nulla est differentia quam in pronun ciandis vocibus, et quibusdam in detrahendis vocalibus.

The People of Mission San Fernando

Joyous in spirit and swift at dancing and games, the quick ones excel at playing games and offer the spectators a delightful experience. They say that they profess the Catholic faith.

The People of Mission Santa Barbara

The Barbareños, gifted with the same religion and spirit, are more remarkable than the Gabrileños and wear their hair longer.

I said little about the spirit and innate character of the Californians. Now [I'll address] something of the differences of languages, insofar as this is reported to me.

The Affinity and Differences of Languages

1. Leaving aside the Apaches, whom I was never able to hear speaking in any formal context, let me begin by considering the Yuma. Concerning them I asserted that the Yuma and Diegueños use a related language, just as the French and Italians, for whom it is affirmed that there is a difference. The Yuma, as I myself have perceived, pronounce their words softly and exhibit a certain harmony and flow in speaking. The Diegueños, in contrast, [speak] harshly and roughly. They have different vowel sounds but a certain affinity.

2. The Luiseños and Juaneños use the same [language], they differ from each other in pronunciation, which Luiseños do with a greater and more emphatic breath; I have mentioned the latter ones [Juaneños] with a sort of footnote [about pronunciation]: *Temet po yobbacala,* namely, certainly the sun falls from heaven to earth, [it being] the case that the earth works this way. Here it is indeed truly observed without hindrance that the pronunciation did not strike me as especially agreeable to them, nor when said in Latin.

One can see that this *h* does not exist before vowels, as is the case of *homo horribilis,* in the same way that it could be stated *hinsidias,* one would be surprised.* These [Juaneños] strip off a vowel, while they [Luiseños] redouble the breaths; there is no difference other than in pronouncing sounds, and in leaving out certain vowels.

---

*I.e., *insidiae* is spelled without an *h*.

3. Gabrileñi et Fernandini mihi videntur adhibere eadem, hoc enim invicem audiri loqunter com me ad illorum pagum contulissem, quemam differentia interfit me ingenue latere fateor, sic de Fernandini num propriam, et Fernandinorum cum lingua affinitaten habeant tamen multum differe sentio ~~quam affiner~~ audiri enim quosdam Barbarenos qui ita verba dictabant, ut vix possen distinguere vocales portem distinguere tanta erat celeritas pronunciandi, et verborum turba, et minum sana mihi videbatur, et mente minime perresponder poteraa, hace pauca de linguis unde posset intelligere quot californienses uterentur, dubito, et picereto habere non possum, utrum quattuor, an tres confundae sint, vel plures, quibus veluti parentibus reliquae eriantur, hoc certe ni genere affirmare possum, summam inter et Sanluiseñam, et Barbareños talem esse differentiam, ut Romanam inter et Angliam esse videatur.

Suam hic Em^e, de Californiensium indole, deque linguarum differentia (quoad videbatur mihi vera videbatur) sententiam protuli. Si quis forte peritus veram esse negaverit, vel addenda, vel detramenda videri sibi quam plurima dinerit, hujus ego sententiae supiento veluti, atque vendi cae parebo, et meam mutaba sententiam.

De Californiensibus.

Apaches.

Parvo corpore, sed maximo sunt animo praediti pauca coma et si rumori eredemus parte capitis posteriori sima, caperata frente, immamtatem quae et crudele nescio quid indicat, Arden tibus oculis, pauca barba et nulla interdum. Yumos praecipue insectantur, et odio mutuo capesunt arma, manusque acriter, ancipitis tan Marte conferunt, modo enim Yumi prae viribus, modo Apaches depertare solent triumphum. Novum prope marimum et sonoram habitant, Catholicae nondum religioni parent.

3. The Gabrileños and Fernandinos seem to me to exhibit the same [language]. They spoke this way to be heard by each other when I went to their country, although I admit that naturally the difference happened to escape me. So among the Fernandinos themselves, and Fernandino as a spoken language, there is affinity.* So far great differences are indeed felt when hearing Barbareños, for they articulated words in such a way that I could scarcely distinguish the vowels. Let me cover so much as [I could] distinguish: there was the speed of pronunciation, the multitude of words, and it seemed to me only barely understandable. I was hardly able to respond. These few things about the many [languages] the Californians use, [I offer] hesitatingly and I cannot [be certain] whether four or three [languages] have been confused or brought together, or many more exist, the rest straying as if from their parents. This I can certainly affirm, that in general, the greatest difference is between the Luiseños and Barbareños, such as there seems to be between Roman and English.

Your Eminence, I have put forth an individual opinion on the characteristics of the Californians, down to language differences (insofar as it seemed to me to be true). If some expert will perhaps deny it to be true, whether by adding or subtracting as much as seems to him wrong, I regret it and shall accede to their claim, go by whatever is said, and change my opinion.

Concerning the Californians

153r

The Apache

They are known as small in body but very large in spirit, with little hair, and we also chose to laugh a bit about their hair behind their heads and furrowed brows, fiery eyes signaling fierceness and ignorance, scant beards and often none. They attack the Yuma especially, and with mutual hatred; they fiercely take arms and the bands engage in war of great danger, for the Yuma are preeminent in strength, but the Apache are accustomed to carry off the utmost victory nearly every time. They inhabit Sonora. They do not yet comply with the Catholic religion.

---

*People from various tribal and linguistic groups made up the population of Mission San Fernando. The populations came to form part of new collectivities at the missions. Those called Fernandinos were one such collectivity; its members came to speak a new or dominant native language, in this case named for the mission.

Yumi

Ingente corpore, capillatiores quam ceteri, nigriore colore sunt Yumi.
Animo vero ut multis rebus judicare possamus pacato potius quam
belligero, pereiti tamen vel suorum nece, re vel eliqua illis quae
nocumentum afferat arma gerunt animumque praeseserunt virilen et
flagrantes Martis numine hispanorum minime arma terrent, partim
quod jam illos non fugit, dirinitatis scilicet arma nihil, ut olim nescii
arbitrabantur, habere, partim quid ipsimet hisetiam peritia quadam
armis utantur. Etenim vel inopia rerum ~~vel~~ olim, vel odio ni hispanes
impulsi illorum plurimos necarunt. Centum licet et decem ~~licet~~ equiter
Olypeo, hostis ensibus igneisque armis obsistere conarentur. Copia
tamen dicendum potuirrema gis quam superare virtute, tria enim ferre
millia fuisse Yumorum hispaniarum auctoritate constat, prope So-
norum morantur si hac voce potius quam vagari licet uti, nondum
Cath. fidei Atemperantes.

Diegueñi

Cato Animo, et constantia et tali fide conati, ut eorum ut quisque no
sana mente amicitiam atque foedus quin ample fatur non dubitet, hoc
vero laborant, ut lacessiter ardeant, aeternumque vulnus animo
inhaeareat animo quid memoria saepius repetunt vel insidiari horti
machinantur, aut melius, ut illi putant diga homine palam fugulant.
Sed modo eo cui religioni parent edocti, convicia temnunt et suis facile
ignesunt hostibus.

Sanluiseñi

Hilari animo libertatem expetunt maximopere eorumque potentiam
ferre minime possunt imperio qui suos cohibere aveant atque com-
primere, obstiterunt Dieguinorum armas temporeque antiquitar

The Yuma

The Yuma, large in body, darker in color, have longer hair than the others. We could attribute, however, as with other things, in peace rather than with a belligerent spirit, the death of their own people experienced together, for example, [is] something that brings about the spirit of Mars, arms and virility, as the arms of the Spanish diminished [intimidated] them somehow but frighten them little. Partly because [it] does escape them to have such arms, with the arms apparent not at all set aside, as they once thought to do in their ignorance, and partly because they themselves also use these arms with a certain skill. As a matter of fact, whether motivated by want of things (now) or before, or by hatred toward the Spaniards, they killed many of them. Although there were one hundred and ten horsemen in Olypeio, they tried to resist the enemy with swords and firearms. Plenty could be said about the affair beyond winning by strength.* It is agreed that there were almost three thousand of the Yuma under Spanish authority. They stay near Sonora, if it is permitted that I use this word instead of "roaming." They are not yet tempered by Catholic faith.

153v

The People of the Mission San Diego

With a clever spirit, both in constancy and in such a faith of undertaking, that no one of sound mind would doubt their friendship and an alliance that is abundantly spoken. They are distressed and exasperated regarding this; a wounded spirit animates their memory eternally. By which spirit they go back on whatever earlier agreement, or they conspire to lie in ambush in the field. Or better, as they deem worthy of a man, they openly run away. But in that way, fully indoctrinated, they give in to whatever religion. They scorn outcries, and they easily flare up at their enemies.

The People of Mission San Luis Rey

They cheerfully aim for freedom with the greatest effort, and whoever desires to surround their possessions and press them in are little able to do so. The persistence of the Diegueños in using arms prevented it.

---

*During the Yuma revolt of 1781, Kw'tsa'n and Mojave warriors attacked Spanish settlements in Yuma territory and effectively closed overland passage to California until 1822.

cum his bellum gesserunt, virtute minores, valebant numero, nunc autom conjuncto foedere religionis causa, una caritate, eodem ni pago morantur.

Sanjuaneñi

Pacato animo acutiores ingenio et sua indole libertatem reliquir anteponunt, janumut hii hispanorum ope fanum ni california erigerent audacia ronpulit audacia crebiore licet california terrae motu agitetur, confectum portentum tale diu nemini videtur portentum, et enim terrae motu labans, majore derique motu multorum nece concidit tertia pars templi eonicidit.

Gabrileñi

Miti animo libertatis atque otii cupidi magiores quam Sanluiseñi strieir praesertim videntur pudere, non enim irasuntur facile, et si aliquando id contigerit, intuis placantur ample et Antur fidem Catholicam.

They have been at war with Diegueños since before, succeeding less by virtue than by number. However, now unified by reason of religion, they occupy the same district as one in charity.

The People of Mission San Juan Capistrano

Peaceful in spirit, sharper in genius and in their character, their notion of relinquishing freedom comes before [when the mission was settled]. With daring and with the help of the Spaniards, they built an arched passageway and sanctuary in California. [They seemed] compelled more by daring, given that California is shaken by earthquakes. With such a finished portent [showpiece] no one saw it as a portent [prediction of threat], and so shaking with an earthquake, finally with a greater quake, a third part of the church fell down [in 1812]. It collapsed, killing many.

The People of Mission San Gabriel

With a mild spirit of freedom and more prone to leisure than the San Luiseños, they especially seem to appear not to have shame, as they do not get irritated easily, even if at times it happens. They are not fully reconciled among themselves about being given over to the Catholic faith.

Pablo Tac's Luiseño-Spanish Dictionary, *A–Cu*

The contents of Tac's three dictionary booklets are listed below, with folio numbers of the manuscript given in the margins of the page. We preserve Tac's format of listing Luiseño on the left followed by a dotted line to Tac's Spanish translation. English translations of Tac's Spanish have been added on the right. We have also retained his order, which is not strictly alphabetical, and his occasional repetition of entries.

Tac's Spanish orthography is inconsistent; sometimes he spells the same word differently within a long example. Spanish grammar systematized the placement of accent marks during the nineteenth century. Tac is not uncommon as a writer of his era in leaving many accents off words that would carry them today. Tac's conjugation of verbs also does not follow a single rule but rather shows wide variation in comparison to modern Spanish.

107r
Acuotaj	aliviado	relieved
Ababais	bermejizo	reddened
Abiis	bermejear	to redden
Abicat	el que bermejea	he who reddens
Abimoquis	el que bermejeó	he who reddened
Abiniabiniis	~~mandar que se bermeje~~	~~to order that one redden oneself *or*~~ that it be reddened

Abiniicat	el que comanda que se bermeje	he who orders that one redden oneself *or* that it be reddened
Abiniimoquis	el que ha mandado que se bermejesse	he who has ordered that one redden one-self *or* that it be reddened
Àbabis	bermejear muchas veces	to redden frequently
Àbabicat	el que mucho se bermejea	he who reddens himself frequently
Àbabimoquis	quien mucho se bermejeò	person who reddened himself frequently
Abibiniabinis	mandar muchas vezes que se bermeje	to order frequently that one redden oneself
Abajis	bermejearse	to redden oneself
Abajimoquis	el que se ha bermejeado	he who has reddened himself
Abajis	el bermejarse	the reddening of oneself
Abiniabiniimoquis	quien muchas veces ha mandado que se bermejese	person who has frequently ordered that one redden oneself
Abiniabiniicat	quien muchas veces manda que se ber[me]je	person who fre-quently orders that one redden oneself
Aiàlis	saber	to know
Aiàlis	sapiencia	knowledge
Aiàlicat	sapiente	knowledgeable person
Aiàlimoquis	el que ha sabido	he who has known
Aiàliniis	hacer saber	to make known
Aiàliniicat	quien hace saber	person who makes known
Aiàliniimoquis	quien hizo saber	person who made known
Aiàliniis	el hacer saber	the act of making known
Aiàl-aialis	saber siempre	to always know

107v

Luiseño	Spanish	English
Aiàl-aialis	el saber siempre	the fact of always knowing
Aiàlaialicat	quien siempre sabe	person who always knows
Aiàlaialimoquis	quien siempre ha sabido	person who has always known
Aiàliniaialiniis	mandar que sepan muchas veces	to order them to know frequently
Aiàliniaialiniis	el mandar muchas veces que sepan	the act of ordering them to know frequently
Aiàliniaialiniicat	el que manda que sepan muchas vezes	he who orders them to know many times
Aiàlinialiniimoquis . . .	quien ha mandado de saber muchas vezes	person who has ordered to know many times
Aiàiais	gracioso, bufon	clown, buffoon
Aiaiais	graciosidad	humorousness
Aiaiacat	gracioso	humorous
Aiaiàmoquis	quien fué gracioso	person who was humorous
Aiaàlis	componer	to compose/repair
Aiaàlis	componimiento	composing/repairing
Aiaàlicat	componedor	composer/repairer
Aiaalimoquis	quien compuso	person who composed/repaired
Aiaàlaiaaliis	componer de nuevo	to compose/repair once again
Aiaàlaiaàliis	el componer de nuevo	the act of composing/repairing again
Aiaàlaiaàlicat	el que compone de nuevo	he who composes/repairs again
Aiaàlaiaalimoquis	el que compuso de nuevo	he who composed/repaired again
Aiaàliniis	mandar que componga	order that one compose/repair
Aiaaliniis	el mandar que componga	the act of ordering that one compose/repair
Aiaàlinicat	quien mando que componga	person who ordered that one compose/repair

108r

Aiaàliniimoquis	quien mando que componese	person who ordered that it be repaired/ that one compose oneself
Aiot	ladron	thief
Aiànnis	coger muchas cosas a un tiempo	to take many things at once
Aiànnis	cogedura de muchas cosas	the taking of many things
Aiànicat	el que coge muchas cosas	he who takes many things
Aiannimoquis	quien ha cogido muchas cosas	person who has taken many things
Aiannaianniis	coger muchas veces muchas cosas	to take many things many times
Aiannaianniis	coger muchas veces muchas cosas	to take many things many times
Aiannaianniis	la cogedura de muchas cosas	the taking of many things
Aiannaiannicat	quien coge	person who takes
Aiannaiannimoquis . . .	quien ha cogido	person who has taken
Aianiaianiis	mandar que cogen	to order that they take
Aianiaianiis	el mandar que cogen	the act of ordering that they take
Aianiaianiicat	quien manda que cogen	the person who orders that they take
Aianiaianiimoquis	quien mando que cogessen	the person who ordered that they take
Aiiis	recibir	to receive
Aiiis	recibo	receipt; I receive
Aiiicat	quien recibe	person who receives
Aiiimoquis	quien ha recibido	person who has received
Aiaiiis	recibir muchas veces	to receive many times
Aiaiis	el recibir muchas veces	the act of receiving many times
Aiaiicat	quien muchas veces recibe	person who receives many times

108v (margin, before *Aiiis*)

Aiaiimoquis	quien muchas vezes recibido	person who received many times
Aiiiniis	hacer recibir	to make one receive
Aiiiniis	el hacer recibir	the act of making one receive
Aiiiniicat	quien hace recicbir	person who makes one receive
Aiiinimoquis	quien hizo recibir	person who made one receive
Aiiinimoquis	quien hizo recibir	person who made someone receive
Ajajot	sabroso	delicious
Ajis	saborear	to savor
Ajicat	quien prueba el sabor	person who tests the flavor
Ajimoquis	quien ha saboreado	person who has savored
Ajajis	saborear muchas vezes	to savor many times
Ajis	el saborear	the act of savoring
Ajajis	el saborear muchas veces	the act of savoring many times
Ajajicat	quien saborea muchas veces	person who savors many times
Ajajimoquis	quien ha saboreado muchas veces	person who has savored many times
Ajiniis	hacer saborear	to make one savor
Ajiniis	el hacer saborear	the act of making one savor
Ajimicat	quien hace saborear	person who makes one savor
Ajiniimoquis	quien hizo saborear	person who made one savor
Ahicho	pobre y tambien orfano	poor and also orphaned
Aiot	ladron	thief
Aiotois	robar	to rob
Aiotocat	robador	robber
Aiotomoquis	quien ha robado	person who has robbed
Aiotois	el robar	the act of robbing

109r

109v

Aiotaiotois . . . . quien siempre roba		person who always robs
Aiotaiotois . . . . el robar siempre		the act of always robbing
Aiotaiotocat . . . . quien siempre roba		person who always robs
Aiotaiotomoquis . . . . . quien siempre ha robado		person who has always robbed
Aiotoniis . . . . hacer robar		to make one rob
Aiotoniis . . . . el hacer robar		the act of making one rob
Aiotoniicat . . . . quien hace robar		person who makes one rob
Aiotoniimoquis . . . . . . el que hizo robar		he who made one rob
Aiotoniaiotoniis . . . . . hacer siempre robar		to always make one rob
Aiotoniaiotoniis . . . . . el hacer siempre robar		the act of always making one rob
Aiotoniaiotoniicat . . . . quien hace siempre robar		person who always makes one rob
Aiotoniaiotoniimoquis	quien ha hecho siempre robar	person who has always made one rob
Añis . . . . dar un golpe abajo la barba		to strike a blow under the chin
Añis . . . . el dar golpe abajo la barba		the act of striking a blow under the chin
Añicat . . . . quien da golpe abajo la barba		person who strikes a blow under the chin
Añimoquis . . . . quien dió el golpe abajo la barba		person who struck the blow under the chin
Añañis . . . . dar muchas veces el golpe abajo la barba		to strike a blow under the chin many times
Añañis . . . . el dar golpe muchas veces abajo la barba		the act of striking a blow under the chin many times
Añañicat . . . . quien da el golpe muchas veces abajo la barba		person who strikes a blow under the chin many times
Añañimoquis . . . . quien dió el golpe muchas veces abajo la barba		person who struck a blow under the chin many times

110r

Añiniis	mandar de dar el golpe abajo la barba	to order that the blow be struck under the chin
Añiniis	el mandar de dar el golpe abajo la barba	the act of ordering that a blow be struck under the chin
Añiniicat	quien manda de dar el golpe abajo la barba	person who orders that a blow be struck under the chin
Añiniimoquis	quien mandó che diese el golpe abajo la barba	person who ordered that a blow be struck under the chin
Añolaj	boracho	drunk
Añàpit	pato	duck
Al	pecho	chest
Aluiis	mirar arriba	to look up
Aluiis	el mirar arriba	the act of looking up
Alùicat	quien mira arriba, astronomo	person who looks up, an astronomer
Alùimoquis	quien ha mirado arriba	person who has looked up
Alùalùis	mirar arriba muchas veces	to look up many times
Alùalùis	el mirar arriba muchas veces	the act of looking up many times
Alùalùicat	quien mira arriba muchas veces	person who looks up many times
Alùaluimoquis	quien miro arriba muchas veces	person who looked up many times
Alùiniis	mandar que mire arriba	order that one look up
Alùiniis	el mandar que mire arriba	the act of ordering that one look up
Alùiniicat	quien manda que mire arriba	person who orders that he look upwards
Alùiniimoquis	quien hizo mirar arriba	person who made one look up
Alùinialùiniis	hacer mirar muchas veces arriba	to make one look up many times
Alùiniialùiniis	al hacer mirar muchas veces arriba	upon making one look up many times

110v

Alùiniialùiniicat	el hacer mirar muchas veces arriba	the act of making one look up many times
Alùinialùiniimoquis . . .	quien hizo mirar muchas veces arriba	person who made one look up many times
Al-Uot	el chico cuervo	the little crow
Alauis	liberal	liberal
Alauis	liberalidad	liberality [political position]
Alauimoquis	quien fué liberal	person who was liberal
Anat	hormiga	ant
Anāmmat	pescado	fish
Anò	coiote	coyote
Anquis	simil	similar
Anquis	semejanza	similarity, resemblance
111r *Amaiamal*	muchacho	boy
Ammis	descargar	to fire; to unload
Ammis	descargo	the firing/unloading
Ammicat	quien descarga	person who fires/unloads
Ammimoquis	quien descargò	person who fired/unloaded
Amamis	descarga[r] muchas veces	to fire/unload many times
Amamis	el descargar muchas veces	the act of firing/ unloading many times
Amamicat	quien descarga muchas veces	person who fires/ unloads many times
Amamimoquis	quien descargò muchas veces	person who fired/ unloaded many times
Amminis	hacer descargar	to order the firing/ unloading
Amminiis	el hacer descargar	the act of ordering the firing/unloading
Amminiicat	quien hace descargar	person who orders the firing/unloading
Amminiimoquis	quien hizo descargar	person who ordered the firing/unloading

Amminiamminiis	hacer descargar muchas veces	to order firing/unloading many times
Amminiamminiis	el hacer descargar muchas veces	the act of ordering firing/unloading many times
Amminiamminiicat . . .	quien hace descargar muchas veces	person who orders firing/unloading many times
Amminiamminiimoquis . . .	quien hizo descargar muchas veces	person who ordered firing/unloading times
Amù	ja, hace tiempo	some time ago
Amuejñai.	mañana por la mañana	tomorrow morning
Amulo.	adelante, y tambien el primero	ahead, and also the first
Amulinis	adelantar	to get ahead
Amuliniis.	el adelantar	the act of getting ahead
Amuliniicat	quien adelanta	person who gets ahead
Amuliniimoquis.	quien ha adelantado	person who has gotten ahead
Amulocat.	quien [e]stà adelante	person who is ahead
Appache	Appache, una casta de Gente	Apache, a caste of people
Amoiaj	descansado	restful or rested
Appàpais.	amplio	plentiful or wide
Aràc	es un sobrenombre de un hombre	it is a man's nickname
Aràcquis	rajar, dividir, hender	to cleave, split, or slice
Aràcquis	hendura, rajadura	cleavage or slice
Aràcquicat.	quien raja, hende	person who cleaves or slices
Aràcquimoquis	quien ha rajado	person who has sliced
Aràcaràcquis	rajar muchas veces	to slice many times
Aràcaracquis	el rajar muchas veces	the act of slicing many times
Aràcaracquicat	quien raja muchas veces	person slices many times
Aràcaràcquimocuis . . .	quien muchas veces ha rajado	person has sliced many times

111v *Amulo*

Aràcquiniaracquiniis . . mandar muchas veces de rajar	to order slicing many times
112r	*Aràcquiniaràcquiniis* . . el mandar muchas veces para que raje	the act of ordering many times that something be sliced
	Aràcquiniaràcquiniis . . el mandar muchas veces para [que] rajen	the act of ordering many times that they slice
	Aràcquiniaràcquiniicat quien manda muchas veces para que rajen	person who orders many times that they slice
	Aràcquiniaràcquiniimoquis . . quien ha mandado muchas veces para que rajen	person who has ordered many times that they slice
	Aràcquiniis . . . . mandar para que rajen	to order that they slice
	Aràcquiniis . . . . el mandar para que rajen	the act of ordering that they slice
	Aràcquiniicàt . . . . quien manda para que rajen	person who orders that they slice
	Aràcquiniimoquis . . . . quien ha mandado para que rajassen	person who has ordered that they slice
	Aràcajot . . . . rajado	sliced
	Assajis . . . . bañarse	to bathe oneself
	Assajis . . . . el bañarse	the act of bathing oneself
	Assajimoquis . . . . bañado	bathed
	Aś . . . . animal	animal
	Asnis . . . . bañar	to bathe
	Asnis . . . . baño	bath
	Asnicat . . . . quien baña	person who bathes
	Asnimoquis . . . . quien ha bañado	person who has bathed
	Assassajis . . . . bañarse muchas veces	to bathe many times
	Assassajis . . . . el bañarse muchas veces	the act of bathing many times
112v	*Assassajimoquis* . . . . . quien muchas veces se baño	person who bathed many times
	Asnis . . . . bautizar	to baptize
	Asnis . . . . bautismo	baptism

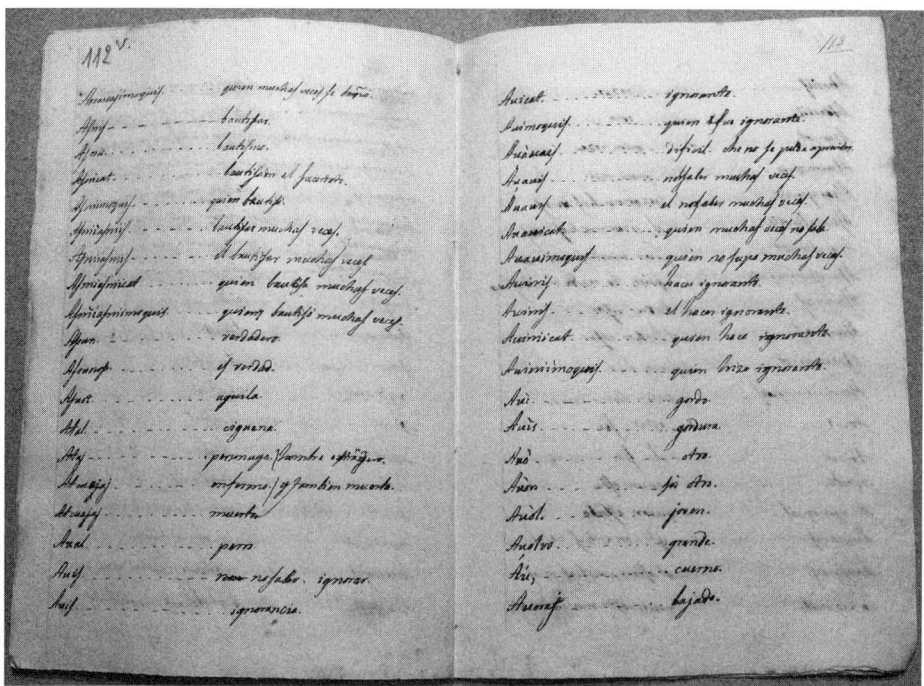

FIGURE 22. Tac's dictionary, fols. 112v–113r.

Asnicat	bautizador, el sarcerdote	baptizer, a priest
Asniimoquis	quien bautizò	person who baptized
Asniiasniis	bautizar muchas veces	to baptize many times
Asniiasniis	el bautizar muchas veces	the act of baptizing many times
Asniiasniicat	quien bautiza muchas veces	person who baptizes many times
Asniiasniimoquis	quien bautizò muchas veces	person who baptized many times
Assun	verdadero	true
Assunop	es verdad	it is true
Assuot	aguila	eagle
Atal	cigueña	stork
Ataj	personage, hombre estranjero	foreign figure, man
Atcuaiaj	enfermo y tambien muerto	sick and also dead
Atcuaiaj	muerto	dead

Aual .... perro	dog
Auis.............. no saber, ignorar	to not know, to be unaware of
Auis.............. ignorancia	ignorance
113r *Auicat* .... ignorante	ignorant
Auimoquis.......... quien fue ignorante	person who was ignorant
Auàuais .... dificil, che no se puede aprender	difficult, that which cannot be learned
Auauis............. no saber muchas veces	to not know frequently
Auauis............. el no saber muchas veces	the act of not knowing frequently
Auauicat .... quien muchas veces no sabe	person who frequently does not know
Auauimoquis........ quien no supo muchas veces	person who frequently did not know
Auinis .... hacer ignorante	make one ignorant
Auinis .... el hacer ignorante	the act of making one ignorant
Auiniicat .... quien hace ignorante	person who makes one ignorant
Auiniimoquis........ quien hizo ignorante	person who made one ignorant
Auì .... gordo	fat or thick
Auis.............. gordura	fatness
Auò............... otro	other/another
Auòn.............. soi otro	I am another/different
Auòl .... joven	young
Auolvo .... grande	big
Áú................ cuerno	horn
Auoraj............. bajado	lowered or descended
113v *Assariis* .... rezar	to pray
Assariis .... rezo	prayer
Assarcat............ quien reza	person who prays
Assarmoquis .... quien rezò	person who prayed
Assarassariis .... rezar muchas veces	to pray many times

Assarassariis	el rezar muchas veces	the act of praying many times
Assarassarcat	quien m. v. reza	person who prays many times
Assarassaramoquis . . .	quien ha rezado m. v.	person who has prayed many times
Assariniis	hacer rezar	to make one pray
Assariniis	el hacer rezar	the act of making one pray
Assariniicat	quien hace rezar	person who makes one pray
Assariniimoquis	quien hizo rezar	person who made one pray
A-uis	estar, ser	to be
A-uis	el ser	the being
Aucat	quien està	person who is
A-uimoquis	quien estubo	person who was
Aauaauis	estar muchas veces	to be many times
Aauaauis	el estar muchas veces	the act of being many times
Aauaauicat	quien está muchas veces	person who many times is

114r	*Et*	pié	foot
	Cai	no	no
	Cachiis	torcer la boca	to twist one's mouth
	Cachiis	el torcer la boca	the act of twisting one's mouth
	Cachiicat	quien tuerce la bocca	person who twists his mouth
	Cachicachiis	torcer muchas veces	to twist many times
	Cachicachiis	el torcer muchas veces	the act of twisting many times
	Cachicachicat	quien tuerce muchas veces	person who twists many times
	Cachicachiimoquis . . .	quien ha torcido muchas veces	person who has twisted many times
	Calà	un hombre vicioso, que se hace ver	a depraved man, who makes himself seen

Càliis	poner sobre	to place on top
Caliis	el poner sobre	the act of placing on top
Calicat	quien sobre pone	person who places [something] on top
Calimoquis	quien sobre puse	person who placed [something] on top
Càlcaliis	sobre poner muchas veces	to place on top many times
Calcaliis	el sobre poner muchas veces	the act of placing on top many times
Calcalicat	quien sobre pone muchas veces	person who places [something] on top many times
Calcalimoquis	quien sobre puso muchas veces	person who placed [something] on top many times
Caliniis	mandar que sobre ponga	to order that [something] be placed on top
Caliniis	el mandar que sobre ponga	the act of ordering that [something] be placed on top
Caliniicat	quien manda que sobre ponga	person who orders that [something] be placed on top
Caliniinioquis	quien mando que sobre pusiese	person who ordered that [something] be placed on top
Calajis	montar a caballo	to ride a horse
Calajis	el montar a caballo	the act of riding a horse
Calajicat	quien se monta a caballo	person who rides a horse
Calajimoquis	quien se montò a caballo	person who rode a horse
Calcalajis	montarse muchas veces a caballo	to ride a horse many times
Cálcolajis	el montarse muchas veces a caballo	the act of riding a horse many times
Calcalajimoquis	quien se monta a caballo muchas veces	person who rides a horse many times

114v — (marginal folio number beside *Caliniis . . . el mandar que sobre ponga*)

Calucluis	una gula que cae	a glutton who falls
Cajàl	cordoniz, y tambien gallina	quail, and also chicken
Cajanot	una cierta yerba, que les sirve para jabon	a certain herb that they use for soap
Camais	hijo	son
Camiis.	dejar	to leave
Camiis.	el dejar	the act of leaving
Camicat.	quien deja	person who leaves
Camiimoquis.	quien a dejado	person who has left
Camicamiis	dejar muchas veces	to leave many times
Camicamiis	el dejar muchas veces	the act of leaving many times

115r

Camicamiis	el dejar muchas veces	the act of leaving many times
Camicamiicat	quien deja muchas veces	person who leaves many times
Camicamiimoquis	quien dejò muchas veces	person who left many times
Caminiis	mandar para que deje	to order that one leave
Caminiis	el mandar para que deje	the act of ordering that one leave
Caminiicat.	quien manda para que deje	person who orders that one leave
Caminiimoquis	quien ha mandado para que dejasse	person who has ordered that one leave
Caminicaminiis	mandar muchas veces para que deje	to order many times that one leave
Caminicaminiis	el mandar muchas veces para que deje	the act of ordering many times that one leave
Caminicamincat	quien manda muchas veces para que deje	person who orders many times that one leave
Caminicaminimoquis. .	quien ha mandado muchas veces	person who has ordered many times
Camùcmuis	amontonado	heaped
Cànniis	encontrar	to meet, to find
Canniis	encuentro	meeting

Cannicat	quien encuentra	person who meets/finds
Canniimoquis	quien ha encontrado	person who has met/found
Cancaniis	encontrar muchas veces	to meet/find many times
Cancaniis	el encontrar muchas veces	the act of meeting/finding many times
115v *Cancanimoquis*	quien muchas veces encuentra	person who meets/finds many times
Caiauis	lavar	to wash
Caiauis	lavadura	washing
Caiauicat	lavador	washer
Caiauimoquis	quien ha lavado	person who has washed
Caiaucaiauis	lavar muchas veces	to wash many times
Caiaucaiauis	el lavar muchas veces	the act of washing many times
Caiaucaiauicat	quien lava muchas veces	person who washes many times
Caiaucaiauimoquis . . .	quien lavó muchas veces	person who washed many times
Caiauiniis	mandar para que lave	to order that one wash
Caiáuiniis	el mandar para que lave	the act of ordering that one wash
Caiauiniicat	quien manda para que lave	person who orders that one wash
Caiauinimoquis	quien mandó muchas veces para que lavasen	person who ordered many times that they wash
Caiauinimoquis	mandar muchas veces para que lave	to order many times that one wash
Caiauinicaiauiniis	el mandar muchas veces para que lave	the act of ordering many times that one wash
Caiauinicaiauiniicat . . .	quien manda muchas veces para que lave	person who orders many times that one wash
Caiauinicaiauiniimoquis . .	quien mandó muchas veces para que lave	person who ordered many times that one wash
Cachicchis	torcido/làdeàdo	twisted/tilted

	Camis		
116r	*Capacpais*	corto	short
	Cappariis.	romper con los dientes	to tear with one's teeth
	Cappariis.	el romper con los dientes	the act of tearing with one's teeth
	Capparimoquis	quien ha rompido con los dientes	person who has torn with his teeth
	Capparcappariis	romper muchas veces con los dientes	to tear many times with one's teeth
	Capparcappariis	el romper muchas veces con los dientes	the act of tearing many times with one's teeth
	Capparcapparimoquis .	quien muchas veces ha rompido con los dientes	person who has torn with his teeth many times
	Cappariniis	hacer romper con los dientes	to make one tear with one's teeth
	Cappariniis	el hacer romper con los dientes	the act of making one tear with one's teeth
	Cappariniimoquis	quien ha hecho romper con los	person who has made one tear with one's [teeth]
	Capparinicappariniis . .	mandar muchas veces para	to order many times that
	Capparinicappariniis . .	el mandar muchas veces para que	the act of ordering many times that
	Capparinicapparinimoquis . .	quien muchas veces ha mandado	person who has ordered many times
	Cappanniis		
	Cappanniis		
	Cappannicat		
	Cappannimoquis		
	Cappancappaniis		
	Cappancappaniis		
116v	*Cappancappanicat.* . . .		
	Cappancappanimoquis		
	Cariis	alzar una cosa	to raise something
	Cariis	el alzar, alzadura	the act of raising

Cariicat	quien alza	person who raises
Cariimoquis	quien ha alzado	person who has raised
Caricariis	alzar muchas veces	to raise many times
Caricariis	el alzar muchas veces	the act of raising many times
Caricariicat	quien muchas veces alza	person who raises many times
Caricariimoquis	quien muchas veces ha alzado	person who has raised many times
Cariis	tocar, sonar la campana	to sound, to ring the bell
Cariis	el sonar la campana	the ringing of the bell
Carricat	campanero	the bell ringer
Carrimoquis	quien ha sonado la campana	person who has rung the bell
Carcarriis	sonar muchas veces	to ring many times
Carcarriis	el sonar muchas veces	the act of ringing many times
Carcarricat	quien muchas veces suena	person who rings many times
Carcarrimoquis	quien muchas veces ha sonado	person who has rung many times
Carut	es un animal	it is an animal
Camottimoquis	quien fue silencioso	person who was silent
Camottinis	hacer que se calle	to make one be quiet
Camottiniis	el hacer que se calle	the act of making one be quiet
Camottiniicat	quien manda para que se calle	person who orders that one be quiet
Camottinimoquis	quien hizo callarse	person who made one be quiet
Camottcamottiis	muchas veces callarse	to quiet oneself many times
Camotcamottiis	el callarse muchas veces	the act of quieting oneself many times
Camotcamotticat	quien muchas veces se calla	person who quiets himself many times
Camotcamottimoquis	quien muchas veces se callò	person who quieted himself many times

117v

Catiis. . . . . Roer	to gnaw
Catiis. . . . . el Roer	the act of gnawing
Caticat. . . . . quien Roe	person who gnaws
Catimoquis . . . . quien ha roido	person who has gnawed
Catcatiis . . . . Roer muchas veces	to gnaw many times
Catcatiis . . . . el Roer muchas veces	the act of gnawing many times
Catcaticat . . . . quien Roe muchas veces	person who gnaws many times
Catcatimoquis . . . . quièn ha roido muchas veces	person who has gnawed many times
Catiniis . . . . hacer roer	to make one gnaw
Catiniis . . . . el hacer roer	the act of making one gnaw

118r   *Catappiis*

Catappiis

Catappimoquis

Cataptatappiis

Cataptatappiis

Catapcatapimoquis

Catappiniis

Catappiniis

Catappiniis

Catappinimoquis

Cau-uis

Cau-uis

Cauimoquis

Caucauis

Caucauis

Caucauimoquis

Cauiniis

Cauiniis

Cauiniimoquis

118v   *Cauattis*

Cauattiis

Cauattiicat

Cauattimoquis

Cauattcauattiis

Cauattcauattiis

Cauattcauatticat

Cauattcauattimoquis

Cauattiniis

Cauattiniis

Cauattiniicat

Cauattiniimoquis

Cauattajot

Caualiis

Caualiis

Caualicat

Caualimoquis

Caualcaualiis

Caualcaualiis

Caualauis

119r *Caualcaualicat*

Caualcaualimoquis

Caualiniis

Caualiniis

Caualiniicat

Caualiinimoquis

Caualinicaualiniis

Caualinicaualiniis

Caualinicalinicat

Caualinicaualiniimoquis

Caualajot

Cauacuais

Cauialuot . . . . cuervo   raven

Cauicha . . . . monte   wooded mountain
                                                          or hill

Cauis . . . . monte   wooded mountain or
                                                          hill

Caquis	hacer la voz del cuervo	to mimic the caw of a raven
Caquis	el hacer la voz del cuervo	the act of mimicking the caw of a raven
Caquimoquis	quien hizo como la voz del cuervo	person who mimicked the caw of a raven
Caquinis	mandar que haga como la voz del cuervo	to order that one mimic the caw of a raven
119v *Caquiniis*	el mandar que haga como la voz del cuervo	the act of ordering that one mimic the caw of a raven
Caquiniimoquis	quien mandó para que hiciese	person who ordered that [the caw of a raven be mimicked]
Càccaquis	hacer muchas veces la voz del cuervo	to mimic many times the caw of a raven
Càccaquis	el hacer muchas veces la voz del cuervo	the act of mimicking many times the caw of a raven
Càccaquimoquis	quien hizo muchas veces la voz del cuervo	person who made the caw of a raven many times
Chat	buho	owl
Chabiis	despolvorear	to remove dust
Chabiis	el despolvorear	the act of removing dust
Chabicat	quien despolvorea	person who removes dust
Chabimoquis	quien ha despolvoreado	person who has removed dust
Chabchabiis	despolverar muchas veces	to remove dust many times
Chabchabiis	el despolverear muchas veces	the act of removing dust many times
Chabchabicat	quien despolverea muchas veces	person who removes dust many times
Chabchabimoquis	quien muchas veces ha despolvereado	person who has removed dust many times

Chabiniis	mandar para que despolveree	to order that dust be removed
Chabiniis	el mandar para que despolveree	the act of ordering that dust be removed
Chabiniicat	quien manda para que depolveree	person who orders that dust be removed
Chabiniimoquis	quien ha mandado para despolverear	person who has ordered that dust be removed
Chacquis	cortar una parte sola	to cut a single portion
Chàcquis	el cortar una sola parte	the act of cutting a single portion
Chàcquicat	el cortador	the cutter
Chàcquimoquis	quien ha cortado	person who has cut
Chàcchaquis	cortar muchas veces	to cut many times
Chàcchacquis	el cortar muchas veces	the act of cutting many times
Chàcchaquicat	quien muchas veces corta	person who cuts many times
Chàcchaquimoquis . . .	quien muchas veces ha cortado	person who has cut many times
Chàcquiniis	mandar para que corte	to order that one cut
Chàcquiniis	el mandar para que corte	the act of ordering that one cut
Chàcquiniicat	quien manda para que corte	person who orders that one cut
Chàcquiniimoquis	quien ha mandado para que cortase	person who has ordered that something be cut
Chàccuis	coger, agarrar	to take, to grab
Chaccuis	el coger	the act of taking
Chaccuicat.	quien agarra	person who grabs
Chaccuimoquis	quien ha agarrado	person who has grabbed
Chacuchacuis	agarrar muchas veces	to grab many times
Chacuchacuis	el agarrar muchas veces	the act of grabbing many times
Chacuchacuicat	quien agarra muchas veces	person who grabs many times
Chacuchacuimoquis . .	quien muchas veces ha agarrado	person who has grabbed many times

120r

120v	*Chàcajis*	llorar	to cry
	Chàcajis	lloro	the act of crying
	Chàcajimoquis	quien ha llorado	person who has cried
	Chàquis.	hacer llorar	to make one cry
	Chaaquis.	el hacer llorar	the act of making one cry
	Chaquicat	quien hace llorar	person who makes one cry
	Chaaquimoquis.	quien hizo llorar	person who made one cry
	Chacaiis	el ladear	the act of tilting
	Chacaiimoquis	quien ha ladeado	person who has tilted
	Chacàchaiis.	ladear muchas veces	to tilt many times
	Chacàchaiis.	el ladear muchas veces	the act of tilting many times
	Chacàchaimoquis	quien ha ladeado muchas veces	person who has tilted many times
	Chañilajis	festejar, hacer fiesta	to celebrate, to hold a celebration
	Chañilajis	festejo	celebration
	Chañilis.	hacer fiesta	to hold a celebration
	Chañilcat.	quien hace fiesta	person who holds a celebration
	Chañilimoquis.	quien hizo fiesta	person who held a celebration
121r	*Chanichñis*	Dios	God
	Chàñis		
	Chaññis		
	Chaññimoquis		
	Chaññchaññiis		
	Chaññchaññiis		
	Chaññchaññimoquis		
	Chaññiniis		
	Chaññiniis		
	Chaññiniimoquis		
	Chammiis		
	Chammiis		

Chammimoquis

Chamchammiis

Chamchammis

Chamchammimoquis

Chamminiis

Chamminiis

Chamminiimoquis

121v *Chammij* . . . . nuestro y nuestra our [m.] and our [f.]

Chappis. . . . . acavar de llover to stop raining

Chappiis . . . . el acavar de llover the act of rain stopping

Chappicat . . . . quien hace parar la lluvia person who makes the rain stop

Chappimoquis. . . . . . . el que hizo he who made [the rain stop]

Chapchapiis

Chapchapiis

Chapchapicat

Chapchapimoquis

Chappiniis

Chappiniis

Chappiniicat

Chappiniimoquis

Chappàquis, unir, to unify

C[h]appaquis, el unir, the act of unifying

122r *Chappacquicat* . . . . . . quien une person who unites

Chappacquimoquis . . . quien ha unido person who has united

Chappachappacquis . . unir muchas veces to unite many times

Chappacchappacquis. . el unir muchas veces the act of uniting many times

Chappacchappaquicat quien ha unido muchas veces person who has united many times

Chappacchappaquimoquis . . quien muchas veces ha unido person who many times has united

Chappacquiniis . . . . . . mandar para que una to order that one unite

Chappacquiniis . . . . . . el mandar para que una the act of ordering that one unite

Chappacquimoquicat	quien manda para [que] unan	person who orders that they unite
Chappacquimoquimoquis . .	quien ha mandado para que uniesen	person who has ordered that they unite
Chappacajit	unido	united
Chacquis	Agarar	to grab
Chacquis	el agarar	the act of grabbing
Chacquicat	quien agara	person who grabs
Chacquimoquis	quien ha agarado	person who has grabbed
Charriis	romper	to tear, to break
Charriis	el romper	the act of tearing/breaking
Charricat	quien rompe	person who tears/breaks
Charrimoquis	quien ha rompido	person who has torn/broken
Characharriis	romper muchas veces	to tear/break many times
Characharriis	el romper muchas veces	the act of tearing/breaking many times
Charachariicat	quien rompe muchas veces	person who tears/breaks many times
Charachariimoquis . . .	quien ha rompido muchas veces	person who has torn/broken many times
Charriniis	mandar para que rompa	to order that one tear/break
Charriniis	el mandar para que rompa	the act of ordering that one tear/break
Chariniicat	quien manda para que rompa	person who orders that one tear/break
Chariniimoquis	quien ha mandado para que rompese	person who has ordered that they tear/break
Charrajot	rompido	torn/broken
Chat		
Chauis		
Chauis	desechar	to throw out, to reject
Chauicat	el que desecha	he who rejects

122v (row: *Charriis* . . . romper)

123r (row: *Chauis* . . . desechar)

Chauimoquis........ quien ha desechado   person who has
                                              rejected

Chauchauis ....

Chauchauis .... el desechar muchas veces   the act of rejecting
                                                   many times

Chauchauicat .... quien desecha muchas veces   person who rejects
                                                     many times

Chachauimoquis ..... quien ha desechado muchas   person who has
                                 veces   rejected many times

Chauiniis.......... mandar que deseche   to order that one reject

Chauiniis.......... el mandar para que deseche   the act of ordering that
                                                    one reject

Chauiniicat .... quien manda que deseche   person who orders that
                                                  one reject

Chauiniimoquis......

Chauinichauiniis .....

Chauinichauiniis .....

Chauinichauiniimoquis

Chauinichauiniicat ...

123v   *Chacuot* ....

Chauaiis ....

Chauaiis .... abrir la palma   open the palm

Chauaiimoquis ...... quien la ha abierta   person who has opened
                                              it [the palm]

Chauaichauais....... abrirla muchas veces   to open it [the palm]
                                               many times

Chauaichauaiis ......

Chauaichauaiicat.....

Chauaichauaimoquis..

Chauaiiniis ....

Chauaiiniis ....

Chauaiiniicat........

Chauaiiniimoquis ....

Chauach ....

Chauais...........

Chalat ....

Chalaliis . . . . hacer andar agachado   to make one dance bent
                             bailando   over

124r   *Chalaliis*

       Chalalicat

       Chalalimoquis

       Chalalchalaliis

       Chalalchaliis

       Chalalchalicat

       Chalalchalimoquis

       Chalalajis

       Chalalajis

       Chalalajimoquis

       Chalalchalalajis

       Chalalchalalajis

       Chalalchalalajimoquis

       Chalaquis . . . . despegar   to unstick, to detach

       Chalaquis

124v   *Chalaquicat*

       Chalaquimoquis

       Chalacchalaquis

       Chalacchalaquis

       Chalacchalaquicat

       Chalacchalaquimoquis

       Chalaquiniis

       Chalaquiniis

       Chalaquicat

       Chalaquimoquis

       Chalacajis . . . . depegarse   to come unstuck

       Chalacajis

       Chalacajimoquis

       Chalacchalacajis

       Chalacchalacajis

125r   *Chalacchalacajimoquis*

       Chapiis

       Chapiis

Chapchapiis

Chapchapiis

Chapiniis

Chapiniis

Chapiniicat

Chapiniimoquis

Chapinichapiniis

Chapinichapiniis

Chapiniichapicat

Chapinichapiniimoquis

Chapàquis	unir		to unite, to join
126r	*Chèbiis*	reventar, contar	to burst, to recount
	Chèbiis	el reventar	the act of bursting
	Chebimoquis	quien ha reventado	person who has burst/recounted
	Chèbiniis	hacer reventar	to make something burst
	Chèbiniis	el hacer reventar	the act of making something burst
	Chebiniimoquis	el que hizo reventar	he who made something burst
	Chèbchebiis	reventar muchas veces	to burst many times
	Chèbchebiis	el reventar muchas veces	the act of bursting many times
	Chèchebimoquis	quien ha reventado muchas veces	person who has burst many times
	Chebinichebiniis	hacer reventar muchas veces	to make something burst many times
	Chebinichebiniis	el hacer reventar muchas veces	the act of making something burst many times
	Chebinichebiniimoquis	quien hizo muchas veces reventar	person who made something burst many times
	Chabajis	reventarse	to break
	Chabajis	el reventarse	the act of breaking oneself
	Chabajimoquis	el que se ha reventado	he who has broken himself

126v	*Chebchebajis*	reventarse muchas veces	to break oneself many times
	Chebchebajis	el reventarse muchas veces	the act of breaking oneself many times
	Chebchebajimoquis . . .	el que se reventò muchas veces	he who broke himself many times
	Cheic	daca, dà acà	give that here
	Cheiat	es cosa que ponen en la cabeza para bailar, echa toda de plumas	it is a thing they put on their heads for dancing, made entirely of feathers
	Cheiis	vestir de esta cosa para bailar	to dress in this thing for dancing
	Cheiis	el vestir	the act of dressing
	Cheiicat	quien veste	person who dresses
	Cheiimoquis	quien ha vestido	person who has dressed
	Cheicheiis	vestir muchas veces	to dress many times
	Cheicheiis	el vestir muchas veces	the act of dressing many times
	Cheicheiicat	quien veste muchas veces	person who dresses many times
	Cheicheiimoquis	quien ha vestido muchas veces	person who has dressed many times
	Cheiajis	vestirse	to dress oneself
	Cheiajis	el vestirse	the act of dressing oneself
127r	*Cheiajimoquis*	quien se ha v[est]ido	person who has dressed himself
	Cheicheiajis	vestirse muchas veces	to dress oneself many times
	Cheicheiajimoquis	quien muchas veces se ha vestido	person who has dressed himself many times
	Cheeniis	trasquilar, cortar	to shear, to cut
	Cheeniis	trasquiladura	the shearing
	Cheeniicat	trasquilador	shearer
	Cheeniimoquis	quien ha trasquilado	person who has shorn
	Cheencheeniis	trasquilar muchas veces	to shear many times
	Cheencheeniis	el trasquilar muchas veces	the act of shearing many times

Cheencheeniicat	quien trasquila muchas veces	person who shears many times
Cheencheeniimoquis . .	quien ha trasquilado muchas veces	person who has shorn many times
Cheliis	empujar	to push
Cheliis	empujè	I pushed
Chelimoquis	quien ha empujado	person who has pushed
Chelcheliis	empujar muchas veces	to push many times
Chelchelimoquis	quien ha empujado muchas veces	person who has pushed many times
Cheliniis	hacer que empuje	to make one push
Cheliniis	el hacer que empuje	the act of making one push
Cheliniimoquis	quien ha hecho empujar	person who has made one push
Chepiis	dar fuego a una casa	to set a house on fire
Chepiis	el dar fuego	the act of setting on fire
Chepicat	quien da fuego	person who sets on fire
Chepimoquis	quien ha dado fuego	person who has set on fire
Chepchepiis	dar muchas veces fuego	to set on fire many times
Chepchepiis	el dar muchas veces	the act of setting [on fire] many times
Chepchepicat	quien da muchas veces	person who sets [on fire] many times
Chepchepimoquis	quien da muchas veces	person who sets [on fire] many times
Chepiniis	hacer dar fuego	to make one set on fire
Chepiniis	el hacer dar fuego	the act of making one set on fire
Chepiniimoquis	quien hace dar fuego	person who makes one set on fire
Chepéquis	pegar	to hit
Chepéquis	el pegar	the act of hitting
Cheqepuicat	quien pega	person who hits
Chepequimoquis	quien ha pegado	person who has hit
Chepeqchepequis	pegar muchas veces	to hit many times

127v (beside *Chelchelimoquis*)

128r (beside *Chepéquis*)

Chepeqchepequis. . . . . el pegar muchas veces	the act of hitting many times
Chepeqchepequicat . . . quien pega muchas veces	person who hits many times
Chepeqchepequimoquis . . quien ha pegado muchas veces	person who has hit many times
Chepequiniis . . . . hacer pegar muchas veces	to make one hit many times
Chepequiniis . . . . el hacer pegar muchas veces	the act of making one hit many times
Chepequiniicat . . . . . . quien hace pegar muchas veces	person who makes one hit many times
Chepequiniimoquis . . . quien ha pegado muchas veces	person who has hit many times
Chepequinichepequiniis . . hacer pegar muchas veces	to make one hit many times
Chepequinichepequiniis . . el hacer pegar muchas veces	the act of making one hit many times
Chepequinichepequiniimoquis . . quien hizo pegar muchas veces	person who made one hit many times

128v   *Chejñais* . . . . lado   side

Chiuis . . . . vencer	to vanquish, to defeat
Chiuis . . . . victoria	victory
Chiuicat . . . . victorioso	victorious
Chiuimo . . . . quien ha vencido	person who has vanquished
Chiuichiuis . . . . vencer muchas veces	to vanquish many times
Chiuichiuis . . . . el vencer muchas veces	the act of vanquishing many times
Chiuchiuicat . . . . quien vence muchas veces	person who vanquishes many times
Chiuchiuimoquis . . . . . quien ha vencido muchas veces	person who has vanquished many times
Chiuiniis . . . . hacer vencer	to make one vanquish
Chiuiniis . . . . el hacer vencer	the act of making one vanquish
Chiuiniicat . . . . quien hace vencer	person who makes one vanquish

Chiuiniimoquis . . . . . . quien hizo vencer		person who made one vanquish
Chidiis. . . . . sonar un strumento para que bailen		to play an instrument so that they may dance
Chidicat . . . . quien toca		person who plays
Chidiis. . . . . el instrumento		the instrument
Chidiis. . . . . el sonar		the act of playing [music]
Chidicat . . . . el sonador		the player
Chidimoquis . . . . quien ha sonado		person who has played
Chidchidiis . . . . sonar muchas veces		to play many times
Chidchidiis . . . . el sonar muchas veces		the act of playing many times
Chidchidicat . . . . quien sona muchas veces		person who plays many times
Chidchidimoquis . . . . . quien ha sonado muchas veces		person who has played many times
Chidiniis . . . . mandar que suene		to order that one play
Chidiniis . . . . el mandar sonar		the act of ordering that one play
Chidiniimoquis. . . . . . quien ha mandado		person who has ordered
Chilcuat . . . . vaso (es echo con ciertas yerbas y les sirve para beber agua y otras cosas liquidas)		cup (it is made of certain herbs and they use it to drink water and other liquids)
Chiliis . . . . rociar		to sprinkle with liquid
Chiliis . . . . el rociar		the act of sprinkling liquid
Chilicat . . . . quien rocia		person who sprinkles liquid
Chilimoquis. . . . . quien ha roceado		person who has sprinkled liquid
Chiliniis. . . . . mandar para que rocee		to order that one sprinkle liquid
Chiliniis. . . . . el mandar para que rocee		the act of ordering that one sprinkle liquid
Chiliniimocuis . . . . . . quien ha mandado para que rocease		person who has ordered that one sprinkle liquid

129r

129v

Chilchiliis	rocear muchas veces	to sprinkle liquid many times
Chilchiliis	el rocear muchas veces	the act of sprinkling liquid many times
Chilchilimocuis	quien muchas veces ha roceado	person who has sprinkled liquid many times
Chilqquis.	desgranar	to thresh (remove the grain)
Chilicquicat.	quien desgrana	person who threshes
Chiliquimocuis	quien ha desgranado	person who has threshed
Chilichilicquiis.	desgranar pronto	to thresh quickly
Chilicchilicquiis.	el desgranar pronto	the act of threshing quickly
Chilicchilicquimocuis	quien ha desgranado pronto	person who has threshed quickly
Chilicquiniis	hacer desgranar	to make one thresh
Chilicquiniis	el hacer desgranar	the act of making one thresh
Chilicquiniicat.	quien hace desgranar	person who makes one thresh
Chilicquimoquis	quien hizo desgranar	person who made one thresh
Chicquis	partir	to depart
Chicquis	el partir	the act of departing
Chicquicat.	quien hace partir	person who makes one depart
Chicquimoquis	quien hizo partir	person who made one depart
Chicchiquis	partir muchas veces	to depart many times
Chicchiquis	el partir muchas veces	the act of departing many times
Chicchiquimoquis	quien ha partido muchas veces	person who has departed many times
Chiquiniis	hacer partir	to make one depart
Chiquiniis	el hacer partir	the act of making one depart

130r

Chiquiniimoquis . . . . . quien hizo partir	person who made one depart
Chippiis. . . . . quebrar	to break
Chippiis. . . . . el quebrar	the act of breaking
130v	*Chippimocuis* . . . . quien ha quebrado	person who has broken
Chippiniis . . . . hacer quebrar	to make one break
Chippiniis . . . . el hacer quebrar	the act of making one break
Chippiniimocuis . . . . . quien hizo quebrar	person who made one break
Chippchippiis . . . . quebrar muchas veces	to break many times
Chippchippiis . . . . el quebrar muchas veces	the act of breaking many times
Chippchippiimocuis. . . quien ha quebrado muchas veces	person who has broken many times
Chippilippis. . . . . hacer todo en pedazos	to shatter
Chippilippiis . . . . el hacer todo en pedazos	the act of shattering
Chippilippimocuis . . . . quien hizo en pedazos	person who shattered
Chippajis. . . . . quebrarse	to be broken
Chippajis. . . . . el quebrarse	the act of being broken
Chippajimocuis . . . . . . lo que se quebrò	that which broke
Chippchippajis . . . . . . quebrarse muchas veces	to be broken many times
Chippchippajis . . . . . . el quebrarse muchs veces	the act of being broken many times
131r	*Chippchippajimocuis.* . lo que muchas veces se quebrò	that which was broken many times
Chicaajis . . . . arrodillarse	to kneel down
Chicaajis . . . . el arrodillarse	the act of kneeling down
Chicaajimocuis . . . . . . arrodillado	kneeling
Chicaachicaajis . . . . . . arrodillarse muchas veces	to kneel down many times
Chicaachicaajis . . . . . . el arrodillarse muchas veces	the act of kneeling down many times
Chicaachicaajimocuis	quien se ha arrodillado muchas veces	person who has knelt down many times
Chicais . . . . arrodillar	to kneel

Chicais . . . . el arrodillar	the act of kneeling
Chicaimocuis. . . . . quien ha arrodillado	person who has knelt
Chicàchicais . . . . arrodillar muchas veces	to kneel many times
Chicachicais . . . . el arrodillar muchas veces	the act of kneeling many times
Chicachicaimocuis. . . . quien ha arrodillado muchas veces	person who has knelt many times
Chicachacquis . . . . hacer arrodillar	to make one kneel
Chicachacquis . . . . el hacer arrodillar	the act of making one kneel
131v *Chicachacquimocuis* . . quien hizo arrodillar	person who made one kneel

Chicalaajis

Chicalaajis

Chicalaajimocuis

Chicalàchicalaajis

Chicalàchicalaajis

Chicalàchicalaajimocuis

Chicalais

Chicalais

Chicalaimocuis

Cittis

Chittis

Chittimocuis

Chittiniis

Chittiniis

132r   *Chittiniis*

Chittiniimocuis

Chitchittiis

Chitchittiis

Chitchitimocuis

Chiuuis . . . . vencer, ganar	to vanquish, to win
Chiuuis . . . . victoria, ganancia	a victory, a win
Chiuuicat . . . . vencedor	the victor
Chiuuimocuis . . . . quien ha vencido	person who has vanquished

Chiuuiniis . . . . hacer que venza	to make one vanquish
Chiuiniis . . . . el hacer vencer	the act of making one vanquish
Chiuuiniicat . . . . quien hace vencer	person who makes one vanquish
Chiuuimocuis . . . . quien hizo vencer	person who made one vanquish
Chiuchiuuis . . . . vencer muchas veces	to vanquish many times
Chiuchiuuis . . . . el vencer muchas veces	the act of vanquishing many times

132v	*Choccajot* . . . . cargado	loaded
	Choon . . . . todo	all
	Chocquis . . . . cargar	to load
	Chocquis . . . . el cargar	the act of loading
	Chocquicat . . . . quien carga	person who loads
	Chocquimoquis . . . . . . quien ha cargado	person who has loaded
	Chocquiniis . . . . hacer cargar	to make one load
	Chocquiniis . . . . el hacer cargar	the act of making one load
	Chocquiniicat . . . . quien hace cargar	person who makes one load
	Chocquiniimocuis . . . . quien hizo cargar	person who made one load
	Chocchoquis . . . . cargar	to carry
	Chocchoquis . . . . el cargar	the act of carrying
	Chocchoquicat . . . . . . quien carga	person who carries
	Chocchoquimocuis . . . quien ha cargado	person who has carried
	Chorquilais . . . . lugar endonde se juega alla rueda; billarda	place where one plays with the hoop or wheel; game with sticks

133r	*Chorriis*
	Chorriis
	Chorrmocuis
	Chorchoriis
	Chorchoriis
	Chorchorimocuis

Choriniis			
Choriniis			
Choriiniimocuis			
Choròiis	medir	to measure	
Choròiis	el medir	the act of measuring	
Choròiicat	quien mide, geometra	person who measures, geometer	
Choroquilais	barra, geometria	bar, geometry	
Choròimocuis	quien ha medido	person who has measured	
Choròiniis	hacer medir	to make one measure	
133v *Choròiniis*	el hacer medir	the act of making one measure	
Choròiniimocuis	quien hizo medir	person who made one measure	
Choròchoròis	medir muchas veces	to measure many times	
Choròchoròis	el medir muchas veces	the act of measuring many times	
Choròchoròimocuis	quien ha medido	person who has measured	
Chori-iis	cortar	to cut	
Chor-iis	el cortar	the act of cutting	
Chor-imocuis	quien ha cortado	person who has cut	
Chor-chor-iis	cortar muchas veces	to cut many times	
Chor-chor-iis	el cortar muchas veces	the act of cutting many times	
Chor-chor-imocuis	quien ha cortado muchas veces	person who has cut many times	
Chorrajis	ir como la rueda	to go like a wheel	
Chorrajis			
Chorrajimocuis			
Chorchorrajis			
134r *Chorchorajis*	ir como la rueda	to go like a wheel	
Chorchorajimocuis			
Choon	todo	all	
Choruot	animal del agua que corta	water animal that cuts	

Chojajis . . . . aparecerse	to appear
Chojajis . . . . aparecimiento	appearance
Chojajimocuis . . . . aparecido	appeared
Chojchojajiis . . . . aparecer muchas veces	to appear many times
Chojchojajis . . . . el aparecer muchas veces	the act of appearing many times
Chojchojajimocuis. . . . quien es aparecido muchas veces	person who has appeared many times
Chojiniis . . . . hacer que aparezca	to make one appear
Chojiniis . . . . el hacer que aparesca	the act of making one appear
Chojiniimocuis . . . . . . quien hizo que apareciese	person who made one appear
Chojinichojiniis . . . . . . hacer muchas veces aparecer	to make one appear many times
Chojinichojiniimocuis quien hizo muchas veces que apareciese	person who made one appear many times
134v *Chojis* . . . . hacer que aparezca	to make one appear
Chojis . . . . el hacer que aparezca	the act of making one appear
Chojicat . . . . quien hace aparecer	person who makes one appear
Chojimocuis . . . . quien hizo que apareciese	person who made one appear
Chocorrajot	
Chocorris . . . . hacer como monte	to make like a mountain or wooded hill
Chocorris	
Chocorrimocuis.	
Chocorchocorris	
Chocorchocorris	
Chocorcho[cor]rimocuis	
Chorrajot . . . . redondo	round
Chuñis. . . . . mamar	to suckle
Chuñis. . . . . el mamar	the act of suckling
Chuñicat . . . . quien mama	person who suckles

FIGURE 23. Tac's dictionary, fols. 134v–135r.

135r			
	Chuñimocuis	quien ha mamado	person who has suckled
	Cuñchuñis	mamar muchas veces	to suckle many times
	Chuñchuñis	el mamar muchas veces	the act of suckling many times
	Chuññchuñimocuis . . .	quien ha mamado muchas veces	person who has suckled many times
	Chuññiniis	hacer que mame	to make one suckle
	Chuññiniis	el hacer que mame	the act of making one suckle
	Chuññiniimocuis	quien hizo para que mamase	person who made one suckle
	Chujis	escupir	to spit
	Chùjis	gargajo	phlegm
	Chujimocuis	quien ha escupido	person who has spit
	Chujchujis	escupir muchas veces	to spit many times

Chujchujis	el escupir muchas veces	the act of spitting many times
Chujchujmocuis.	quien ha escupido muchas veces	person who has spit many times
Chujiniis	hacer que escupa	to make one spit
Chujiniis	el hacer que escupa	the act of making one spit

135v *Chuppiis*

Chuppiis

Chuppimocuis

Chupchuppiis

Chupchuppiis

Chupchuppimocuis

Chuppiniis

Chuppiniis

Chuppiniimocuis

Chupuis.	cerar los ojos	to close one's eyes
Chupuis.	el cerar los ojos	the act of closing one's eyes
Chupùimocuis.	quien ha cerado los ojos	person who has closed his eyes
Chupùchupuis.	cerar muchas veces los ojos	to close one's eyes many times
Chupùchupuis.	el cerar muchas veces lo ojos	the act of closing one's eyes many times
Chupùchupùimocuis . .	quien ha cerado muchas veces los ojos	person who has closed his eyes many times

136r *Chupùajis*	el cerrarse dellos ojos	the act of closing one's eyes
Churrajis	ir abajo	to go underneath

Churrajis . . . .

Churrajimocus. . . . .

Churchurrajis . . . .

Churchurrajis . . . .

Churchurrajimocuis. . . .

Churris	echar algo de arriba	to throw something from above

Churris . . . .

Churris . . . .

Churiimocuis. . . . .

Churchurris. . . . .

Churchuris . . . .

Churchurimocuis. . . . .

Churiniis . . . .

136v   Churiniis

Churiniis

Churiniimocuis

Churecquis . . . . quitar el hilo al arco   to remove the string
                                                             from a bow

Churecquis

Churecquimocuis

Churecchurecquis

Churecchurecquis

Churecchurecquimocuis

Churecquiniis

Churecquiniis

Churecquiniimocuis

Chureccajot

Chuiis . . . . quemar   to burn

Chuiis . . . . el quemar   the act of burning

137r   Chuiimocuis . . . . quien ha quemado   person who has burned

Chuichuiis

Chuichuiis

Chuichuiis

Chuichumocuis

Chuiniis

Chuiniis

Chuiiniimocuis

Chuiajis. . . . . quemarse   to burn oneself

Chuiajis

Chuiajimocuis

Chuichuiajis

	Chuichuiajis		
	Chuichuiajimocuis		
	Chuiajot . . . . quemado		burnt
137v	*Cobbajis* . . . . caerse		to fall
	Cobbajis		
	Cobbajimouiuiom		
	Cobbhobbajis		
	Cobbebajis		
	Cobcobajimociom		
	Cobbis. . . . . hacer caer		to make one fall
	Cobbiis,		
	Cobbiis,		
	Cobbimocuis		
	Cobbiniis. . . . . mandar que alcuno haga caer		to order that someone fall
	Cobbiniis,		
	Cobbiniimocuis		
138r	*Cobcobbiis* . . . . hacer caer muchas veces		to make one fall many times
	Cobcobiis . . . . el hacer caer muchas veces		the act of making one fall many times
	Còis. . . . . morder		to bite
	Còis. . . . . el morder		the act of biting
	Còimocuis. . . . . quien ha mordido		person who has bitten
	Còocòis. . . . . morder muchas veces		to bite many times
	Còocòis. . . . . el morder muchas veces		the act of biting many times
	Còocòimocuis . . . . quien ha mordido muchas veces		person who has bitten many times
	Còiniis. . . . . hacer que muerda		to make one bite
	Còiiniis . . . . el hacer que muerda		the act of making one bite
	Còiniimocuis. . . . . quien hizo morder		person who made one bite
	Coiniconiis . . . . hacer que muchas veces muerda		to make one bite many times
	Coiniconis. . . . . el hacer que muchas veces muerda		the act of making one bite many times

Coinicoiniimocuis	quien hizo que muchas veces mordiese	person who has made one bite many times
Còchis	cocer	to cook
Còchis	el cocer	the act of cooking
Còchicat	quien coce	person who cooks
Còchimocuis	quien ha cozido	person who has cooked
Còchcochis	cocer muchas veces	to cook many times
Còchcachis	el cocer muchas veces	the act of cooking many times
Còchcochimocuis	quien muchas veces ha cocido	person who has cooked many times
Còchiniis	hacer cocer	to make one cook
Còchiniis	el hacer cocer	the act of making one cook
Còchiniimocuis	quien hizo cocer	person who made one cook
Colauot	palo	stick
Colauquis		
Colauquis	traher madera	to bring lumber
Colauquicat.		
Colauquimocuis		
Colanuiniis		
Colanuiniis		

138v (left margin, at *Còchicat*)

139r (left margin)
Colàuiniimocuis

Colajis

Colajis

Còlajimocuis

Colcolajis

Colcolajis

Colcolajimocuis

Coliis.	hacer caer lagrimas de los ojos por el hume	to make tears fall from one's eyes because of smoke

Còliis

Colimocuis

Colimocuis

Coliniis

Coliniis

Coliniimocuis

Colcoliis

Colcoliis . . . .

139v *Coiouot* . . . . ballena   whale

Conòcnois . . . . verde   green

Conniis . . . .

Conniis . . . .

Connimocuis . . . .

Conconnis . . . .

Conconnis . . . .

Conconnimocuis . . . . .

Cononis . . . . hacer que sea verde   to make it green

Cononis . . . . el hacer que sea verde   the act of making it
                                                               green

Cononimocuis . . . . quien hizo que fuesse verde   person who made it
                                                               green

Cononcononiis . . . . . . hacer muchas veces que   to make it green many
                            sea verde   times

Cononcononiis . . . . . . el hacer muchas veces que   the act of making it
                            sea verde   green many times

Cononcononimocuis . . quien hizo muchas veces   person who made it
                         que fuesse verde   green many times

Comale . . . . pizarra   slate, chalkboard

140r *Corrorajis* . . . . levantarse   to rise, to get up

Corrorajis . . . .

Corrorajimoquis . . . . .

Coppiis . . . . golperear la cabeza   to strike one's head

Coppiis

Coppimocuis

Coppimocuis

Copcoppiis

Copcoppiis

Copcoppimocuis

Coppiniis

Coppiniis

Coppiniimocuis

Coppajis

Coppajis . . . . golpear la cabeza   to strike one's head

140v   *Coppajimocuis*

Corrorcorrorajis

Corrorcorrorajis

Corrorcorrorajimocuis

Cossajot . . . . dulce   sweet

Cosis . . . . endulzar   to sweeten

Cosis

Cosimocuis

Cocosis

Coscosis

Coscosimocuis

Cosiniis

Cosiniis

Cossiniimocuis

Cubatis . . . . limpiar   to clean

141r   *Cubatis*

Cubaticat

Cubatimocuis

Cubiis . . . . limpiar   to clean

Cubiis

Cubimocuis

Cubatiniis

Cubatiniis

Cubatiniimocuis

Cucubis

Cubcubis

Cubcubinimocuis

Cubatcubatiis

Cubatcubatimocuis

141v   *Cuijiis*

Cuijiis

Cujisnacuis

Cujcujis

Cujcujis

Cujcujimocuis

Cùiis

Cùiis

Cùimocuis

Cùicuiis

Cuicuimocuis

Cuicuiis

Cuicuiis

Cuicuiniimocuis

Cuiajot

142r	*Cuñis*	esposo	husband
	Cuña	en el fuego	in the fire
	Cuñauis	del fuego	of the fire, from the fire
	Culaclais	hombre sin verguenza	shameless man
	Culajot	sacada	removed
	Culiis	sacar	to remove
	Culiis	el sacar	the act of removing
	Culimocuis		
	Culuculiis		
	Culuculiis		
	Culuculamocuis		
	Culiniis		
	Culiniis		
	Culiniimocuis		
	Culajis	sacarse	to remove oneself
142v	*Culajis*	el sacarse	the act of removing oneself
	Culajimocuis	quien ha sacado	person who has removed
	Cuaat	mosca, gusano	fly, caterpillar
	Cualmais	debajo el brazo	below the arm

Cupuajis	dormir	to sleep
Cupuajis	el dormir	the act of sleeping
Cupuajimocuis	quien ha dormido	person who has slept
Cupùcupùajis	dormir muchas veces	to sleep many times
Cupùcupùajis	el dormir muchas veces	the act of sleeping many times
Cupuis.	hacer que duerma	to make one sleep
Cupuis.	el hacer que duerma	the act of making one sleep
Cupùimocuis.	quien hizo dormir	person who made one sleep
Cupùcupùis	hacer muchas veces dormir	to make one sleep many times
Cupùcupùis	el hacer muchas veces dormir	the act of making one sleep many times
Cupùcupùimocuis	quien hizo muchas veces dormir	person who made one sleep many times

Index

Italic page numbers indicate illustrations.

TEXT
10/13 Sabon Open Type

DISPLAY
Sabon Open Type

COMPOSITOR
Integrated Composition Systems

INDEXER
Alexander Trotter

PRINTER/BINDER
Sheridan Books, Inc.